The Bed I Made

The Bed I Made

A JOURNEY OF FULFILLED HOPE, FIFTY YEARS IN THE MAKING

Robert M. Lynch

With Christopher B. Lynch

Edited by Marilyn Murray Willison

THE BED I MADE is a true story. Some names have been changed in the interest of privacy and, in some cases, in order to allow for the faltering memory of an octogenarian Old-Corps Marine.

THE BED I MADE Copyright © 2017 by Robert M. Lynch. All rights reserved. No part of this book may be used or reproduced in any manner without permission.

Published in the United States by Ó Loingsigh Press

ISBN: 1979771480
ISBN 13: 9781979771481

For my mother and father, Barbara P. and Joseph A. Lynch. Thank you for being such loving parents and for teaching me that love expressed equals love received. I love you from the bottom of my heart.

For my siblings, Matthew Lynch, Ellen Ferraro, Marianne Landau, Joseph A. Lynch, Jr., Kathleen Lynn, Schanna MacDonald, Christopher Lynch, and Mark Lynch. THE BED I MADE is our story. I am so lucky to have shared it with you all.

In Memory of my dad's friends—his Brothers—who gave their lives while he was in Korea. You were the mighty Cannon Cockers of Able Battery, 1st Battalion, 11th Marines. You were each a hero to Dad and will forever remain a hero to every citizen of South Korea. I wish you could see what has become of the place.

CPL Edward Allen *Denny* Flom
March 27, 1929 – August 20, 1950

PFC Donald Miles
December 15, 1928 – November 30, 1950

CPL Bryan Eugene Simmons
August 19, 1928 – December 2, 1950

Cpl Patrick O'Brien Parrish
March 17, 1931 – December 4, 1950

SSgt Donald Sylvester Foster
September 10, 1925 – December 5, 1950

PVT Leland Clair Godfrey
September 28, 1930 – December 9. 1950

CPL Eugene Di Stefano
October 21, 1929 – February 3, 1951

To Stanley Jerry Zabodyn (March 20, 1930 - July 6, 2017) and Harold Digger O'Dell (November 30, 1928 – October 28, 2017). You will never fully know what your friendship has meant to my dad or the deep love he feels for you to this day.

This book is dedicated to all combat veterans of the United States of America who have sacrificed so much for so little in return. But for you, freedom's ring would fall flat.

Contents

Introduction

A HUMBLE MAN DOES NOT think, *I have done great things*, and then choose not to speak of them. Instead, a humble man thinks that the great things he has done are of little consequence. He does not see the greatness in himself.

Like many men of his generation, my father, Joseph Andrew Lynch, Sr., rarely—if ever—indulged in self-aggrandizement. After all, a medal for valor received during a horrific war means little to a humble man when he has seen other men sacrifice their lives for the same cause.

Also, a truly strong man is one who has taught himself to hold close his doubts and fears and sorrows. My father—who is now well into his ninth decade—is merely one member of the legions of *Everyman Heroes*. They are the quiet unsung warriors who have buried their experience of war. For years, they have cloaked themselves in a finely-crafted disguise of ordinary emotional wellness.

As a professional videographer, I have spent my career peering through layers of finely-cut glass as delicate layers of hidden truths of countless subjects revealed themselves. All the while, I remained insulated from, and ignorant to, my own father's extraordinary, and sometimes harrowing, experiences and achievements. I have traveled the country in order to meet with and film great heroes of American wars, politics, and sports, while, unbeknownst to me, the real-life hero of any man's imagination—my father—sat at home in quiet anonymity.

I thought I knew him as well as any child could know a parent after fifty years. I knew that he'd become a Marine at the young age of sixteen, and I had sketchy details of his service in the Korean War. And even though I have never served in the military, I could certainly imagine the horror of combat, and formulate my own understanding of what he had probably experienced without the benefit of his input.

Additionally, I did not need to be a police officer in New York City in order to understand the difficulties and dangers of protecting and serving the citizens of the largest city in the country, which he had also done. And it doesn't take an economic wizard to realize the struggles he faced in order to make ends meet for a family of thirteen on a patrolman's salary. I thought I knew my father.

Then, at the age of fifty-two, while visiting my father in the modest San Diego home where he and my mom have lived for over thirty years, I sat in front of this then-seventy-eight year old man—whose full head of salt-and-pepper hair was in need of its bi-weekly trim—and I listened to the remarkable story of his life. Two hours later, with glistening eyes, I almost felt as if I'd been sitting in front of a complete stranger.

My reluctant confession is that it took me almost a thousand conflicted, confusion-filled days to process the story that he'd quietly and somberly shared with me. Eventually, I enlisted the help of my brother, Christopher, in what turned out to be the three-year quest to share my father's story with the rest of our large family, our friends, and you. The process began with a video camera in my father's small home office, where for scores of hours, over a period of six months, Christopher and I poked and prodded into every corner of this stranger's (our father's) life.

The candor with which he patiently answered every question, and offered stories neither Christopher nor I even knew to ask about, both surprised and humbled us. What slowly and painstakingly emerged was a real-life story of courage, strength, sadness, joy, fear, and—most of all—hope. More importantly, he revealed a story of triumph against seemingly insurmountable odds. What eventually unfolded before us was an eye-opening portrait of my real father.

From a hardscrabble childhood filled with conflict and fear, he—as a sixteen-year old boy—left his home in Brooklyn, NY and found a new family in the United States Marine Corps. Where other young men loathed the strict discipline of boot camp, Dad savored the structured lifestyle that had eluded him both in school and at the unforgiving hand—and belt buckle—of his father. The letter he'd received from his mother, whom Dad cherished, when she'd learned that he was at Parris Island, had been blunt:

Joey, You've made your bed. Now, you can sleep in it.

"Well," Dad told me during the interviews with him, "The bed I made was easier to sleep in than the one I had at home."

In order to keep up with the older recruits, and not have his young age revealed, Dad pushed himself hard and he excelled. Although Marine Corps expectations had been rigorous, he savored the lifestyle and, after graduation, plunged himself into life as a Marine. At Camp Pendleton in California, he joined forces with the men of the 11th Marine Regiment, and created bonds that those of us who have never served cannot begin to understand. Those friendships would last their lifetimes—some of them shorter than others.

As I pieced Dad's stories together, I had the pleasure to visit with Harold *Digger* O'Dell, one of Dad's best friends from his Marine Corps days. We discussed their time together at Camp Pendleton, and Digger's gentle, eighty-seven year old eyes filled me with second-hand nostalgia. Then he told me something that reminded me his old friend was not the same man who'd raised me. Recalling their days together, Digger told me, "Joe was always so carefree and happy. Always quick with a smile."

Although I'd often witnessed my father's handsome smile, "carefree and happy" are words I would have never used to describe Dad. Digger was saddened to hear the unwelcome news that something had changed for his long-ago best friend. It would take decades for my father to comprehend that the personality change he'd experienced had been a direct result of his meritorious service in the Korean War.

When faced with the gut-wrenching decision whether or not to go to Korea, Dad chose to voluntarily fight alongside his brother Marines.

"I didn't want anyone to think I was a coward," Dad told me. "I didn't want my friends to face the war without me."

That statement *did* speak to the father I knew. I grew up knowing that Dad would not hesitate to put his life on the line for others. Although I had no details, I was aware that he'd received the Bronze Star with the combat "V" for Valor during the Korean War, but I'd never actually laid eyes on that medal. As a child, I'd been at New York City Hall when then-mayor, John Lindsay, pinned the Catherine O'Dwyer Medal for Lifesaving—the highest honor the city bestowed upon a police officer at the time—on his chest (This coveted award had quickly been stashed away with the Bronze Star). And I'd also witnessed in his civilian life when he stepped out of himself to protect others at great risk to himself.

But at home, I'd also seen episodes of repeated, inexplicable, explosive anger and deep depression, all of which now flies in the face of Digger O'Dell's characterization of my father as "carefree and happy." Like my eight siblings, I'd been unaware of the horrific nightmares that had plagued my father for over five decades. The debilitating depression he suffered seemed—to me—like quiet anger. He'd hidden his feelings of guilt, self-doubt, and self-loathing. The once-carefree and happy young Marine had morphed into a husband, father, and neighbor who endlessly struggled with anger, stress, and turmoil.

When it comes to his brave actions during the war, my father will tell you without hesitation that he is no hero. Once, when I suggested otherwise, he shook his head and said, "I'm not a hero. No." Then he told me, "The fellas who gave their lives, they are the heroes."

Dad lowered his head, and with solemn eyes stared at the bookshelves behind me. I suspected that what he saw there were friends—brothers—he had lost in that long-ago war. Then, he seemed to realize that I was waiting for him to continue his story, and he said, "I didn't know this was going to happen. None of us knew. We had fun at Pendleton. We worked hard, but we had fun. Then we went to Korea and everything changed. We found out we could die, and some of us did."

It all caused me to wonder: What does it mean to give one's life? Death on the battlefield is easy to identify. But what of the combat Marine who is chased by that battlefield for fifty years. Has another casualty occurred when the demons of Post Traumatic Stress Disorder (PTSD) alter the course of that life for decades? After learning my father's story, I am convinced it has. In the name of service to his country, my father sacrificed his capacity to have a life of joy and sanity, and did so on the many battlefields of the Korean War. He is the epitome of a hero because he showed great strength, fortitude, and valor during the brutal challenges of combat. But, perhaps even more heroic was his decision, at the age of seventy-two, to embark on a journey of recovery that—after a five-decade struggle—continues today. The young Marine who Digger O'Dell knew over sixty-five years ago, is now the almost fully gray-haired man I know today—a loving parent who is once again carefree and happy.

During the process of writing this book, I have embarked on my own journey. It has been one of discovery, not only of my father, but also of military life, veterans' issues, and the heartbreaking complexities of PTSD. Through friendships that developed during my research, and as I assembled chapter after chapter, I have learned that Dad's story is remarkable in its commonality. It is a tale that has been repeated countless times through the numerous— yet small percentage of—American men and women who are our combat veterans.

I have found heroes like Joe Lynch all around us. Like my father, they live their lives in quiet anonymity, their medals for bravery carefully tucked away with their fears, guilt, and uncertainty. Without understanding who they are or what has affected them, we see these humble heroes in our malls and grocery stores, on our highways and jetliners, and at our theaters and amusement parks. Sometimes we even see them at busy intersections where we avert our eyes so that we do not feel obligated to pass our loose change to them through our car windows.

They each embody a story of the *Everyman Hero* that has not been streamed across headlines or blared from our television screens. They are the quiet heroes who cling to their shrink-wrapped stories so that their true selves remain hidden from us. In each, there is a story of a private war that rages beyond the battlefield and our ability to see. But in each, there is also a story of hope that they may have yet to write.

In the six years since my father began to share his story with me, I have learned that Joe lives in your neighborhood—perhaps in your home. He is your grandfather or maybe your dad. Joe is your uncle or your nephew. Joe may very well be your brother or your husband. And do not be shocked to learn that *Josephine* may be your sister or your aunt.

By helping my father share his personal story, I hope to convey some of the immeasurable value that lies within each of these personal and, as yet, untold, stories. If the fates are kind, we will all learn to better understand the true sacrifices that our combat veterans have made on our behalf. Perhaps my father's hard-earned triumph over adversity will serve as a signpost toward recovery for others who have trudged in his combat boots.

It has been a privilege to have the opportunity to spend hundreds of hours listening to my father as he brought his past to life. Thanks to this project, I have learned more about him than I could have ever imagined. Unlike most men of my generation, I have been given the opportunity to create a new, deep, and unique relationship with my father that we both treasure.

There has never been any doubt regarding the deep love that I have felt for this remarkable man throughout my entire life. But with each story, each admission, and each confession, my love for him has expanded exponentially. Just as I have loved him, and in spite of a firm-handed upbringing, I have always known his love—something he never knew from his own father. I recognize now, that his love was a gift that I all too often took for granted.

I have spent countless hours re-watching and re-listening to my father's recorded interviews, and I never fail to be floored by the honesty, introspection, and poignancy found within them. Therefore, I have chosen to write this story through his voice, so that you may also experience the power of my humble father's clear and eloquent words.

Hope is not something that you conjure up in your own mind. Hope is an inspiration you get from the people you are around. Hope has to be shown and seen. Hope is something that is developed, that's learned. You must see the opportunity for hope.

Ravenell Williams, IV

CHAPTER 1
Cheese Sandwich

I MUST HAVE BEEN PRETTY close to the youngest Marine to ever wear the uniform—the youngest Marine to become a rifle instructor on the range at Parris Island. Fortunately, I wouldn't be the youngest Marine to see a dead Marine in Korea. That wouldn't happen until a few days past my nineteenth birthday. Time would pick me up and race me there soon enough.

On this particular day, I was only ten years old. I stood in front of my father, Walter Lynch, with a bright red handprint across my left cheek and fought the need to piss my knickers at the thought of what might happen at any moment. Maybe a sudden backhand propelled by his long spindly arm that would drop me on my ass and leave a mark on my right cheek that'd surely get my mind off what was on the left. Perhaps a few hard-booted kicks to the thigh or back while I was still down, because I hadn't stood when spoken to. He demanded to know what the hell had happened.

My lips trembled and my breath failed me, as I looked around the small living room for the right answer. Wearing a well-worn housedress, my mother, Anna, sat on her bed—the living room doubled as my parent's bedroom—and offered no help. There was nothing she could say or do, anyway. I understood that. At forty-five, with streaks of gray and a few extra pounds, she looked more like my friends' grandmothers than like their moms. She didn't like to see us get hit, but seemed to accept the fact that kids needed discipline, which she left to her husband—willingly or not, I can't be sure.

"Tell your father what happened, Joey."

So, I looked the old man square in his plaid-shirted stomach, and I told him.

It had happened at school. I'd been eating my lunch—the free meal that the school had been giving us ever since the war had started. World War Two had caused many hardships on the home front, and for a family like ours, one that had perfected the art of hardship long before the war had broken out in Europe, that free lunch meant a lot. Even a dumb kid like me recognized a cheese sandwich when he saw one. This one, however, barely qualified. Two slices of white bread and one thick slice of cheese—condiment free. I was happy for it, though. The other kids had already finished eating and were gone. I guess I was savoring mine, which didn't endear me to the teacher who had the arduous task of reading a book while she waited for me to finish.

She looked up from the book and said, "You're finished, Joe."

I looked down at close to a half sandwich in my hand and said, "I'm not finished yet."

She slapped the book down on the desk and walked over to me. "Yes you are. Don't talk back to me."

I guess I was a little slow on the uptake with the whole talking-back thing, and explained, "I'm not talking back to you. I'm not finished. Look, my sandwich is here, and my milk is here."

That's when I obtained my cheek adornment in the form of her open-fingered hand. It came fast and stinging-hard. At first, I was stunned. Then I cried. I stood up and left, no longer concerned about my remaining protein-rich sustenance. As I walked home, shock turned to anger, which turned to fear. I had wished that the anger could have lasted longer, because it felt good. I still had a whole lifetime ahead of me, however, to develop my anger staying-power skills. Besides, the fear would put me in the right frame of mind to prepare for my father, if he happened to be home, which, of course, he was.

Actually, a little of that fear might have been a good thing back in the classroom. I could have skipped the whole shock phase and hightailed it out to the playground—happy with my anger at that bitch teacher for making me skip out on my unfinished lunch. Not to mention that I wouldn't have had to explain why I got hit by a teacher (which was typically a beating offense) to my father.

Having finished the story for my father, and with the realization that my feet were still squarely planted on the floor, I nervously lifted my gaze to my father's eyes. His face had turned as red as the handprint on mine. He raised the cigarette that had been dangling at his side, took one last drag from it, and then squashed it in an ashtray that sat on a second-hand table in front of the old sofa.

"Let's go."

I couldn't believe what was happening. We were going to the school. My father was going to make this right. I could barely keep up with him during the three-block walk up Hoyt Street to PS 32 in Brooklyn. His five-ten, slender frame had been built for effortless speed, and I didn't dare ask him to slow down, nor did I care to. The pride I felt at my father, who was about to vindicate me, propelled my legs to a blur. Maybe I just liked the taste of anticipated vengeance. Either way, we were on a mission.

I was about to witness the man I feared more than anything else in the world take his anger out on someone else, *on my behalf.* It was mind-boggling. Instead of getting the hardware end of his belt across my back, he was about to defend me. What I felt at that moment is difficult to explain. It wasn't love. By the age of ten, I had already given up trying to love this man years before, so that couldn't be it. Maybe it was respect. Looking back now, I guess it's possible to respect one action of a man I otherwise had little or no respect for. Whatever I felt, it was—where my father was concerned—a new sensation for me.

We raced by President Street and flowed through the front door of the school on a conveyor of air and adrenalin. I couldn't feel my feet touching the cement floor below them. In the office, my father introduced himself as Walter Lynch and demanded to see the teacher. In those days, such a demand was followed by an audience with the subject of one's ire. If a teacher pissed off a parent, it was her problem to deal with and make it right. It was obvious to the secretary that said teacher had pissed off this parent. The layers of protection that we know today, between the outside world and the teacher, just didn't exist back then. Of course, no teacher in her right mind would consider bitch-slapping a ten-year-old kid today. Mrs. Corizzo was about to learn a lesson.

In the presence of her red-faced (with a hint of soured-alcohol and cigarette breath), bulging-eyed interrogator, Mrs. Corizzo portrayed a self-assured smugness that I knew would only piss off my father even more. When she insisted that she had never laid a hand on me, the confrontation was over in a flash that manifested in a backhanded slap across my right cheek—that day's penalty for lying. Stunned again.

With my father's attention turned onto me, Mrs. Corizzo added a hint of a smirk to her arrogant countenance. Her steadfast eyes told me everything I needed to know—*I'm watching you, kid.*

She glanced up at my father and said, "If that's all."

Without waiting to find out if that was actually all, she abruptly walked out of the office. My father shoved me out behind her, as she turned right into the bowels of the school, emboldened by power-affirming encounter. We went to the left toward the school exit and an uncertain immediate future for the unlucky kid who had *lied* to his father.

The silent walk home to 388 Hoyt Street contrasted sharply with the earlier walk to the school in that—this time—I easily kept up with the old man. The pace alone set my mind at ease. He was cooling off, and the heat in my face began to dissipate. I optimistically assumed that he was not anxious to get me to the apartment where he could remove his belt and continue my punishment.

Gradually, my fear subsided. I knew to leave the issue alone, and to keep my mouth shut. There was no point in trying to defend my good name. That would only push my father's delicate buttons. When we got to the apartment, I went straight to the bedroom that I shared with my four older brothers—three, actually, since my oldest brother, John, was by this time somewhere in Europe fighting the good fight.

I used to wonder how it happened. How a carefree day could explode into madness without warning. How a cheese sandwich could cause the development of an enemy at a place where enemies were already plentiful, and allies were scarce. That day encapsulated everything I'd felt about school and my father. The two loomed large as powers to fear and, in the case of my father, avoid whenever possible. By this time in my life, school offered nothing more than anxiety. My mornings brought consistent sick feelings caused by trepidation of what lay ahead of me for the school day. The knots in my stomach overwhelmed me, and classroom hours dragged on as I sought to not be noticed by the teacher. To be called on to answer a question that I *knew* the answer to filled me with dread and left me standing in a speechless slump. *You know the answer.* Nothing. My days filled themselves with thoughts of the eight years of school that still lay ahead of me, which seemed like a century to a ten-year old. I wanted to be in Europe with my brother, John. At least with him, I'd know that my back would be secure.

And what I had to look forward to when that bell rang in the afternoon—when all the other kids ran through the doors, giddy screams and laughter for the excitement of home and games and carefree existence—was *my* home, where *He* might be. I'd walk down Hoyt Street, sometimes with a classmate, sometimes alone, wondering if my father would be there when I got home. My footfalls spaced themselves farther apart in time, closer together in space, with the passing of each short block between school and our apartment. The fear was usually vague, because most times I had done nothing wrong. Theoretically—in anyone else's world—I had nothing to fear. But, for me, the uncertainty had been an expanding monster in my life and proved more than enough to fear in its own right. Uncertainty about the mood I would find, the perception of right and wrong that I might encounter, the annoyance that could erupt at the sound of the door closing or me talking with my mother. *Had he—or had he not—been drinking?* Uncertainty was my enemy.

On that particular day, when my father backhanded me in front of Mrs. Corizzo, everything became crystal clear. I knew with certainty that my father was a man to hide from rather than someone I could count on to hide behind. He would never be my protector, my friend, or my hero. I could no longer concentrate on schoolwork, and my fear of doing poorly in school became self-fulfilling. I essentially stopped learning. I continued on to the next grade, but soon realized that I could not keep up. At times, I hadn't a clue what the teacher was talking about. I may as well have been deaf. For that matter, I may as well have been mute, because I told no one.

I began to think, and then to believe, that I was stupid. The time to care had slipped away, and so had my chances for success. That backhanded slap from my father spelled defeat to me, and—at the early age of only ten years old—I had given up. I believed that the school continued to pass me, just to get me through the system and out of their lives. Well, the feeling was mutual.

CHAPTER 2

Lavender Lake

It usually doesn't take a genius. And that's a good thing, because nobody ever accused my buddies and me of being geniuses. And I say *usually,* because it applies to so many of the situations life throws at us—or the situations we plunge ourselves into. I can't tell you how many times one of my children stood in front of me and said, *I didn't know.* And I'd answer, *That's because you didn't think.* I'd say it pretty much the way you might think: sharp, with the taste of venom. Think *before you do something.* Think *before you open your mouth.* Think, *and you'll know.* It made me crazy when they acted without thinking. It's a good thing I always thought when I was a kid.

Scratch that.

The Gowanus Canal is an approximately two-mile long waterway in Brooklyn that runs from just north of Douglas Street, and ends in Gowanus Bay to the south. It was built in the late 19th century in order to tame a great marshland that Gowanus Creek fed from the bay. Six-foot tides forced salt water up through those marshes that made the creek near-useless to commercial endeavors. But with the dredging of the canal, the marshes had been backfilled, and property values skyrocketed. Industry sprang up along the new waterway, and boat traffic increased commerce. It was all very tidy.

And it was a shithole. Literally. Every drop of raw sewage from the Borough of Brooklyn made it's way through an intricate maze of sewer pipes to the Gowanus Canal. This epically-proportioned toilet bowl was flushed twice daily by those same six-foot tides that had flooded the marshlands in another era. There were days that my limited imagination could conjure nothing worse than the occasional smell that would drift the quarter-mile from the canal to the fire escape of our apartment on 3rd Street where we now lived. The locals called the canal Lavender Lake.

The second big issue with the canal lies at its murky depths. Skeletons. Or so I assumed. It was common knowledge—or perhaps local lore—that guys with monikers like, Louis *Lepke* Buchalter, Albert *The Mad Hatter* Anastasia, and Jack *The Dandy* Parisi used the Gowanus Canal as a convenient dumping ground. The press giddily referred to these goons as "Murder, Inc." When your murder business is so large that you need to incorporate—they were believed responsible for up to one thousand murders in the thirties and early forties—you need someplace to get rid of the evidence. In this case, the evidence was any unfortunate who had unwisely crossed the Mafia in some way. The reasonable thinking by Murder, Inc., was that nobody in his right mind would go in Lavender Lake looking for a body. Nobody.

Mr. Saranelli had built a salvage yard on a small lot on the other side of the canal, right at the 3rd Street Bridge, only two and a half blocks from my parents' apartment. He took in junk that was being shipped back from the war. There was an awful lot of stuff coming back from Europe and the Pacific. Shipwrecks were coming in and he was collecting scrap metal trying to make himself a millionaire—I'll bet he succeeded. One fine Sunday, four of my buddies and I walked across the bridge, and we spotted a big military life raft on his property. Junior Sheehan, who was two years older than me, said, "Let's go for a ride."

A simple suggestion like this can sometimes be confused with a dare. I guess that's the way this went down, because we all looked at each other, and I sensed that we each waited for one of the others to express all the reasons that we should not *go for a ride*. None stated, it was then our obligation to set sail.

We slid the raft into the water, which was about four feet below the top of the bulkhead. Tommy, Junior, and I jumped down, and then Joe Farrow passed down a couple oars before he and Tony joined us. The raft was pretty big, about five feet by eight feet. We sat on the inflated sides, while Junior and Farrow pushed the oars through the water. We were all happy for the sturdy, netted, raised floor that allowed any filthy water splashed by the oars to drain below our feet.

We floated down the canal and soaked in the sun, as well as the new-to-us views of the neighborhoods. Boats from the war that were destined for the scrap yards lined some sections of the bulkhead. The vibrating sound of tires on thick steel mesh bounced off the calm water around us as cars sped by on the bridges above. The farther we floated, the more inconsequential the smell of the water became. Surprised at our effortless passage, we drifted for large portions of the trip down to Gowanus Bay, and used the oars more for steering than propulsion.

For me, this was the adventure of a lifetime. I'd never done anything even remotely comparable. At the time, I wasn't much of a reader, but I do remember feeling like that kid in the Mark Twain story—Sawyer, or Finn, or something like that. Occasionally, we'd spot someone on the bank of the canal who watched us float by. I was certain that I could smell the envy of people who could only imagine what the life of the other-half must be like. We waved to them in the nonchalant manner of passengers on a luxury yacht who were accustomed to a life of leisure. It was perfect.

We explored a section of the bay, where boats had turned into ships. The heavy smell of oil permeated the air. The damage to the once great and powerful warships boggled the mind. I could easily imagine the sailors somewhere in the Pacific racing around the deck and manning their gun stations, as the bombs or torpedoes ravaged their vessel. How I wished I could have been with them. What I hadn't thought about was the gruesome deaths that so many of them had suffered.

When we realized how far the sun had moved in the sky, we prepared for our leisurely float back to Saranelli's, where we would return the raft, leaving no one the wiser about our afternoon excursion. By the time we had reached the mouth of the canal, however, we discovered that the oars would now have to earn their keep. We took turns digging in and pulling the oars through the water. We worked harder, only to make much slower progress on the return trip. When my arms began to feel like stretched rubber, I'd pass my oar back to Junior, who sat right behind me. We continued alternating this way, working in rotations that seemed to get shorter and shorter, with the oars cycling back to me faster and faster. We'd had no idea what caused the difference. It wasn't as if we were navigating a running river, where we'd rationally expect difficulty on the northerly trek.

With the light at the end of the tunnel—the 3rd Street Bridge—within striking distance, my eyes locked on the bulkhead. A large dark area—maybe five feet in depth—that had not been there before, had materialized. I saw that each of my boat mates were interested in the same strange phenomenon. Each of us wore a similar "Oh-shit" expression. The tide had gone out. I didn't know. *That's because you didn't think.*

On cue, the two current oarsmen dug in and paddled harder than ever. We needed to get back to Saranelli's before another drop of water left the canal. The oars had made another rotation through the ranks in quick succession, yet—by the time we reached our landing—the water level had dropped almost another foot. The top of the bulkhead was now a full nine feet or more above the water line. *Shit.*

Without a word, I got a handhold in the rough, wooden surface of the bulkhead, and shoved my feet in hard between the floor netting and the inflated side of the raft. It was a snug and secure fit. In this way I was able to hold the vessel steady, while Junior and Farrow boosted, first Tommy, and then Tony to safety. Then Junior gave Farrow a shove from below as the others pulled him from above. The teamwork had been impressive. Junior told me to go next, but my grip was firm.

"You go, then pull me up," I said.

What a hero. Junior stepped up on the side, and his hands met those of Tony and Farrow. He made quick work of getting up top. My turn.

I held on tight to the bulkhead and loosened my feet from the raft. I could feel it slide on top of the water a little, so I pulled it back in. My right foot—and then my left—made it up onto the side of the raft, where I'd been sitting all afternoon. The raft wasted no time floating away from the bulkhead. I could see the fear in Junior's face. He dropped down on his stomach and reached down as far as he could. Not far enough. The spot I was holding on the bulkhead was about a foot below his reach. Farrow got down next to him, but his even shorter arms held little promise.

"Reach up, Joe!" That was Junior. His voice carried the same fear I felt in my thumping chest. I was too scared to let go. The raft drifted farther. It was now or never. I let go with my left hand and reached up. The raft shot out from under me like ice skates on a dog, and our hands never made it to within eight inches of each other. *Shit.*

There followed, a moment in time so small as to be immeasurable, when detail became crisp, and my mind saw with perfect clarity what I had just gotten myself into:

There is a man, he is quite large, and he wears a sleeveless undershirt that reveals tufts of sweat-matted hair that covers his chest, arms, and shoulders. He needed a shave four days ago. The cheap cigar he thrusts into his mouth has been chewed to a gnarly stump. His boxer shorts are around his ankles and his thighs have large red marks from the pressure of his elbows as he reads the Daily Mirror. There are no slacks to be seen, and on his feet, only black socks. In a fluid motion, he stands and pulls his second-day shorts over his hips. A line of hair on his stomach points to the area where, on a slighter man, you'd be able to see the waistband. A roach scurries along the baseboard behind the toilet, and the man pushes the handle to send the bowl's contents on its remarkably-fast journey under the streets of South Brooklyn to Lavender Lake.

And then:

Pools of yellowish light from widely-spaced overhead lamps, and the occasional nightlight of a nearby warehouse illuminate the late-night darkness of the canal neighborhood. A 1946 Cadillac Coupe, with a black paint job so shiny it looks like you could walk through it, swerves into a lot alongside the canal. The car's headlights fade away before the car comes to a full stop. Two men with long overcoats and fedoras that may as well be neon signs that read *Gangster*, rush from the car and pull a large, thrashing, canvas sack from the trunk. Mugsy cuts open the sack, and Bugsy lifts his tommy gun. The man from the bag is shoved to the edge of the canal and Bugsy levels the gun. I can hear the man pleading for his life. "I didn't know. I swear, I didn't know!" Mugsy is disgusted by such a lame excuse. "That's because you didn't think!" Ra-ta-tat-tat. A few short bursts from the gun and the man from the sack is airborne in agonizing slow motion above Lavender Lake.

After this moment of undignified clarity, time resumed its relentless march. My arms thrashed at the air as if I could grab hold of it and pull myself up. My legs kicked in search of the invisible steps that would lead me to dry land. Splash. I hit the canal in a fit of terror. My mouth closed in time to allow only a rain barrel's worth of filthy water through. It tasted like— I don't need to tell you what it tasted like. I would have sworn I'd seen the tortured face of the man from the sack floating up toward me just as I sank down. I scrambled to the surface like a cat thrown into the deep end of a pool. When I broke the sloshing plane between watery excrement and relatively fresh air, water, and pieces of lung (I refused to believe it was anything else), as well as unbridled profanity flowed from my mouth. My friends could not get me out of there fast enough. Truthfully, they could not have been much slower about it.

Just as I imagined the man from the sack reach up to grab my ankle and pull me back to my soupy Mafia grave, my four friends did their best Three Stooges-plus-one routine, and tried to *think* of a way to get me out. In the span of about twenty seconds—during which I spent a week imagining how to kill each of them—Tommy had found a bundle of heavy nautical line (rope to us) and tossed it down to me. Fortunately, he'd held on to the other end. I snaked my end around my right forearm and held on for Mother Ireland and my own sanity with both hands. Three of them pulled while I ran up the side of the bulkhead like a sprinter in the fifty-yard, vertical dash—good training for the Marines, which I wouldn't need for another eight months. I just didn't know that at the time.

When I finally reached solid ground, I fell to my hands and knees, where I coughed, hacked, spit, gagged, and invented some new swear words. I looked up at my friends, who stared back at me in utter disbelief. Each of them stayed well beyond my drip line, for fear of contracting whatever disease would surely take hold of my body, melt my skin away, and cause large tumors to develop on my face. I was with them on this. God, I had never felt so awful in my life. I was terrified, but at least I wouldn't die in the canal. The thought did take hold, however, that I now might die at the hands of my father. I was certainly not out of the muck yet.

Then it happened. My friends' faces revealed a slight change. They tried so hard to hold it back, but once the first laugh escaped, it raced through the lot of them like the cholera that had certainly made its way to my vital organs. Contaminant-laced water dripped from my eyes as I, too, let some laughs slip past my tongue, which felt numb. Then Junior Sheehan stepped out of himself and to my side. With little regard for his own safety, he helped me up to my feet.

"C'mon. We gotta get you home before that fuck of an old man gets there."

He put an arm around my shoulder as we set off for the bridge and the short walk home. Junior Sheehan was a good friend. But a few short months in the future, he would reconsider that friendship, when I persuaded him to join the Marines with me, and he got his first taste of boot camp.

We walked across the bridge together, and the guys recapped the closing scene of our cruise on the River Shit. Junior looked off the south side of the bridge at the canal, and the rest of us followed his gaze. There went Mr. Saranelli's raft. It softly bounced off a boat, and made gentle spins before it found another boat to kiss in its aimless journey. At that moment, I felt a certain kinship to the untethered raft.

CHAPTER 3

Broken Record

"I'M GOING INTO THE SERVICE."

"No, you're not."

"I'm going into the service."

"No, you're not."

"Yes, I'm going into the service."

"No, you're not. Leave me alone!"

The conversation was always the same. Everyday, without fail, I'd tell my mother, "I'm going into the service." And she'd always say, "No, you're not."

It was a broken record, but I refused to lift the needle. I haunted her.

"I'm going into the service."

"No, you're not."

A few months before this go-nowhere conversation had begun, I'd shown up at the Metropolitan Vocational High School Main Building on James Street for the first day of eleventh grade. It was an easy subway ride from Brooklyn—9th Street to a transfer at Hoyt-Schermerhorn, and under the river to the first stop at Fulton Street in the lower east side of Manhattan. I was in the Merchant Marine program with my sights set on hitting the high seas as soon as I graduated. That's when I would put Brooklyn and my father as far behind me as possible. I spent half of my school day in this building pretending to learn math and English and the others. The rest of the day was spent on the S.S. John W. Brown, a real-deal Merchant Marine ship that was tied up close by at Pier 4 on the East River. When she'd been decommissioned

15

after the Second World War, the New York City Board of Education got their hands on her as a loaner from the government. The ship was used as a floating high school for go-getters like me who wanted to learn the Merchant Marine business in order to put Brooklyn and their fathers as far behind them as possible. Good plan.

Schooling on the ship was all right, I guess. We actually learned something there, because we did real work. It felt good. But, frankly, anything I learned there, I could have learned on the job as an actual Merchant Marine. Problem was, at sixteen years of age, I couldn't get the job. There's not much you *can* do at that age. But at least it got me out of class for a half day, every day. So I figured I'd stick it out. And, had I reported straight to the ship that first day of school in 1947, I might have done just that. Instead, I had to report to the Main Building.

As I walked down James Street, I was aware of other students converging on the grand stairway entrance up ahead, but they may as well have been the breeze off the East River for all I actually saw them. The wide sidewalk narrowed, and the smooth stone wall of Metropolitan Vocational High School began to crowd me to my right, and lean over me from above. The familiar closed-in feeling of school filled me before I'd reached the front doors. As I climbed the wide cement steps to the ornately framed doors, my legs became heavy. From two or more miles away, the phantom stench of the Gowanus Canal filled my nostrils. The familiar school-induced stomach knots twisted and tightened. I looked at my hand on the doorknob—*What the hell am I doing here?* There was no need to wait for an answer. A couple of students parted as I rushed down the stairs.

One of my schoolmates who I had not even noticed called after me, "Where ya goin', Joe?"

His voice and his words floated through my head. Halfway down James Street to Madison, my feet slowed, which gave good sense an opportunity to catch up to me. It was a close call, but I got my feet back on pace and managed to avoid rational thought altogether. I was good like that.

I knew the underground alphabet by heart—I'd learned it early. When I was just a kid, my oldest brother, John, kept his spare pennies in one of his two dresser drawers. Five boys in one bedroom, with one bed and two dressers. So, we each had about two drawers. The bed was more complicated. I'd snitch a few coins, get a piece of candy or two down at the corner store, and then put one of those pennies on the trolley track in order to stretch it to the size of a nickel. That make-do nickel would get me into the subway, where I could go anywhere in the city. Maybe the F line out of Brooklyn to Washington Square and the C up the West Side to 145th Street. Or I could ride the D line to Bryant Park and hop over to Grand Central on the S. It didn't matter; it was all about the ride—the feeling that I had somewhere to go and important things to do. It was all about the escape. I'd disappear for a couple hours or the whole damn day—sometimes on my own, others with a neighborhood buddy or two. We'd follow the commuters into Manhattan in the morning and back to Brooklyn before supper. As long as I didn't step out of the system, I could ride the trains for as long as I pleased. *A nickel a ride—follow the tide.* I loved it.

The first day of the eleventh grade that never was, I'd taken the G line to Hoyt-Schermerhorn and transferred to the A line into Manhattan to get to the school. After turning my back on education, I descended below the city streets, this time at Canal Street, and rode the Q to Herald Square in silence. I never bothered to look at any of the people on the platforms at Prince Street, or the others from 8th through 28th—normally a highlight of this subterranean world. The names of the stops and the letters of the lines strobed past at the stations we blew through. With no shopping money in my pocket, I skipped the urge to ascend to Macy's at 34th Street, and—instead—jumped on the D which took me up the west side of Central Park. Of course, I didn't see the park. No stop for me at the Museum of Natural History on 81st Street. *It's all about the ride.*

In the past, the hours had always slipped away—as did Brooklyn, Queens, The Bronx, Manhattan, and my life. But on this day, I couldn't imagine how I'd last down here until mid-afternoon when I would be expected home from school. The normally soothing rumbles and jolts of the train were, this day, annoying. The flickering lights through windows of the opposite-direction trains that used to hypnotize me, frazzled. The smell of piss filled my nostrils. *Why hadn't I noticed that before?* I was back on the platform at 9th Street in Brooklyn before noon.

Junior Sheehan saved the day. Or, at least, he'd occupied it. A couple years older, Junior didn't have to worry about school anymore. He needed only to worry about what to do with his life. On this day—lucky for me—he was only concerned with making up the three-run deficit his three-man, sewer-to-sewer ball team had gotten themselves into.

"Hey, Joe! Get down to the Packard. You're the outfield."

It was just what I needed. No questions from Junior, even though he knew I should be at school. No questions from the guys we were playing against about adding another player. I slipped into the game seamlessly, and killed the better part of the afternoon. We lost. Three times. *Who cares?*

After the game I knew I'd have time with Junior. I looked up to him, and figured he'd have some direction for our lives. He'd be going places, and I'd go along for the ride, with much of the same comfort I'd always derived below the streets of New York City.

But Junior had nothing. He talked about some of the factories and warehouses in the neighborhood—many of them lining Lavender Lake—with little enthusiasm.

"Hey, maybe Saranelli'll give us a job over the scrap yard," he suggested.

Our futures smelled like shit. But the day would come soon enough, when we would put our heads together and develop a plan to get out of Brooklyn altogether. Actually, I'd put the plan in his head, and he'd be the one going along for the ride. He'd realize a little too late that it was no Alphabet-Soup subway adventure.

Days and weeks passed. Stickball, football in the street with a tightly wadded paper ball—none of us could afford the real thing—and subway rides that had lost the old luster. Whenever I walked across the 3rd Street Bridge, I'd think about the raft and how great that business had been (I did my best to block out the dip at the end). I'd see that raft floating down the canal with the tide—an endless cycle that mirrored my life. I had a plan, though. It had always been there, tucked away in the back of my head, in the beat of my heart, and in the breaths that sustained me.

It had started years before when my brothers had gone to war—John to Europe with the Army Air Corps, and Wally (followed by Jimmy) to the Pacific with the Navy. I'd kept track of the war with a ravenous appetite as a kid. The newspaper brought glorious reports of victories as well as heartbreaking tales of setbacks, and I soaked up every word. I wanted to be there. My brothers, whom I honored beyond measure, had been saving the world without me, and I'd yearned to join them. It was a foolish child's dream. At the time, I didn't know that John had shrapnel embedded in his head, and that he'd gone deaf in one ear due to the injury. I wouldn't find out about that for a lifetime—his lifetime. It wouldn't have mattered; my pride in—and admiration for—him would only have elevated.

When they all returned in one piece—John's Purple Heart tucked away where even he didn't have to think about it—Bobby joined the Navy after the war had just ended. Even though my father had successfully dodged the draft throughout the First World War, and bragged about it at every opportunity, I'd come to believe that military service was the Lynch way of life—at least the means to get life started. So, I'd do the same. I'd join the service. So far with my brothers, it was three to one—Navy over Army—so I'd just stick with the winning team. There was just that one small issue of my age—sixteen.

One afternoon, the neighborhood kids were hoofing it home from bus stops and train stations, so I made my way to our apartment for some make-believe homework. My mother was in the kitchen slow-cooking tomato sauce.

"Joey."

I hated it when she called me that. Now, I only wish I could hear it again.

"Joey."

Something in the tone of her call put me on the defensive.

"Shit."

"What did you say?"

"Nothing, Ma."

The aroma of the sauce on the stove and my lack of lunch may have spurred the empty feeling in my stomach, but I'd have to put my money—if I'd had any—on whatever else was in the air.

"Why haven't you been to school?"

"I've been to school. I just got home."

She dropped the wooden spoon into the pot and wiped her hands on a cloth as she turned to catch my eye.

Shit. That expletive managed to stay in my head.

"You've never been a liar, Joey. Don't start now."

One Mississippi, two Mississippi, three—

"Why haven't you been to school?"

"I quit."

"No, you didn't. You get your knickers to that school tomorrow, and you beg them to let you come back."

"Ma, I don't wear knickers anymore."

"You'll be back in knickers, you want to act like a child."

"Ma, I can't go back."

"And just what do you think you're going to do?"

"I was thinking about going into the service."

The apartment door opened and shut.

"Shit."

"And watch your mouth, boy."

My father had three moods: beer, boilermaker, and no money for the drink. The safest mood was the one he'd settle into when he'd been drinking beer. He was usually happy, maybe whistling or even singing. I'd heard neither from down the hall. What I wouldn't have given for a few verses of *How Much is That Doggy in the Window.* Boilermakers—the combination of beer and whisky—made him mean and ugly. He'd come in quiet, and you'd do well to keep your distance, because he'd backhand you just for being in his space. Silence was deadly, and you could have heard a pin drop after the door had shut. There was a little hope, though. No money for the drink meant quiet and somber. The lack of sound could mean quiet and somber. *Don't do anything stupid and you might be okay.* He would speak in this mood, but always short and to the point.

He walked into the kitchen to find my mother and me faced off. I didn't dare turn.

"What's this?"

He spoke. No money for the drink. *Don't do anything stupid.* Too late.

"Joey quit school."

"Is that right?"

I didn't know how to answer. If he punched me, I was fully prepared to beat the crap out of him. I told myself that, anyway. I'd dreamt of doing it, but I guess I knew that it'd never happen. I just needed to get out. At least he never hit my mother, so I didn't have to worry about that.

"Turn around."

I did as he said.

"Is that right?"

"Yes, sir."

He searched my eyes and then looked down at my hands. They curled into squirming fists. In reality, I was just wiping the sweat from my fingers with my palms. Maybe he'd read my thoughts about taking him on. More likely he'd resigned himself to his not finishing school, followed by my four older brothers not finishing.

"Why should this one be so special?"

He turned and walked to the living room—his bedroom.

"Get a job," was the last thing he said to me that day as he disappeared around the corner.

My mother had lost, and the hurt in her eyes filtered straight to my heart. It was the first time I'd ever disappointed her in a big way. I didn't know it then, but I'd do it again soon enough. This time in a way so big that she would stop speaking to me.

For now, I was filled with hate. Hate for the school system that I felt had pushed me away. Hate for my father who was pushing me away, even from my mother. But most of all, hate for myself, because I did not have the guts to reconcile the first two in order for her to have one freaking kid finish school.

It wasn't going to happen, though. She turned to her saucepot, and I disappeared into my room. My brother, Raymond, six years my junior, was going to have to be the one to get a diploma. Me? Somehow I'd find a job and figure out how a sixteen-year old could join the service.

My brother Jimmy turned out to be the *somehow*. When he got out of the Navy, he'd landed a job with a window blinds company. They manufactured custom blinds, and he was one of their installers for homes and offices. A magician with his hands, Jimmy could do just about anything, and do it well. Show him once, and he was an expert. Don't show him, and he'd figure it out himself, and *then* he'd be an expert. He'd pretty much used up that entire gene, passed down from our father, leaving none for me. Actually, I may have been the only son *not* to get a piece of it, so I guess Jimmy had at least taken my share.

"Hey, kid, I got you a job at the factory."

Jimmy had come by the apartment to give me the good news. *Great.* He took a drag from his cigarette.

"Come in with me in the morning, and they'll get you set up."

"Doing what?"

"Putting the blinds together." He squinted through the drift of smoke in his face. "Whadda ya think?"

Great. He gave me a little slap to the head and I brushed his hand away. It was brotherly love.

"And you better do a good job. I spoke for you. And I don't wanna have to fix the damn things before I install them."

Great.

"Be out front at seven." He brushed away a dropped ash on the floor with his shoe, and left.

Jimmy could be a real asshole at times. Mostly, though, he was my hero. He was closer to me in age—five and a half years my senior—than my other brothers who had gone to war. So, when he had shipped out, I was older and more mature—a solid twelve—than when John and Wally had. I felt more ready to follow Jimmy than when our older brothers had gone.

While he was away in the Navy, I'd received a school assignment to write a short report about my hero, and I had written about Jimmy. That was, in no small part, due to the rifle he'd sent me from Okinawa. As I said before, I held all my brothers in high honor, but a rifle? Are you kidding? You bet he was my hero. When he returned home, he took it to the hockshop. *Asshole.*

I'd been fifteen then and still fumbling through school as well as everything else in my life. My mother was happy that Jimmy had made it home safe. She had no favorites, and each of us was her baby. Jimmy was the last one to get home from the war, and she couldn't have been happier.

He lived back at the apartment, and Ma let him know that he'd have to contribute to the household. He was receiving the 52/20 unemployment benefits from the government—$20.00 per week, for up to fifty-two weeks. Everyone with World War Two credit was eligible for it. I think Jimmy's plan had been to stay out of work for that first year back.

"What happened to all that money I sent ya while I was gone?"

What the hell kind of question was that for him to ask his mother? And to do it while she's cooking him supper. I was already pissed. He knew the situation here.

"I spent it. I have a household to run."

"Well, I sent ya money for three years. Now, I need money."

Yeah, he needed money. He'd developed a taste for booze just like the old man. He must've worked on that over in Okinawa. Now, he was running up to Mannix's Bar early in the day, and getting out before my father got there for the second shift. A quart bottle or two of Ballantine would be in his fist when he came in to sit at the kitchen table and watch my mother cook or clean. When my father would come in, they'd give each other a knowing look. *I know what your drunk feels like.* A bottle-born kinship. Between the two of them, they spent another fortune on their cigarettes. Pall Mall for the old man, and Lucky Strike—*Luckies*—for Jimmy. Truthfully, Ma and I were the only ones in that house who never smoked or drank. The apartment always looked like it was on fire.

So, Jimmy did need his money. How else was he going to kill himself? I could see how hurt my mother was. *Fucking asshole.* I lunged from my chair and slammed him into the china cabinet. It took him a few beats—in which I'd landed a couple of good punches to his ribs and one to his face—to realize what was happening. Then he tossed me off and kicked me around like my father on a boilermaker buzz. I was just a scrappy, pissed off, fifteen-year old, and he was a twenty-two-year old war veteran. He kicked my ass pretty good, but—I'll tell you this—he knew he'd been in a fight when we were done. So did Ma's china cabinet. We broke it pretty good. First, he'd landed on it, and then I'd been slammed into it a couple of times before she could get between us and bring the madness to an end. The china cabinet was a cheap piece of crap—like everything else in the place—but it was the only china cabinet she had. We didn't make life easy for her back then.

"Talk to her like that again, and I'll break your damn neck."

Jimmy faked with a right, looking for me to flinch. I didn't. I was physically spent, breathing heavy, and ready to give it another go anytime he was.

"Get outta here, kid," was all he had to say. As far as I know, he never gave my mother another dime. *Asshole.* But I loved him. And I still do today. We'd help each other out a lot over the years, and we'd go at it a few more times, as well. Today, he and I are the last survivors of the whole messed-up lot.

So, I met him downstairs at seven the next morning and went to work assembling blinds with the parts other people had made. The blind-manufacturing cycle would start and end with my brother. He'd go out, take the measurements, place the order, then the parts would get punched, cut, bent, and formed, then I'd put the puzzle pieces together, and hand off the finished product to Jimmy, who would install them. God help me if any of those blinds came back for imperfections. I was slower than the other assemblers, more methodical, and only slightly more likely than them to have a return. In time I got pretty damn good at the job. I hated it.

"I'm going into the service."

And so it began.

"No, you're not."

It'd usually start when I came in from the factory. "I'm going into the service."

Ma would be fixing supper, and usually had her attention on the stove, or her face in the pantry. "No, you're not."

I knew how to win this argument—persistence. "Yes. I'm going into the service."

But she'd always end the back and forth with a slam of the cabinet, or the crash of a saucepan on the table. "No. You are not! Get outta here."

I'd get out of the kitchen and storm to my room. "I'm going."

Another slam—this time the oven. "You're not!"

Weeks of this insanity passed. Every day I'd come home and start it. Sunday mornings before mass. At night when she was sending me off to bed. Walking out the door to take trash to the alley. Always the same.

"I'm going into the service."

Sometimes she'd try gentle reasoning. "Joey, how are ya gonna join the service? You're only sixteen. They won't take ya, Joey."

"I don't know. But I'm joining."

Reasoning over. "No, you're not."

Sometimes she'd get out ahead of it. I'd bound through the front door one evening and found her in the living room folding clothes. She was in no mood.

"Don't you even say it, mister. You're not going any place, and I don't want to hear a word."

Sometimes you have to read the situation. I walked away. But this was far from over.

"I'm going into the service."

It was a couple days later, and the round-robin was getting dizzy. But I learned that this wasn't as far from over as I had thought.

"I don't give a damn what you do. Go!"

There it was. Permission. I judged my mother's eyes, and knew that it was certainly *not* permission. It was a worn out, pissed off, abused woman, giving up—telling me what I wanted to hear just to shut me up. I walked to my room in shame, but with the plausible deniability I needed to do whatever the hell I wanted. She'd said it: "Go!" So, I went.

CHAPTER 4

Understated Confidence

THE PUTRID WATER OF THE Gowanus canal seeped out of my pores and soaked my undershirt. Drops glistened on my forehead and above my upper lip. I licked away the sweat around my mouth—it tasted like salty shit (the tide must've been coming in). In front of me, the seal of the United States Navy loomed large on the glass door. *You can do this.* I could almost feel the hand of the man from the cloth sack below the surface of Lavender Lake tug at the back of my shirt as I reached for the door. A mental shrug released the grip, and the sun glinted off the words "Recruiting Station" below the seal as the door swung outward and I slipped through it.

Man the Guns—Join The Navy! Give The World The Once Over in The United States Navy. The Navy Wants MEN. The recruiting posters lined the drab-gray walls. Graphic drawings of sailors waving the flag, battle ships on turbulent seas, and storm clouds churning purple skies offered motivation to lesser men who were unsure of their call to duty. Uncle Sam pointed a steady finger directly at me. *I WANT YOU TO JOIN THE U.S. NAVY. ENLIST NOW!*

"That's what I'm here for."

"What?" The voice came from below the last poster.

I needed to learn to keep my thoughts inside my head.

"Whadda ya need, kid?"

He walked over, and inserted a book among several other enormous books on a shelf. He was probably twenty-two or twenty-three years old. The patch on his shoulder—an upright eagle with wings spread proudly, crossed anchors, and single chevron—identified him as a petty officer third class. E-4. I knew my Navy ranks.

"I wanna join the Navy."

"Well, have a seat, and let's talk."

He planted himself behind the metal desk that would have blended right into the wall had he not been between the two. My undershirt clung to my sweaty chest, and I felt it tighten around me. A second voice to my right stopped me two steps from the offered chair.

"Why do you want to join the Navy?"

Triple chevron—petty officer first class. E-6. This guy walked around his desk against the perpendicular wall to the right. He couldn't have been any older than twenty-five or twenty-six, but my mind projected the image of an admiral. He seemed much older. *Is that gray in his hair? No.*

He asked me again, "Why do you want to join the Navy?"

I knew the answer: *I want to serve my country.* But I was in fourth grade again—too afraid to open my mouth. E-4 tightened his brow, and looked over at E-6, who leaned his ass against the front edge of his desk, and folded his arms across his hard chest.

"Does your mother know you're here?"

E-4 looked back at me—his brow lifted in anticipation.

"I want to serve my country."

I sounded as though I'd just hit puberty at that very moment. A half grunt, half laugh slipped from the throat of E-4. He turned his attention back to E-6 who stared me down.

"You want to *serve* your country."

He looked down at his shoes and examined the one on the right. It lifted from the floor, and slid behind his left calf where he buffed it lightly with a few slow strokes against his sharp-pressed slacks.

"You see that shoe, kid?"

He held it out for me. My eyes were glued.

"If you're not outta here in five seconds, I'm gonna *serve* that shoe to you right up your ass. We'll need to take you to the hospital to have it removed."

E-4 looked at me. I stood frozen in wide-eyed, slack-jawed stupor. Given the opportunity, I knew I could reason this through—convince E-4 and E-6 of my resolution to serve my country and make the Navy proud. My throat tightened as I forced what felt like a paper football through it. All of the oxygen had left the office.

"GET THE HELL OUT OF HERE!"

E-6's ass pulled away from the desk and I tripped over myself as my feet spun and stumbled me toward the exit. My chest hit the door. I'd been moving too fast to spin the knob fully. The cool air of the outside world hit me hard when I'd finally figured out the complicated device that would separate me from a rectal exam by a shiny, black size-ten.

"Fucking kids."

That was the last thing I'd heard before the door shut behind me. A glance through the large, plate-glass window revealed E-4 and E-6 pissing themselves at my expense. I gave them a steady finger that I was certain Uncle Sam would only have shown the Japs a few years before. *Where the hell was that confidence when I'd strolled in?* It didn't matter. I now knew I would never get past that guy. *Screw the Navy.* I understood that the Marine Corps was looking for a few good men. Better preparation was called for, though, before I headed to the recruiter on Fulton Street in Brooklyn.

"I'm gonna join the Marine Corps Reserves," I said.

Junior Sheehan looked at me like I had two heads. I got the impression he didn't see an eight-pointed, brimmed, Marine Corps-issued utility cover on either one of them. I'd met up with him at the corner of Nevins Street, right on the other side of the Carroll Street Bridge over the Gowanus Canal when he'd checked out of work. Now we made the left on Bond, just two short blocks from his home on 2nd Street.

"Why the reserves?"

"I figure I'll get less crap if I go that way. I can do inactive reserves. They get a recruit and, for the time being, nothing really changes for me."

"Then what's the point?"

"I'll switch to active duty later when nobody's looking up my ass." *Or threatening to put a shoe up it*, I didn't add.

He looked at me with the wisdom of a man with two long years on me. "You're still gonna have to prove that you're eighteen. Which you're not."

I handed him my permission slip. He stopped walking and examined it closely.

"October 22, 1929? Where the hell did you get this?"

"It's Eileen's."

Junior knew my sister, Eileen. They were the same age and, over the years, had attended many classes together.

He looked back down at the birth certificate, and ran a gentle finger across the name.

"That's your name."

We walked again. I so wanted to play it cool, but, despite my best efforts, the smile worked its way across my face.

"Pretty good, huh?"

"Wow, Joe, this might work."

He looked back up at me and his grin faded.

"But, boy oh boy, you still look like a kid. I mean, you look young for your *real* age."

I took the birth certificate back.

"Screw you. I look my age."

"Whatever. That's still not enough."

"That's where you're gonna help," I said as we made the right on 2nd. "I'm hoping some of your age rubs off on me."

"Whadda ya talking about?"

"It's time for you to do something, too. You gonna work at a warehouse on the canal all your life? You gonna live in this shitty place? Join with me."

"You're crazy."

"I'm going down there tomorrow and sign up. If I change my mind, I don't ever have to go active. Nothing changes."

"You're still in diapers. If you change your mind, you can get out. I'm eighteen. I can't change my mind."

"I'm not gonna get out. I need to get out of here."

He sat down on the stoop in front of his apartment. I leaned on the banister.

"Whad'ja do to get that?"

He was referring to the bruise on the side of my head not far from my right eye. I knew he'd seen it as soon as we met up, but he hadn't said anything. Junior was good like that. I had caught him shake his head and purse his lips just the slightest. He wasn't my old man's biggest fan.

It'd happened the night before. Supper had been going pretty well. My father hadn't been drinking, and my mother and I were talking about my sister, Eileen, who was out with one of her girlfriends.

"She spends her money like water," Ma said.

"She's a girl, Ma. She needs those pretty dresses to get a husband." I said this as I reached for my glass, but I'd been looking at my mother. The back of my hand pushed the glass over, and cool milk streamed across the table. The back of the old man's fist came across my face before I'd even seen it coming.

"What the hell is the matter with you? You know what that shit costs?"

"Yeah, I know what that shit costs. I put more groceries on this table than you do."

"Holy shit. You said that?" Junior Sheehan's eyes were wide in disbelief.

"Hell, no. But I thought it. I just looked at him like an idiot. Told me to get the fuck outta there. That's what I'm doing."

"I woulda clobbered that fuck. When are you gonna stand up for yourself?"

"That's what I'm doing tomorrow when I get to the Marine recruiter."

"What you need to do is beat the crap outta that guy."

"He's still my father. I'd love to, but I can't. It'd kill my mother. Honor thy father—ya know?"

"Honor thy father, my ass. That's bullshit. How 'bout eye for an eye? And when's the last time you seen the inside of a church, Mr. High And Mighty?"

At the mention of 'eye,' I felt a throbbing pain behind the one close to where that punch had landed. Junior was right, though; I'd lost interest in church—another thing that would have killed Ma if she'd known. They say converted Catholics are the best Catholics, and my mother was living proof. She'd made the switch from the Protestant faith long before I'd been born, and stuck with it through the loss of four children. If anything, that probably deepened her faith. I don't really know—it'd been well before my time. But as sure as the sun would rise, and my father would spend the grocery money on liquor, I saw her faith as a constant. She'd say a full rosary every night before bed—sometimes two. If she fell asleep before she'd finished, she would wake up with those beads still in her hands, and finish her prayers before getting up. Oh yeah, she was a good Catholic. On Sunday mornings, I'd head out to Church at the usual nine o'clock, but she'd already be home from the six-thirty mass and have us all fed.

Finding something to do in Carroll Gardens (sounds nicer than it is) on a Sunday morning when I was supposed to be at church was easy enough. I'd usually play sewer-to-sewer ball with a broken broomstick and a dimpled rubber ball if somebody had one. There was nothing like the feeling of hitting that ball solid, and running the bases—off the first sewer cap in the middle of the road (home plate), touch a car bumper for first, round the next sewer cap down the street for second, another bumper for third, and back for a home run. That'd get my mind off the potential punishment for skipping church. One time, I'd hit the ball through Joe The Butcher's front window. *Shit.* There was no running and hiding from this. Joe was a good guy—a friend. I had to go face him. I knew that my father was going to kill me three times for this one: Once, for breaking the window. The second, for not running and hiding (which would bring the expense of a new window to our household—even though he'd make me pay, it was money that would have otherwise gone to my mother, leaving him to spend his own on liquor). My third death would come for playing ball while I was supposed to be at church. My father only went to church for baptisms, weddings and funerals. That was a big enough strain on his time. But we kids had better get our asses down there, and pray for our mother, our souls, and his good health, so he could go down to Mannix's Bar on Sunday afternoon.

I had to go get Joe The Butcher from his apartment above the store. We met on the stairs. He'd heard the racket of breaking glass through the open window of his apartment, and had been on his way down to investigate.

"I'm sorry, Joe. I broke your window."

"Okay, Joe. Let's go take a look. What happened?"

"I hit the ball through it."

"Home run?"

"Foul ball."

"Humph. Mighta been worth it for a home run, Joe."

He was making this too easy on me. We reached the storefront where broken glass from the huge window was spread all over the floor. Junior and a couple of the guys leaned against a Ford across the street. They'd kept just enough room between the broken window and themselves to leave the blame for me, while not looking like cowards—a delicate balance.

"Oh, that's a good mess, Joe."

"I'll clean it up, Joe."

"We'll clean it together, Joe."

"I'm gonna pay you for this, somehow, Joe. You gotta tell my dad?"

"This one's on me, Joe. No need to tell your dad."

Joe The Butcher knew my father, and I'm sure he'd also realized what this would have meant for me if my father had found out. Joe protected me that day, and I still love him for it. He'd had the window replaced that afternoon, and never asked for, or received, a dime from me. I should have tried a little harder.

Junior was still sitting on the stoop. I pushed myself off the banister.

"I'm going to the recruiter on Fulton Street first thing tomorrow."

"Okay. Stop here on your way."

"You're going?"

"What else am I gonna do?"

I couldn't believe how easy this was. Then I said the stupidest thing that ever came out of my mouth.

"No. I don't want you to do this for me."

Of course, I did. I wanted him to do it for himself, too, but it certainly occurred to me that having a friend to do it with would make it easier. When the time came to report for active duty, it would be comforting to bring a piece of Brooklyn with me. What better piece to bring than a good friend like Junior Sheehan? I felt instant guilt, though.

"I'll do it myself. Go to work tomorrow."

"Jeez, Lynch, screw your head back on. One minute you're begging, next you're talking me out of it. Do me a favor, and don't think so damn high of yourself. I'm sick of this place. This is for me. My only other choice is American Can. Paddy's brother, Mike, is gonna get me a job over there. Can you imagine?"

"Making tin cans for the rest of your life? Shit, Junior, I may have just saved your life."

He gave a shove to the back of my head.

"Go tell your Mommy the good news, Joey."

I took a few skips backwards toward Bond Street and gave Junior a double, middle-finger salute. We both laughed aloud. Then I turned and sprinted as fast as I could around the block to our apartment. The adrenaline raced through me like no drug I had ever experienced. The Marine Corps Hymn played in my head into the wee hours when I'd finally fallen asleep.

It had been a mild fall season to this point. Now, with the temperature at least ten degrees below that of the previous day, I wondered if we'd have a White Christmas this year. That'd be good by me. I figured it would make my mother happy, too. The thermometer outside Joe's butcher shop read a solid thirty when I shivered past it on the way to Junior's.

"Shit, Joe, you sure this isn't an omen?"

"It'd have to be a cold day in *Hell.*"

"Okay then. Let's do this."

The train was packed this time of day. Junior and I snaked our way through silent commuters headed to offices, factories, construction jobs, and schools (teachers, administrators, and students). We found a spot in the aisle where we squeezed together in between an older woman and a guy in a business suit, and grabbed the overhead handles. The train jerked forward, and I bumped the woman who stood snug against my right arm.

"Pardon me, ma'am."

She pursed her lips into a half smile of acceptance. Older than my mother, she was dressed too nice for factory work, not quite as sharp as I would expect for an office job. Something about her said menial work—maybe housekeeping at a hotel. I didn't spend too much brain energy trying to figure it out. Train etiquette says to act like the others aren't there, even though we all share intimate space. As the train rushed out of the station, I'd steadied myself against the sudden jerks and sways of the car—something you just grow accustomed to as a seasoned rail rider. Below me, a young professional in his twenties sat in the aisle seat staring into space.

For me, there was always a certain discomfort about having a seat when the train was filled, and so many people stood around me in the aisle. It bordered on guilt. It felt nice to sit, but I'd almost rather stand and let someone else take a load off.

"Hey, buddy," I said to Mr. Young Professional.

He continued to look ahead.

"Excuse me, sir."

He looked up, almost in disbelief that I'd broken the rules—maybe that was my imagination. I glanced at Junior whose thoughts I *could* read: *Really? You know the rules.* His expression was unmistakable.

Back to Young Professional: "Maybe this lady would like that seat."

I cocked my head to the woman next to me, and Young Professional turned back to stare at the beehive hairdo in front of him. Not a word. No expression change. No, "Fuck off." The woman looked out the window adjacent to the seat two rows back. Maybe she thought, *Thanks for trying.* Perhaps, *You shouldn't have broken the rules.* Junior smirked and shook his head. *You're a real pisser, Joe.* Again, I'd only needed to read his thoughts.

At the next stop, everyone shifted as commuters circulated on and off the train. The woman next to me squirmed her way past me. Eye contact was short but purposeful.

"Thank you."

Her words were more mouthed than spoken. Acknowledgement feels good.

When the train was off again, I said to Junior, "When we get there, we need to be confident."

"*You* need to be confident," he said. He tapped the folded paper peaking out of his breast pocket. "I've got a legitimate birth certificate. My boss knows why I'm gonna be late. My mom and pop know where I am this morning."

Now, Mr. Young Professional is interested in what I have to say. A short stare-down sent him back to his own world.

"Right. Just back me up if I get in a spot."

"What are you gonna tell him if he asks about the shiner?"

"That I beat the crap out of a couple of Spics."

Junior glanced around the car. "What if he's Puerto Rican, asshole?"

"You think?"

"How the hell do I know? You think all Marines are Irish?"

Junior had a way about him. Without saying it, he'd just call me out. *You don't talk like that. Why now?* I guess I was just working up the confidence.

"How 'bout, I got hit with a baseball—no big deal."

"That's it," he said. "What's the word? Understated. Understated confidence. Don't be a big shot."

"Yeah, okay. I like that. I'll be understated."

The single poster at the Marine Corps Recruiting Station depicted three proud Marines in dress blues. Emblazoned upon it in big block letters was the statement, *ONLY EIGHTY THOUSAND MAY SERVE.*

I mustered my best understated confidence and boomed, "You can take that down now. I'm here." *What a badass.*

Junior was still pulling the door shut behind me. Only I could hear him mutter, "Jesus Christmas."

Shit.

The two Marines shared a sideways glance. As best I could tell, their stripes indicated Sergeant and Staff Sergeant.

"What can we do for you men?" That was Sergeant.

"We're here to enlist in the reserves," Junior said, jumping in to take the lead. "Inactive."

"I'm Sergeant James Skopek. Call me Skopes." Handshakes followed. "This is Staff Sergeant Hector Rodriguez." Now, Junior and I shared a sideways glance.

"You may call me Hector for now."

"Joe and Timothy," Junior said.

"What? Timothy? I thought your name was Junior?" I was dumbfounded.

"It's Timothy, you lug. Timothy D. Sheehan, Jr.—I go by 'Junior.'"

"It's no wonder, *Timothy*. Don't even tell me what the D stands for."

"Okay. Have a seat, men."

Everyone settled in: Skopes behind his desk, and Junior and me in front of it. Hector pulled the chair from behind his desk, and situated himself close to Skopes's. Hector squared on me.

"What happened to your face, Joe?"

That was fast. Junior lightly tapped my shoe with his.

"Um, baseball. No big deal."

Another sideways glance between the recruiters. *Stop that.*

"Yeah. No big deal. I like that. How old are you guys?"

"Eighteen," in unison.

"Good." Hector looked right at me, again. "Of course, we'll need documentation. Birth certificates?"

Junior wasted little time. He snatched his birth certificate out of his pocket, leaned across me, and handed the document to Hector. I pulled mine out, and held it with clammy hands while I watched Hector examine Junior's.

"Good."

He handed it to Skopes who gave it a cursory look, and dropped it on the desk. With another look from Hector, I handed over mine.

Eternity. *Is he taking longer with mine?* The four fingers of his left hand remained immobile on the underside of the birth certificate, but the thumb slid up and down on the front surface. *It's not Braille, mister.* The Gowanus Canal pooled in my armpits. I briefly wondered if the Marines put civilians in the brig. *Do Marines have brigs? Focus.*

"Okay." He handed it to Skopes. "Check them against the birth records."

Both Junior and I remained stoic, and resisted the urge to look at each other. Skopes got up and pulled an impossibly large book from the metal shelves behind him. He dropped it on the desk with what must have been a thick thud, but, to me, sounded strangely like a cell door slamming shut. These guys now resembled uniformed versions of Mrs. Corizzo. I pulled my stomach together. *I got this.*

Skopes allowed large groups of pages to drop from his right hand as he made his way through the bulk of the book. Then, with a glance at Junior's birth certificate, flipped individual pages until settling on one, and scanned the page with his left index finger.

"There we are." A couple of looks between the book and the certificate. "Timothy is good."

Huh! Timothy. You think you know someone. Junior looked at me—a dare to say it aloud.

Skopes moved my birth certificate atop Junior's and flipped a couple of chunks of pages to the Ls, and then to the Lynchs.

"A lot of Lynchs in Brooklyn."

"Yeah, Lynch is like Smith in Ireland."

Junior had to have been surprised by the calm in my voice.

Skopes looked up at me from the book and then continued scanning the names. Flip the page, then back.

"Not here." He looked at me, then Hector, then me. "You're not in here."

Junior leaned in to speak, and I returned his foot tap from earlier.

"Huh. Is Eileen Lynch in there?"

Skopes looked from me to Hector and back to the book. His neck must've been getting sore. Hector leaned in for a look himself.

"Yeah, Eileen Ruth Lynch. October 22nd, 1929."

Now, they both looked at me for meaning. Junior wore an *I'm waiting* expression, as well.

"Eileen is my twin sister." I'd swear that Junior coughed, but I was too far in the zone to care.

Hector took another look at the entry, and then picked up my birth certificate. I had no idea which way this was going to go, but I'd given it my best shot.

"Well, I guess if you and Eileen are twins, you must be at least as old as her. Eh, Joe?"

"At least."

"Okay. Birth Certificate says Oct 22, 1929. Good enough for me."

Skopes shut the book, and we got to talking about our futures.

"He knew!"

"No, he didn't," I said. "Understated confidence."

We made our way back toward the train station after an hour of Marine Corps history, standards, pride, physical requirements, and on and on. I sat through the whole thing, and registered not a bit. Mostly, I wondered about how long to wait before coming back and switching to active. A week? A month? Two months? Tomorrow?

"Oh, he knew. And he let you in, anyway."

"He didn't know, Timmy."

"Don't do that."

"Sorry."

"You knew about the book, didn't you?"

"I seen the books at the Navy office. Made my balls tighten. Never got that far, though."

Junior slapped a hand on my shoulder, and squeezed. "I gotta say, you played it good."

"Thanks for not choking to death."

"Hey, this Marine got your back, pal."

We walked another half block in silence.

"I'm telling you, he fucking knew."

CHAPTER 5

Shitbirds From Yemassee

I DIDN'T FEEL MUCH LIKE a Marine. Junior Sheehan and I had made it through our physicals, and my shady birth certificate had passed muster one more time. Yet, nothing changed. I'd continued to crank out completed window blinds for Jimmy to install, play Alphabet Soup with the trains deep under the city, receive harsh disciplinary action at the hands (and belt) of my father, eat home cooked meals, but as yet, hadn't even been measured for a uniform.

Weeks turned to months, turned to years—seasons came and went. That's the way it had seemed, anyway. In actuality, I'd held out for about forty days. All I'd had to say to Junior was, "Let's go." Maybe it was the weather—it was early February, 1948, and the cold wasn't letting up. It could have been American Can—he'd started working there shortly after we'd seen the recruiter, and he didn't seem too keen on the job. Why would he? Or perhaps it'd been the same routine, in the same neighborhood, with the same run-down buildings, and the never-ending stench of oil, chemicals, shit, and dead bodies emanating from Lavender Lake.

He shrugged and said, "I'm ready."

My secret had remained secure the entire time. Two parents, five brothers, one sister, a bunch of neighborhood friends and Joe The Butcher—no one was the wiser. Junior's family knew he'd joined, but as best as I could tell, he'd kept my secret. I never doubted him.

We made our way back to speak to Staff Sergeant Rodriguez and Sergeant Skopek—as soon as we'd put our John Hancocks on the dotted lines, all familiarity had been done away with, and Hector and Skopes were nevermore.

The sergeants required no explanations.

"We'd like to change our status to active duty."

"Very good. We'll do the paperwork, and you'll be notified in a week or two with a report date."

That was it. All business. Those final weeks were the toughest. Until this point, we had committed to do nothing. We'd enlisted without joining. Had the need manifested, they could have come looking for us at any time, but the end of World War Two was only a couple years behind us, and our country wasn't likely to get itself in another war anytime soon. The United States was tired of war, and so was the world. But, now, we were about to eat the cake we'd already baked a month and a half before.

I quit my job within that week of changing my status with the Marine Corps. Everyday, I made sure that I was at the front stoop when the mail came. Mike, the mailman, had to know something was up—he'd dropped the mail directly in my hands more times in that two-week period than the entire previous year.

"Joe, what are you doing with yourself these days?"

"Not much, Mike."

"Yeah, that's what I figured. Ain'tcha cold out here on the stoop?"

"Nah. I like this weather."

I was freezing my ass off. Good thing it was cold, though, otherwise my mother might be out here with me. She and a couple of lady friends along with her sister who lived across the street liked to pull their kitchen chairs out to the sidewalk for a visit and some gab. That wouldn't happen again for a couple months, thank God.

The Department of the Navy, United States of America—no mistaking that return address. I'd shoved the letter in my jacket and brought the rest of the mail inside. Jimmy hadn't ratted me out yet for quitting the job. He was making a life with his new wife, Pat, and didn't come around for the free meals so much anymore. Neither he nor my parents had a phone. You'd think he'd stop in to say "Hi" to his mother once in a while, but I was glad for his bad manners. Ma hadn't even noticed that I'd been getting home a bit early from *the job*. Until today.

"Why ya so early, Joey?"

"Not as much work at the factory." Not nearly as much.

"Please tell me Jimmy is still working."

"Oh yeah, Ma, he's working. Jimmy's the best installer they got."

"Good. He needs to take care of that pretty wife now. What are you going to do?"

"I'm going to find something else, Ma. Don't worry."

The letter was burning a hole in my chest and weighing heavy on my heart. I hated to deceive my mother, who wouldn't have the first clue about how to tell a lie.

"I'm gonna go talk to Junior about it now." At least that much was the truth.

Junior sat on his stoop with the letter in his hand. When he spotted me coming down the block, he lifted the letter so that it dangled from one corner, in between his thumb and index finger, and waved it like a southern belle waving her handkerchief. It seemed fitting, as we were about to find ourselves under the Banyans—Spanish moss and all—in rural South Carolina.

"25th?"

"25th," I confirmed.

Well, here's another fine mess you've gotten me into. No, he didn't really say that. I guess my recollection of those times brings that oft-used Oliver Hardy line to mind, because, soon enough after that, Junior didn't seem overly pleased with the decision. It had made me feel bad, but I continued to believe it'd been the right choice—even for him. The positive feelings I experienced—even through boot camp—were not, however, shared by my closest friend, and that left me feeling lonely at times. I'd eventually experience similar feelings with my mother, but I'll get to that. I often wonder how Junior Sheehan's life turned out. Sad to say, but we would lose touch during our Marine Corps service. I like to believe that things went well for him.

For the time being, however, we'd be seeing a lot of each other. Our letters were each the same:

You have been accepted as physically qualified for service with the United States Marine Corps. You are requested to report to the U.S. Marine Corps Recruiting Station, 1413 Federal Office Building, 90 Church Street, New York, N.Y., on 25 February, 1948.

Less than two weeks. The letters went on to share a few bits of useful information, such as what to bring: *very little*. And what not to bring: *everything else*.

February 25th showed up in a flash. I walked out of the apartment that morning knowing damn well that I'd not be back for supper. That, alone, was a lot more than my mother knew. It wasn't a good feeling. The plan was to write her as soon as I got to Parris Island in South Carolina. Those had turned out to be the longest three days of my life. I'd find out they hadn't been *her* best days, either. And, even though my father didn't know that I wouldn't be there that evening for him to berate or bruise, I didn't really give a damn.

Junior and I scooted over to the Marine Corps Recruiting Station on Fulton, and Sergeant Skopek drove us into Manhattan in a Jeep. It was the roughest ride I'd ever loved. Until he caught my eye through the mirror.

"Just remember, boys, you're not Marines till you graduate. Until then you're nothing."

And here I'd thought this lug was our friend.

"So, why can't we call you Skopes then?"

"Free advice, Lynch: leave your wisecracking in this Jeep." He hit a pothole on cue.

Soon enough, I'd learn just how sage that advice actually was. Looking back, maybe he *was* our friend.

90 Church Street was a limestone monstrosity that took up a full city block in lower Manhattan, just north of the original World Trade Center site—of course, back in 1948, the World Trade Center wasn't even a dream. Junior and I had already been here once before for our physicals, but things

were a little different this time. Skopes escorted us to the fourteenth floor, where all branches of the military had offices.

"These boys are the real deal, Mickey, take good care of them."

Mickey, another sergeant, went about his business as though we weren't there. Skopes patted my back and leaned in to me.

"Don't screw up."

My head turned as far as my neck would allow, and I watched my buddy Skopes pass through the door like a young mom leaving her kid for his first day of school. When my head made the return trip to front and center, I noticed that Junior wasn't looking too good.

I gave him a nudge with my elbow and said, "Lighten up. This is good."

He pursed his lips and nodded.

Throughout the day, fifty or more guys showed up from various parts of the city, and things did lighten up. After swearing us in, the Marine Corps treated us to a nice chicken dinner, and put us up at a hotel for the night. I was already feeling part of something, and I liked it. In the morning, we had our second of what would be a string of free meals for the next three years, when Sergeant Mickey put an egg breakfast on the government account at the recruiting station's favorite greasy spoon. I'd wondered if this was what a vacation felt like. That'd be my last meal in New York for a couple months. From the diner, we shipped straight up to Penn Station and boarded a train for South Carolina. I was free.

I had been on a train out of the city before, so this experience was not entirely new to me. But I'd never been on a train without the benefit of my mother holding my hand throughout the process.

Sergeant Mickey put us on the train with simple advice that we had no trouble following: "Be on this train when it pulls into Port Royal."

We weren't long out of the city, when New Jersey turned to country-side. Bare trees and evergreens alike alternated with picturesque and partially snow covered farmlands. From my seat next to the window, my attention split between fellow recruits getting acquainted and the vastness of brick- and concrete-less wonder that lay just beyond the railroad tracks. It was 1948. We'd had no television set to show me this other world, and groceries had been more essential than the magazines that might have reminded me that the universe extended beyond Queens or The Bronx. I might have even gotten a glimpse of the bigger world, if the ferry to Staten Island had not cost more than a trolley-flattened penny.

"Hey, Joe, why don't you tell the guys about our trip down the Gowanus?"

The *Guys* were all shits and grins by this time. Junior'd been yucking it up, and the others were ready for another story that ended in some poor schmuck's humiliation—mine.

"I'm not quite over that yet, Junior. You go ahead."

And he did. All the guys laughed at the right parts, and one dubbed me Lavender Lynch. The staying power of this potential new nickname was wholly dependent on Junior, who took one look at me and decided the incident alone had been traumatic enough without the lasting legacy of a new moniker. So, to my relief, he squelched the new name. I'd laughed with the others on cue, despite my lack of rapt attention. I'd been reminiscing about my only experiences away from the endless surfaces of asphalt, concrete, stone and glass—the childhood summers I'd spent in Pennsylvania during my younger days.

The window seat had been the way to travel for any twelve-year old, too. My mother, sister Eileen, youngest brother Raymond, and I rode the rail out of Penn Station, through New Jersey, and halfway through Pennsylvania to Yeagertown. My three oldest brothers had already gone off to war. Bobby was taking care of himself and, I'd guess, keeping his distance from our father, who was otherwise on his own. The trip had begun by way of this same route—south through Jersey to Philly. This time I'd continue on through Baltimore and DC, and all points south. In 1943, we'd changed trains in the City of Brotherly Love, and railed west through Lancaster to Harrisburg. With the subway experience I'd already had by the time I'd taken that trip, I'm confident I could have done it on my own—same concept, broader reach.

The ride through Pennsylvania proved impossibly magnificent. My only preparation for this had been the few movies I'd gone to with my mother over at the Gloria Theatre on Court St. The black and white picture shows had, through no fault of their own, downplayed the vastness and beauty of life outside Brooklyn. At twelve years old, I'd instinctively understood that such sights could only be captured through the eyes God had given us. Hillside after rolling hillside ambled by. Cows and horses—the first live animals I'd seen that were not cats, dogs, or rats—grazed in fields of grass, only to be replaced by farms of corn and grain that were punctuated by idyllic farm houses, barns, and silos.

On the train of would-be Marines destined for the Semper-Fidelis proving ground of Parris Island, I had wished for the opportunity of a quick side trip that would have revisited my journeys of the past. As we approached Baltimore, I remembered pulling into Harrisburg—the state capital of Pennsylvania—four-and-a-half years before. For us, it had been the gritty, industrial crossroad from which we'd cut through hills and mountains, alongside the wide Susquehanna River by bus in order to make our way up to Yeagertown. Small rural towns slid by with the occasional passenger disembarking or boarding—reminders that life did go on, if not thrive, in these otherwise lost places. As the bus labored up steep inclines and glided down gentle slopes, we caught occasional glimpses of the Juniata River, which led us—at last—to Lewiston, where we disembarked at the town square with it's imposing Civil War Memorial as its centerpiece. It was here that we were greeted by my grandfather, and driven the short, four-mile trip into Yeagertown.

Uncle George Anderson, Ma's only brother had died within a year after returning from World War One. A victim of poison gas during the war, he'd survived where sixteen million others had not, only to succumb to the effects of the deadly compound at home. It was the modest death benefit that would eventually give my grandparents the ability to purchase a home in Yeagertown, far from the rigors of life in Brooklyn and the memories of their lost son. A bedroom community to the Standard Steel Mill just across Kishacoquillas Creek in Burnham, Yeagertown's population at present is 1,050, which I'd have to imagine hasn't changed much from the time I'd first visited my grandparents in '43.

The house on Main Street had been built around 1900, along with the rest of the homes on the road that stretched a full mile and marked the length of Yeagertown. My grandparents had converted the second floor into a rental apartment, complete with a new bathroom. That left only the owners of the home (and their family from Brooklyn) to use the outhouse in the backyard. I'd thought that was the greatest thing in the world—until about day two. At least we hadn't visited in the winter.

From the front porch, we could see—through the trees across the street— sections of the massive steel mill right on the other side of the creek. Grandpa had only needed to walk a block to the bridge on Mill Street in order to cross over to his job with the rest of the populations of Yeagertown and Burnham. Before and after the war, the principal product had been train wheels. I'd been proud to learn that my grandfather had produced gun barrels and tank parts at the mill for the war effort. Even this Swedish immigrant from Brooklyn had been doing his part.

It took me a while, but I'd met some other boys my age. We'd do many of the same things that the boys in Brooklyn did—stickball, softball, football— but, it seemed, with much more air to breathe, certainly more trees to climb, and, if I'd happened to fall in the creek, much less crap to smell like. Staying out of trouble seemed best. As the saying goes, *Yes, the boys in Yeagertown do bad things, but they always admit their deeds. That's because everybody knows everybody, and somebody's going to find out anyway.* It was much easier to get away with stupid things—busting lights in the subway stations, steeling rides on the trolleys, nicking an apple off the produce cart—in Brooklyn, where anonymity often enough ruled.

Of my short life up to the time I'd boarded the train for Parris Island, Yeagertown had provided my fondest memories. Two summers out of Brooklyn and away from my father. It was a carefree and stress-free life. I'd spend the better part of my working life under the assumption that I'd go back there to live one day, even if that meant waiting until retirement. Perhaps I'd get a place on Main Street, or closer to town—our reference to Lewiston—where

I'd eaten my first meal in a restaurant and seen the occasional movie at the Embassy Theater. The Embassy was adjacent to the halcyon town square with the Civil War monument that seeded my fascination with that turbulent period in history. Assumptions are like arithmetic problems, though—sometimes they just don't work out the way you'd expect.

We'd arrived at our drop-off point in Port Royal, South Carolina to fanfare—in the form of a blunt, loud, and annoyed drill instructor, who had been expecting us three hours earlier. *Shitbirds.* It seemed this was his favorite word, and we'd hear it an awful lot over the next twelve weeks. Turns out, that's what Sergeant Dean thought we were—*Shitbirds. Shitbirds from Yemassee.* It didn't matter to me, though. I'd been called worse.

CHAPTER 6

The Bed I Made

YEMASSEE, SOUTH CAROLINA WAS THE last stop before Port Royal and the short bus ride into Parris Island. Every Marine recruit came through Yemassee, unless they had second thoughts. In that case, it was their final opportunity to jump the train and get lost in the Lowcountry. We'd picked up several groups along the way: Baltimore, DC, Richmond, Florence, and Charleston—Shitbirds of a feather. Not a one flew the coop.

Sergeant Dean wanted to have his fun with us before he transferred us over to Parris Island by bus, and I'd found it amusing. He'd played the mean-and-nasty routine with us as soon as we stepped off the train, but I was just a kid and I still had my sense of humor (thankfully, I've managed to keep it all my life). I took his harassment for an act. In the end, that's really all it ever was, but I'd learn the act could get personal at times. I'd known enough that day in Port Royal, to keep my laughs to myself.

The New York recruits all bussed over to Parris Island together. There were almost enough of us for a full platoon. It all became real as we lumbered through the main gate. No clowning now. Shitbird silence.

"Get your shitbird asses off that damn bus."

Drill instructors (DIs) were the loudest human beings I'd ever experienced to date. Sergeant Nethery, Sergeant Dean's boss, stormed around us as we ambled through the bus door.

"Good Lawd, they sent me a whole bus loada New Yawkas. What the hell am I supposed ta do with all you New Goddamn Yawkas?"

Shitbirds? New Goddamn Yawkas? I wanted to laugh so badly, and I'd bet dollars to donuts that every other guy I'd just spent the last twenty-four hours on the train with wanted to laugh just as much. Survival instinct, however, held us together. None of us so much as looked at each other for fear of losing it and capturing the attention and ire of the one man who was in uniform.

We got processed in quickly. Our hair was shaved to the scalp. I'd still not been measured for a uniform, and the clothing we did receive had merely been thrown at us by a corporal.

"Get your goddamn uniforms on, you New York shitbirds."

Everything was a size too large, including the hat, but I'd kept that information to myself. We exchanged uniforms later, and most of us ended up with clothes that fit.

"Now, get your shitbird asses in there and write your mamas. You tell her you got yourself a new mama now. You understand me? I said, 'Do you understand me?'"

We understood, and I was anxious to do just that.

The letter had been written dozens of times in my head—while assembling window blinds, walking the cold streets of Brooklyn, in the Marine Corps-provided hotel room in Manhattan, and on and off during the twenty-four-hour train ride to the mosquito-infested swamps of the South Carolina Lowcountry. Now, I sat on my bunk without the slightest clue about how to start. How do I tell my mother I'm gone? How do I tell her that I left without a word, and knew how worried she'd be? How do I tell her that I've joined the Marines, and that I couldn't come home even if I wanted to? And then tell her that I hope she will be proud of her sixteen-year-old kid who is now a man? *Just write it.*

Dear Mom,

I hope you are well. I have joined the Marine Corps, and am at boot camp in South Carolina. I hope you have not been too worried. Junior Sheehan is here with me, and we are excited about becoming Marines. Our drill instructors are swell. I should be able to come

home for a visit after I graduate in twelve weeks. Say hi to Raymond
for me.

With love,

Joe

That wasn't so bad. The truth is, I'd gone to bed more worried that night, and
for the next week—until I'd finally heard back from her—than at any other
time during the entire process of enlisting and getting there. The whole reason I hadn't told her before I'd left, or just set a letter on my bed on my way
out the door, was that she could have stopped me in my adolescent tracks.
My John Hancock on the enlistment papers didn't matter for a hill of beans.
I wasn't old enough to have a John Hancock. One word from her, and that
hill of beans would have crashed down right alongside my short-lived Marine
Corps career. And it still wasn't too late. She could waltz into that recruiting
office on Fulton and guide Hector and Skopes by their ears to a glance at my
real birth certificate. One look from those guys, and Sergeant Nethery would
have chased this Shitbird from Yemassee back to New Goddamn Yawk just as
fast as my scrawny wings could carry me.

I liked boot camp. I'll say that again, because you won't hear it from too
many recruits: *I liked boot camp.* It's true. The drill instructors gave us constant crap. Nothing we did was ever right. They worked us like the shitbirds
they saw us as. Make your bed—they'd pull it apart, and have you make it
again. Drills and physical training before breakfast—you'd better have your
ass down when doing those push-ups. Run a few miles with a sixty-pound
pack on your back, and don't you dare slow down. You got a reason to smile?
"Wipe that shit off your face!" It was a living hell from the first, but I liked it.
I enjoyed the discipline, because it meant something. It had purpose. It shaped
me, and I felt it right out of the box. I was part of something important, and
I knew right away that the work and the grief were all to my benefit. I was
aware that, because of my age, I had better keep up, so I worked hard. The

sense of accomplishment fed me like no food ever could. I stayed sharp and disciplined, and I excelled. These guys thought they could give me crap, but they didn't give me half the crap my father had given me—crap with no purpose. Those DIs didn't know what crap was. I was good with this.

Well, there was that one time…

We'd been in boot camp for almost a week. Our platoon had been marched over to the dental clinic so they could check out our choppers. We'd been lined up in alphabetical order outside the door, and then we waited for an eternity to see the dentists. Nethery and Dean were inside, and with the name *Lynch*, I was somewhere in the middle of the line. As each man finished his examination, he'd come back outside and stand at attention. Every so often, the DIs would check on them. I finally saw a dentist, sat through X-rays, and endured the poking and prodding.

"Next."

I walked outside, squinted into the sun, and replaced my cover. Over half the guys who'd gone through before me were in formation, standing at attention, with eyes front and center. My DIs were inside. Big shot that I am, I walked down the three steps, and offered my compadres some respite.

"Stand down, men." God, I could be funny sometimes.

Now, if this had been a movie over at the Gloria Theater in Brooklyn, a heavy hand would have landed on my shoulder. An awkward pause would have followed, during which my eyes would have popped wide, and I'd have studied the shocked faces of my fellow boots. Some of those men would have shielded their eyes with a hand, and looked to the ground. Other faces would have drawn up in silent, *eek!* And a few would have slowly shaken their heads from side to side. Then I'd have had another second or two during which I'd swallow a big, throaty gulp.

But this was no movie. The hand grabbed my shirt by the back of the collar, and swung me back toward the clinic door in one fluid motion. I'd been dragged up the stairs—stumbling and searching for footing—before I'd even known who had hold of me, or why my body had lost all control. A drill instructor from one of the other platoons in attendance kicked the door open and shoved me through, and my body stopped just short of crashing into

Sergeant Dean. I stood at rigid attention while one DI explained to the other what he had just witnessed.

"Oh, you're a funny shitbird, aren't you, Lynch? You just bring the house down in Yemassee, don't you?"

He tossed me up to the wall, kicked my legs out into spread eagle like a cop about to frisk a perpetrator, shoved my face against the wall, and ordered me to stay there, hands behind my back, for the duration. The longer I stood in this position, the more my nose compressed. The pain increased exponentially until I could stand it no more. I put one hand flat against the wall and pulled my head back for relief. That lasted the better part of a half second. Dean's hand crashed against the back of my head, and my face met the wall with a crack. The blood streamed, and the room silenced. I wondered how these guys always managed to be directly behind me.

"Awww, shit!"

Dean pulled me back, and he and Nethery assessed the damage to my face. Broken nose and a gusher. They laid me down, and stopped the bleeding. Then I cleaned myself as best I could. There was going to be no trip to the medic. Dean knew that—even by the Old Corps standards of 1948—he'd gone too far, and would be in some shit of his own. I could have reported him, but the sergeants had made it clear that I'd be put in another platoon and would be set back at least a week, because I'd be starting over. Besides, Junior was in *this* platoon. I was staying right where I was. So, we had ourselves a stalemate, with only one thing to do: make like it never happened. He sent me out to stand in formation with the rest of the shitbirds. If only I'd listened to my buddy, Skopes, back in Brooklyn and left that great Lynch sense of humor in his Jeep.

The worst form of humiliation is that moment when someone steals your thunder, and rubs your face in it like a dog's nose in his own crap. I came back outside, and my eyes locked with Junior's after he'd seen the blood on my shirt. He'd still been in line awaiting his turn with the dentist. The expression remained stoic, but the eyes said it all: *We're not in Brooklyn anymore, Joe.* It might have been my imagination, but I did feel like we could read each other. Whatever he'd been thinking, he just wanted me to watch myself—reel it in a little. Or a lot. I made my way past the rest of the guys and fell into formation. I didn't look for their eyes, nor they mine. Nobody wanted a piece of this, and I couldn't blame them. So, I lived with that broken nose, and my septum is still deviated today.

I left that experience with the understanding that I'd already seen the worst of it. A lot of the guys got fed up with the bullshit, but—from that point on—everything held less power for me. I found out I could tolerate a lot of crap. A DI screaming in your face means nothing when he's already broken your nose. I knew I could do this and taught myself to stifle the occasional urge to cut up. Everything they ordered us to do, I did to the best of my ability, and then I pushed myself even further.

Sergeant Dean marched us out to a swampy area near the rifle range where the sand fleas were ninety degrees past abundant. The damned things would eat you alive. He had us stand at attention, and a half-million hungry fleas swarmed and feasted. We'd stood there twitching and shaking.

"Don't you dare move."

And we didn't.

"You swat at my sand fleas, and so help me, I will swat you. Those fleas gotta eat too, ya know."

The fleas crawled up my nose, and I managed to sniffle and blow out without moving a muscle. I blinked them out of my eyes, and reminded myself that this was better than a belt buckle across my back. He wanted to see how disciplined we could be, and I think we all handled it pretty well.

During the march back to the barracks, I tried to get Junior's attention, just to give him a wink of acknowledgment for having handled the ordeal like tough guys. He didn't look over at me. *Did he not see me?* Or, maybe he did not *want* any acknowledgment from me? I couldn't tell. He offered nothing to read, and it left me with an uneasy feeling. After we fell out of formation, everyone danced a mangy-dog, slap-and-scratch jitterbug. There'd been quite a number of expletives mixed in with the moans and groans.

"We handled that shit, eh?" I said to Junior.

"Yeah, that was swell, Joe." He tromped into our barracks.

Some of the guys claimed the victory, while others focused on the misery. Junior seemed to be in the latter group. Perception is a personal thing, and I could appreciate his dismay. It had, after all, been a miserable exercise. And Junior had been having a rough time from the very beginning. *Left* and *Right* are, without a doubt, not a matter of perception, and—God help him—that boy could not step off with his left foot for all the tea in my mother's busted china cabinet.

"Forwaaaard hartch!"

Sergeant Nethery gave the command, and seventy-three left feet in platoon 37 stepped off, while one right foot in the formation went along for the ride.

"Your left, your right, your left."

Junior double-skipped in a futile attempt to sync up, only to land on right again when every other man landed on left.

"SHEEEEEEHAAAAN, YOU ASSHOLE! YOU STEP OFF WITH YOUR LEFT FOOT! YOUR LEFT FOOT! YOUR LEFT, GODDAMNED FOOT!" Nethery sidestepped in Junior's face. "THIS IS YOUR LEFT FOOT, SHITBIRD!"

Every time. Day after day. *Your left, your right.* Junior would always do *his right, his left.* It was one of those things that would make a guy laugh, even while he felt pain for his fellow recruit. Some of the others called him *Righty.* I said it once—only once. A fellow didn't have to be Junior's best friend to read the look I got. Shame poured over me, and the forgotten moniker *Lavender Lynch* flowed through my mind.

Junior had not taken well to the realities of boot camp, and it strained our relationship. I don't think he consciously shunned me, but—over time—he'd chummed around with me less. He gradually buddied with the guys who griped the most, which merely served to feed his dislike for the situation. There were times when I'd wanted to break off a broom handle and get him and some of the guys on the parade grounds with a rubber ball—a little taste of Brooklyn. But it was never going to happen at Parris Island. Nethery would have broken that stick across my back.

Nethery's drinking made matters worse. He'd been a sharp drill instructor, and I'd respected him from the start. He was good—he was really good. But he was a drunk. Sometimes, in the middle of the night, Nethery would part with his rye long enough to come in the barracks and rouse us from our sleep for no other reason than to make our lives miserable. When we did our exercises, if he saw a push-up ass too high, he'd throw a rock at it.

"Get that shitbird ass down!"

The rock would never hit the offending ass, though—his aim couldn't find it's bearing through the booze-induced haze. Sometimes, that rock would find Junior's ass, or elbow, or back, even though he'd had some of the sharpest push-ups in the platoon.

Junior did, however, make it through boot camp with the rest of us, and he became a Marine. He'd learned how to subdue his natural inclination to lead off with his right foot, and, finally—on that glorious graduation day—had made everyone proud when seventy-four left feet showed their best stuff to the brass in the reviewing stand and to the visitors in the bleachers. I'd swear an audible sigh of relief could be heard throughout Platoon 37. But everything that Junior Sheehan and I shared as best friends from Brooklyn had faded. We'd each get our orders and go our separate ways as *used-to-bes*. Three years later, I'd reconnect with Junior again on our old battleground of Parris Island. I'd been sent back there to taunt and teach young shitbirds of my own, and he'd been in Intelligence at the time. We'd caught up, had a couple of laughs, shook hands, and patted each other's backs as might be expected of old friends. But that was the last time I would ever see or hear from Junior Sheehan. We all have a small bag of sad stories to tell. This one takes up an excessive amount of space in mine.

Early on at boot camp, though, my sad-story bag overflowed with images of my mother. Eight days after I'd written to her, I received her return letter. I'd spirited away to my bunk with it. As long as she was proud of me or happy for me, I knew I could handle anything else she had to say. She'd been worried, yet so filled with pride when my brothers had enlisted, so I looked forward to my piece of that. I opened the letter and read:

Joey,
You've made your bed. Now, you can sleep in it.

My heart pounded in my throat. I flipped the single page over, and then back. That was it: *You've made your bed. Now, you can sleep in it.* She hadn't even signed it. No, *Love, Mom.* No, *Love always,* which is how she'd always sign a letter. I was devastated to learn that I'd hurt her so badly that she'd be that cold. I'd felt her pain through my own. The only bright spot in her terse note, was that she didn't seem inclined to get me out of there. *You've made your bed. Now, you can sleep in it.* Well, the bed I made was easier to sleep in than the one I'd had at home.

No other letters came from my mother until shortly before graduation. In her defense, I hadn't written to her again, either. Mostly, it'd been in the name of avoidance. I'd best avoided her anguish by hearing no more of it. And unwritten pleas of forgiveness wouldn't spur her to turn me in. Her sister, my Aunt Charlotte, did write to me a couple times. She'd obviously known that my mother was upset, and wanted me to have some word from home—one of the great pleasures for anyone doing their time at boot camp. I loved her for it. She, too, avoided the conflict and never wrote of it.

One night, I'd thought it was all over. Nethery walked through the barracks to my bed. Unlike the theatrics of other times—when he'd blast the door open and scream his way through the dorm—this time, he let everyone sleep until he'd reached me. He had new theatrics in store. He jumped on my bed, straddled me, and repeatedly slapped both sides of my face.

"Get your shitbird ass outta this bed."

He reeked of alcohol. Through my confusion, I prayed that he not puke on me.

"I got some papers in my office for you to sign. You better have your ass there in two minutes."

Every wide-awake eye in the room was focused on him as he stormed off, and then they watched me get dressed—in a New Yawk hurry.

Oh, shit. He knows. I'd thought it while he was still atop me, and I thought it as I shoved my legs through my slacks. One look at Junior confirmed it.

Oh shit. He knows. Junior didn't have to say a word.

She told. Shit! He knows I'm sixteen.

Nobody else in the platoon knew. Their expressions said, *What the hell did you do, Joe?*

Then, as I'd passed him, Pete Sampson said, "See ya, kid."

I spun back to Junior, and he became suspiciously interested in his blanket. He'd told Pete. How many others? I surveyed the eyes on my way to the door, but got nothing. Had one of these rats turned me over? Did Junior? The thought was too much. I'd gone from sweet dreams to paranoid nightmare in about a minute-thirty flat.

Shit, shit, shit, shit, all the way to Nethery's office. I rapped on his door.

"What?"

Jesus Christmas! How many other recruits did he slap the shit out of at two-thirty in the morning? I snapped to attention—as well as my rubber legs would allow—in front of the closed door, and boomed louder than necessary, "Sir, Private Lynch reporting as ordered, sir!"

"Get your ass in here."

When I opened the door, Sergeant Nethery took a sip of his beloved rye. As calm as a nun in the confessional, he said, "Here, I need you to sign these discharge papers. Come over here."

My throat closed. Pleading, begging—pouring him another drink—wouldn't change a thing. He couldn't let a sixteen-year-old kid stay in the Marines. I'd sign it, go back and get my things, and wait for my ride to the train station somewhere far from Junior Sheehan, Petey Boy, and all the others. I stepped up to the desk and took the papers in one hand, the proffered pen in the other, and read the heading at the top: *Discharge from the United States Marine Corps Reserve.*

Confusion set in. "Reserves, sir?"

"You think you're getting outta the goddamned Marines, shitbird? Them assholes who bagged you up in New Yawk City never got you to sign the discharge. Just do it, and get outta my sight. Got no business being outta your bunk this time a night."

"Yes, sir!"

Inside of five seconds, my ass was out the door with my copy of the discharge in hand. *Discharge from the Reserves. Jesus Christmas!* As soon as they'd been sure that Nethery hadn't followed me back, every guy in the platoon sat up in his bunk.

"What happened?"

"Everything okay?"

"What'd you do?"

"What'd he do?"

I held up the paper. "I got discharged."

Not a word. Nothing on Junior's face—he was stunned.

"From the reserves! Ha! They never got me to sign the discharge."

Tony Bledsoe says, "Nethery's an ass. Coming in here like that for such a stupid thing."

I nodded to the door. "Hope he don't have his ear to it." I glanced around then. "But it's true. The jerk coulda waited till morning."

After we'd all settled back in and I had my head back on the pillow, Junior squatted by my bed.

"Pete's the only one, Joe. I swear. And I told him I'd break every bone in his body if he told anyone."

"It's okay, Junior."

"I'm gonna have words with him tomorrow. I should bust his lip."

"Go easy on him."

"Really, I'm sorry, Joe."

"We're good, Junior. Get to bed." And we were good. Nobody'd ever had my back like that guy. We were good as pie.

As graduation grew near, I had decided that there'd be no reason to go home for the ten-day leave we'd earned. I felt that I wouldn't be welcome. With no place else to go, I'd planned on staying at Parris Island until I got my orders. Missing out on what was possibly the most important and exciting break any young Marine would ever experience was a hard pill, but, if my own mother wouldn't have me, there was no point to it. The loneliness of slowly losing my best friend had been dwarfed by the thought of losing my mother. Then, straight from God's hands, the letter came. There was no talk of the past—the hurt. *Happy* and *Proud* jumped off the page. *My Boy Marine* were not words I'd have chosen, but they punctuated the former nicely. There was no mention of forgiveness, yet every word spoke it. Aunt Charlotte must have broken her down—something else to love about her. This sixteen-year-old Marine was going home.

CHAPTER 7

Semper Fi

OTHER THAN BIRTH AND THE occasional stickball game, I'd never completed anything in my life. I came close a couple times with homework, but you know what they say about horseshoes and hand grenades. Yet, here I was with the Eagle, Globe, and Anchor, a symbol of accomplishment that very few *men*—never mind sixteen-year-old kids—get to wear. It meant I was a Marine.

I savored the very moment the train descended below ground—I was home. The dark tunnels, the strobing lights and platforms, the squeal of brakes, the jolts to the left and to the right with each turn, the musty smell that rushed through the opening doors, the commotion of commuters at Penn Station, all filled me with an emotional rush that saturated me to the bones. Until now, I hadn't been aware of the deep sense of homesickness I'd felt. When the G Line emerged south of 3rd Street in Brooklyn, the anticipation I felt was electricity coursing through my conduit veins like the Streamliner through the subway tubes. The neighborhood that rumbled by below looked the same with it's run-down buildings and painted signs, yet it also seemed more beautiful than I'd ever noticed. *God, I must be homesick.* I stepped off the train at 9th Street, and stood in the bright springtime sun, where the pungent odor of the Gowanus Canal assaulted me. *Yeah, I'm home.* That was okay, though, it was all part of the experience.

At the apartment, I struggled for my breath, with my face buried in my mother's neck. That woman could hug. The pain and fear she'd lived with at my leaving flowed down my face in the form of her warm tears. I'd been grateful for her to use the opportunity to get it out. So I let her hold me as long as I could bear, and then pulled back from what today could only be described as the original form of water boarding. With her calm demeanor, Aunt Charlotte's welcome presented a sharp contrast. She'd been in the kitchen with my mother preparing a nice welcome-home meal when I'd arrived. A proud smile, a gentle embrace, and a kiss on the forehead had been the perfect complement to the chest-crushing hold and salt bath from Mama Bear.

"Sorry I made you worry, Ma."

"Oh, my Boy Marine is worried about his mother." She pulled me back in to finish the job.

Three days after returning to Brooklyn, there'd been important business to attend. I laid out my Dress Blues, and put each piece on with careful attention to detail. Before stepping out the door, my mother had inspected me with single-tear-on-the-cheek pride.

"So handsome. Go show'em, Joey."

"Thanks, Ma."

I stepped out on the sidewalk, squared my cover on my head and began the three-quarter mile walk. Joe The Butcher leaned against the jamb in his open door and watched me approach. When I'd gotten close, he took two steps out onto the sidewalk to greet me.

"Well, look at you, Joe. Your ma told me you joined up."

"Hi, Joe." We shook hands.

"She wasn't so happy about it," he said.

"She's good now, Joe."

"Ha! How could she stay mad when she sees you in that get up?"

He slid an index finger under the medal hanging on my chest and examined it.

"Rifle Expert. The neighborhood hooligans should watch out for this guy."

Even Joe The Butcher seemed proud of me, which was more than I could say about my father, from whom I hadn't heard "Boo"—neither while I was in boot camp, nor even since I'd gotten home. If I'm going to be honest, maybe I just hadn't paid attention. He certainly knew he didn't have me to punch around anymore, though.

The salamis hanging in Joe's window seemed to welcome me.

"I finally got some money for that window, Joe."

"You're money's no good here. Unless you need some pork chops. Get something for your ma with that money, big shot."

"Thanks, Joe." I walked on.

"Hey, Joe," He called. When I turned back, he asked, "Where you headed, all pretty and all?"

"I just got some business to take care of while I'm home."

"Oh, business. Gotcha. Go take care of your business, Mr. Marine." He disappeared back into the shop.

The last time I'd been to Nathan Hale Junior High School (PS 6) on Warren Street had been two years before. Ninth grade seemed like another lifetime ago. That should have been a carefree time, but, in reality, it'd been filled with stress and fear. With all the good intentions of a teacher who wanted the best for her students, Mrs. Davis—my English teacher—had only added to my fears of an uncertain future.

"Joseph, you will never amount to anything."

She'd never said it as a put down. Mrs. Davis had wanted me to prove her wrong. For my own good, she'd tried her damnedest to push me to get on the stick and do the work she'd felt me capable of. It'd been too easy, however, for a kid whose self-esteem had been sliding the slippery slope for so long to take her words as prophecy and, therefore, believe them. I'd needed this visit for my own good, as much as to show her she'd been wrong about me. The hall was silent as I'd made my way to the staircase at its center. I glanced in an open classroom door as I passed, and a teacher I hadn't known interrupted her lesson to watch me walk by. There's a natural tendency to walk straighter and taller when wearing the Blues, but I caught myself reaching for a bit more. Riding inside that uniform is indescribable. And that is what it's like—*riding*.

It's as though the uniform does the effortless work of carrying its occupant through time and space. Impossibly shiny shoes walk a cushioned floor, the air in front of the Blues separates so that you slip through fluidly, and the warmth sought by a child fills you through its soft, comforting touch. I could have lived in that uniform.

Taking the stairs two at a time seemed too easy. Perhaps I should have asked the uniform to go for three. When I'd slinked down the second-floor corridor two years before, Mrs. Davis's classroom had been to the left and then through the second door on the right. She still occupied the same space. A firm knuckle to the door, and a quick tuck of my stark-white cover beneath my right arm, presented a classroom-silencing figure of grace and pride. Well, I'd enjoyed that thought, anyway. The classroom, at least, did go silent.

It took Mrs. Davis a good two seconds to study me before her head cocked like a treat-anticipating dog. "Joseph?"

"Yes, ma'am"

She smiled and stood up from behind her desk. Any self-doubt about my mission that had lurked at unreachable depths by the empowering Blues had vanished. As I approached her, I felt the eyes of twenty-two students follow me. My operational objectives had nothing to do with them, so I kept my own eyes on the prize. I learned at a later date that I should have given that classroom a better inspection. There had been a young lady at one of those desks whom I once had a bit of a safe-distance crush on. I know: Here I am a Marine, and I'm talking about having a crush on a Junior High-aged girl. But I was sixteen and she was fourteen—not so creepy.

Barbara Chattman lived across the street from me on 3rd Street. The first time I'd noticed her was in December of 1947, about the time I'd been chased out of the Navy recruiter's office, and afraid that his shoe was going to make contact with my ass. She'd been walking down 3rd Street with a girlfriend who may as well have been a cocker spaniel on a leash for all I'd noticed her. The girl who had caught my attention, however, was stunning, and I could only wonder how I would be able to meet her. I'd always been a shy kid when it came to girls. I'd followed her to her home at number 66 on the corner of Hoyt. A stoop across the street made for a convenient spot from which to watch the second-floor window above the grocery store. I guess I'd been one of the original stalkers. Fortunately, my payoff came soon enough. She'd come to the window, reached out, and pulled something out of a box on the fire escape. I didn't know what she picked out, but I knew about the box. Decembers in Brooklyn had been cold enough to let most folks stop their ice deliveries for the kitchen icebox. Instead, they stored food and drink in an outdoor box to keep them cold. Much later, I'd discover that she'd been retrieving beers—one for each of her parents. I'd stuck around long enough to see her one last time that day at the *refrigerator door*. It was well worth the cold-stoop chill that seeped into my body just to get a glimpse of the young woman who would one day take my name.

Standing in the classroom in front of Mrs. Davis, I'd fought the urge to smile, but I failed miserably.

Unbeknownst to me, fourteen-year-old Barbara had been whispering to the girls around her, "I know that boy. He lives across the street from me. They have a lot of kids." Again, I'd find out about that sometime later.

Mrs. Davis surveyed my uniform. "My goodness, Joseph, you're in the Marine Corps?"

She had always used my proper name, *Joseph*. Even though I was comfortable with the shortened version—everyone but my mother called me *Joe*—I'd always liked the sound of *Joseph* when it rolled off her tongue. In the uniform, I'd felt like a proper *Joseph*.

"Yes, ma'am. Private first class."

"Private First Class, Joseph Lynch. It looks good on you." Then she showed her puppy-dog head cock again, this time accompanied by an expression of concern. "You couldn't have finished school…"

"No, ma'am. But I've completed basic training, and I wanted you to know that I have made something of myself."

The look of concern deepened. "So young for the Marines, Joseph."

My shoes felt tighter as my insides sagged to my feet. Teacher first, of course she would expect nothing less than completion of my education. Who was I kidding? I knew then that this had been an ill-conceived mission. As my heart raced to catch up with the rest of my guts, which had slid down to my lowest extremities, a surge of heat rose to my face. I became aware of all the students who watched.

And then Mrs. Davis smiled. She ran a gentle hand over my single stripe and said, "Sometimes, Joseph, a man must recognize his calling. You cut a fine figure of a Marine, and I know you will excel. I can see that."

The rush of relief left me feeling dizzy. "Thank you, ma'am."

"I was wrong about you. You really have done something with yourself. And I am overjoyed that you chose to come and tell me, Joseph."

I sucked in. My chest expanded. "I... I just wanted you to know, Mrs. Davis. Thank you."

I turned and, with no desire to appear hurried, rushed to the door.

Mrs. Davis's voice caught up. "Thank *you*, Joseph."

I didn't look back.

The rest of the ten days flew by. There were a couple games of stickball with the gang, at least one visit from each of my siblings (who all had their own lives to live now), as well as time spent with my mother and Raymond. Those events chewed up the remaining days, and spit me out on a train back to South Carolina. Ray was only eleven years old, and he'd already started to get the military bug—just as I had done at his age. "Finish school first, kid," was the prudent advice he'd gotten from this seasoned military man who himself wasn't even old enough to have finished getting his own education. Oh well—easier to tell than to do. I don't remember ever noticing my father during that short visit.

When I got back to Parris Island, I received my first orders as a real-deal Marine: Parris Island. *Parris Island?* I'd been assigned as the newest rifle instructor on the range at the toughest training facility in the US Armed Forces. *Rifle instructor?* During boot camp, I'd scored near or at the top of my class with weapons. The truth is, most guys earn that rifle expert medal. We were taught right out of the gate that a Marine is a rifleman first, and that everything else is secondary. So, if you want to be a Marine, you'd better be good with your rifle. But I had excelled, turning in near-perfect results when put to the test. *But still.* I wanted to ask, "Why the hell would you want a sixteen-year-old kid to be your Rifle instructor?" I held my tongue.

Private first class, fresh out of boot camp, and I was treated like a drill instructor. Corporals and sergeants—who had done their time and earned their rank—dealt with me as near-equal. Recruits talked to me like I was a general, just as I had done—only weeks before—when I was in their shoes. I had earned the respect others had spent much more time struggling to attain. *I could get used to this.* But I never did. Although I believed I did the job well, the responsibility stressed me out. While I'd never have admitted to myself that my young age was a factor, the uneasy feeling that I was barking orders at my older brothers was always there. Men who were twenty years of age and older called me "Sir," and it never felt right.

When Platoon 37 had completed our graduation, an astonishing number of the men had pulled out, and pinned on, service ribbons from previous service. As boots, those awards meant nothing to the Marine Corps. As Marines, they were once again permitted to wear them with the honor they deserved. During my twelve weeks at camp, I'd no clue that I'd shared drills with former corporals and sergeants from the Army and the Army Air Corps, or that I exercised and studied with erstwhile petty officers from the Navy. Their previous colors had not been shown until we'd each become Marines. But as an instructor on the rifle range, I understood that within the ranks, there lurked previous non-coms who now bowed to my whim. My biggest fear was that they would peg me for a fraud. I felt fraudulent.

I gave myself a chance to settle in, and did a total of three months at the range, where I worked beside instructors who had—only months before—taught me. I never did settle in. Maybe I'd consider this assignment again in a year or so, but for the time being, this job was best left to the grownups. So, I put in a request for transfer to the Fleet Marine Force, which I knew they'd never refuse. The Marine Corps is always looking for a few good men who are prepared to storm the beaches of distant lands in the event of war. The plan was that they'd send me to Camp Lejeune in Jacksonville, North Carolina, where the fourteen miles of beaches on the base made it the perfect spot for amphibious-assault training. That'd be the optimum assignment, because I'd easily be able to make the occasional trip up to Brooklyn. Who would have guessed that California had beaches, too?

CHAPTER 8

Pendleton

IN AUGUST OF 1948, SHORTLY after my seventeenth birthday, I'd made my new home at Camp Pendleton in San Diego County, California—the farthest possible location in the Continental United States from Brooklyn that they could possibly have chosen for me. And they put me in Artillery. The Marines could be funny that way.

At Pendleton, I became a cannoneer assigned to the 105mm Howitzer. I'd left a cushy job on the range at Parris Island to become a grunt on another range, twenty-five hundred miles due west. Right away, they sent me down to Camp Elliott, for cannoneer school. Elliott is a small piece of what is now Marine Corps Air Station Miramar—also in San Diego County—about fifty miles south of Camp Pendleton. It'd felt like a two-hundred mile motor march. I sat in the back of a truck that traveled sandy, rocky, dusty, bumpy, dirt roads almost the entire distance, and by the time we'd reached Elliott, I felt as though the Navy recruiter had made good on his promise. It hadn't ever appeared that we left Camp Pendleton, because everything looked the same north of the city of San Diego back then. Today, we'd be stuck in traffic on Interstate 15, and it probably wouldn't be that much of a better ride.

At the time, the Korean War was still two years away, and whether they saw it coming or not, the Marines had been getting us ready for it. We'd never dreamt that we'd actually go to war one day. We didn't think about them preparing us for war. We just did what we were told, and we did it to the best of our ability. Our days had been filled with training—drills, marches, runs, and Howitzers—that had been like a continuation of boot camp, minus the *shitbird* comments. We were treated with the respect afforded a Marine. They trained us hard, and, if for no other reason, that training made me a better man. The Marine Corps made me feel proud.

Once we'd been assigned to a gun back at Pendleton, many of us became fast friends. Harold *Digger* O'Dell, Patrick Parrish, Paul Kreiger, Stanley Zabodyn, Jerry Levan, Sam Findley, Bryan Simmons, and I became inseparable. We'd shared a gun, and, although some of us may have been unsure of our purpose, we'd shared that, too. When you are fourteen or fifteen years old, you think that the people who are close to you then are the ones who will be there for your entire lifetime. You think they are the only people who will matter forever. The friends you make and the experiences you share during that time, are life, attitude, even personality molding relationships that surely cannot be undervalued. Boot camp friendships, as important as they are, proved to be momentary relationships that merely served to get us through our toughest test to date.

When I'd started my Marine Corps life at Pendleton, though, the imprint of true friendships had been stamped in a way that is difficult for others to understand. This is where I'd learned who my friends were, who I could count on, and who would be by my side both in good times and in bad. This is where the groundwork had been laid for lifetime friendships—long and short lifetimes. The Marine Corps prepared us for many things, not the least of which was surviving a gruesome war that none of us knew was on the horizon. But they did not prepare us for the reality of witnessing the end of those short lifetimes. They hadn't readied us to see one friend cover the body of another, willing to give his own life in order to save the one he didn't realize was already dead. The Marines hadn't told us about the horror of seeing your best buddy—legs black from frostbite—roll from the bed of a truck with two bullets in him while calling your name. They teach you what to do in any situation that might arise, but fail to inform you of the guilt you'll experience when you are one of the only two survivors of an ambush that had injured or killed eleven others. You thank God you know how to protect the surviving injured, but you are unprepared for the lonely feeling of spending a long, dark, cold night praying for the rumble of an approaching convoy that you know is out there. Every Marine knows that the next guy has got his six, but until the real bullets fly, we have no clue what it's like to realize we have failed to have his. We will always be friends, though, through long lifetimes and short.

And that's what Pendleton created: men who prepared for war and understood, to a degree, the meaning of relationships that required we each give ourselves for others. This concept alone forged bonds that might only be replicated in the ranks of first responders who know that they have to trust the man beside them with their lives. The day would come when those bonds would be put to the test in Korea, but for the time being, we languished in our ignorance of the future while we soaked in the California sun. Sometimes, we even had fun.

"Got a rosebush full of diamonds,"

We were in the enlisted men's slop chute on Pendleton—the beer hall. Paul Kreiger had the floor. Most of the guys drank beers, while I sipped my Coca Cola. Paul sat on a stool with his back leaned against the bar. He had the pads of his thumb and forefinger pressed together against his tightly puckered lips. He inhaled deeply with a loud hiss.

"Got six Cadillacs,"

He leaned his head back, blew imaginary smoke to the ceiling, and then looked around our circle to each man.

"Don't bother opening the door, man,"

He took another satisfying toke.

"I'll just float through the keyhole."

We all busted up. Kreiger was the funniest man in the Marine Corps, and I hadn't even known what the Hell he'd been talking about. Must've been something he'd picked up in Los Angeles—his hometown. He'd bring that Keyhole routine to Korea with him and pull it out anytime we needed a break from the harsh realities we'd been living with. I bet he even did it for the medics, too, when they'd carried him off from the forward observer post that he'd volunteered for. His was a sense of humor that would never be squelched by frostbite and a near-fatal bullet wound. And in Korea, every bullet wound that didn't kill a guy was near-fatal.

Every once in a while, we'd get off base for a little fun. We could go into Oceanside, which was the closest town. It'd been just a military town back then and not very nice. The only thing Oceanside wanted from us was our money, and if you weren't spending, you might as well stay on base. If we were prepared to fight with the sailors, we could take the bus or train down to San Diego. They'd laid claim to the city, and we were not welcome. It was an ill-conceived idea for three—or a dozen—Marines to show their faces at a bar in San Diego. Once in a while, we'd take the bus or a train north to Los Angeles, which was a big and exciting city even back then. The first time we'd gone, though, we should have taken Kreiger along to show us around. Patrick Parrish and I had been walking around minding our own beeswax, when a police car pulled up alongside us.

"Hey! What are you guys doing?"

"Just looking around."

"Get in the car before you get yourselves killed."

Apparently, we'd not been in the best *looking-around* neighborhood. Thanks to that cop, Patrick would just have to wait till we got to Korea to get himself killed. Anyway, we'd spent most of our free time at the slop chute staying out of trouble, having a few laughs, and—speaking for myself—feeling homesick.

A soon as I'd arrived at Camp Pendleton, I put in a request for my first leave. Christmas was still four months away, and I'd figured my early request would better my chances.

"Christmas?" The staff sergeant looked over my request. "That'd be swell, kid."

Turned out, he didn't actually think that was so swell.

"Everybody and the dishwasher wants Christmas, kid. Gotta do your time to get Christmas. How 'bout Thanksgiving? Your ma will like that."

So, Thanksgiving it was. By the time November rolled around, I'd been glad not to have to wait another month to go home. I hadn't known it yet, but when I got home, I'd have to suck up all the courage I possessed to do something that terrified me.

My mother sent me over to Katie's, the grocery store on the corner, for a few things she needed for the next day's feast. Katie sold a lot of candy in that shop, and we all just called it the candy store. While in there, the girl from number 66 right across the street walked in. I didn't even know her name, but I had it covered.

"Hi, Blondie." I was smooth—very smooth.

She turned around, looked right at me, and then looked at this other guy who was standing slightly behind me.

"Oh, hi Glenn. How are you?" Then she turned back to Katie at the counter.

There was only one way to handle the situation.

"Hi, Blondie." I said it louder. I really had a good thing going there with my silky tongue. My face warmed up. She finished her business and walked out, which left me with Katie and Glenn—whoever the hell he was—waiting for my next move. The thought of collecting the vegetables my mother had sent me for and getting out of there occurred to me, but I set it aside and followed Blondie out the door.

"Excuse me, Miss, I'd like to meet you."

She stopped. "Well, who are you?"

She knew darned well who I was. Maybe not by name, but I knew she'd seen me around, just as I'd seen her. She'd caught me on that stoop across the street looking up at her when she'd retrieved the beers for her parents. And, although I didn't know it at the time, she'd seen me at the school when I'd gone to visit Mrs. Davis. I introduced myself as Joe Lynch, and told her—with a gesture toward our apartment—that I lived across the street from her.

"Oh, yes. The big family."

"That's right."

"I'm Barbara Chattman."

The fire in my cheeks subsided, and I plunged further. "I'd like to take you to a movie or something."

She looked down at her feet. Oh God. Even I knew that meant "No."

"I'll have to ask my parents."

"Okay! I'll go up with you."

"You will not. I'll go ask. Wait here." So, she went upstairs to ask. She'd told her father that I was a Marine.

"You're not going out with any Marine."

"Daddy, he's only seventeen. I'll be sixteen in February."

I'd waited on the sidewalk for a five-minute eternity before she'd returned with the good news. Apparently, Boy Marines who were only a year-and-a-half older than Barbara had been acceptable. We had our first date the very next day—Thanksgiving. I wanted to impress her, so I wore my dress blues. After we'd each had supper with our own families, I took her to see *High Noon* at the Gloria Theater. *Do not forsake me, oh my darling...* it was jazzy. I'd loved it so much, I went out and bought the record. It was on this date that she told me she'd seen me in Mrs. Davis's classroom.

I saw Barbara a few more times before I left for California. We corresponded often. There really wasn't much to say, because we were just getting to know each other. I'd already known everything I needed—she was beautiful and I was in love. I didn't mind if she dated other guys (I never dated anyone else), so I never asked. She had her life to live, school to attend, and I was in California. The first photo she'd sent was from Easter Sunday in 1949. She was standing in front of the candy store wearing a sharp and pretty green skirt suit. Beautiful.

Eventually, she'd marry me, love me, give me a house full of kids, and stick with me through thick and thin. I would repay her with undying love, overshadowed by more than five decades of grief, fear, and emotional hardship. *Thick and thin* would merge over time into a blurred line of day-to-day uncertainty.

By June of 1950, I'd been well into the deck-of-cards countdown that motivated every one-term serviceman through his final year. Throw away one card from the deck with each passing week of the final fifty-two. My enlistment would be up in about eight months, and, even though I'd known I made the right decision about joining the Marine Corps, I'd begun to feel The Itch. The day-to-day crap of military service had begun to pile up, and—while the

Marines had made me a better man—I was ready to strike out and become my own person. Besides, Barbara was waiting for me at home, and there is no better motivation for a serviceman to move on and make a life for himself than a long-distance sweetheart. I'd be getting out at the age of nineteen, which is close to the age most guys are coming in. That head start, along with the experience obtained through my three years in the Marine Corps, would propel me into a secure future in which I could one day follow my brother onto the New York City police force. I could then marry Barbara (I figured I had a good shot at this), and start a large family. In one of my letters, I had confided in Barbara that I wanted a large family, and it hadn't scared her off. Left out, for the time being, was that by "large," I had meant twelve children—one more than my mother. There'd be plenty of time to share this plan before any nuptials—or at least before we'd reach that lofty number.

I'd managed to keep a good attitude as I watched my deck of cards dwindle to thirty-eight. Thirty-eight more weeks. When you are counting in weeks, the time seems less powerful. After all, I was only twelve cards away from the halfway point. Time's momentum seemed to have built, and the cards had taken on a life of their own. I dropped the five of spades into my drawer (hey, why waste them?). June 25th—thirty-five weeks remaining.

N. KOREA REDS DECLARE WAR
Invade South by Land and Sea

That headline, in one form or another, blared from every newspaper across the country. WAR. I didn't know much about South Korea, but I did know that we'd had a small military presence there since the end of the Second World War. They were called Advisors. I wasn't entirely sure what advisors were, but I hoped those boys were keeping their heads down. I sat rigid at the edge of my bunk, and looked from the newspaper to my deck of cards on the small nightstand. *Shit.*

It only took two days for the United Nations Security Council to form the U.N. Forces in Korea. The United States was going back to war only five years since World War Two had ended, and thirty-two years after the good guys had won The War To End All Wars. I went into my quarters and held my remaining thirty-five cards. Three fives—Diamond, Heart, Club—and every suit of the remaining cards through King. Truman had declared our involvement a Police Action. *I was gonna be a cop, anyway. No time like the present.* I found a rubber band, stretched it around the diminished deck, and tossed it in my footlocker.

Work to prepare for deployment began immediately. In the days that followed, my crew had been tasked with readying everything the battery had for the move down to San Diego and loading on ships. Every detail was double-time, because we'd be shipping out on July 13th—two weeks. The Army was already moving into Korea from their stations in Japan, but reinforcements were critical. Word was that these boys were in for a tough time as the Reds pushed their way through the South on a murderous rampage. As I worked beside the others to prepare for war, the put-aside deck of cards had left my consciousness. Then I was called to the principal's office.

"Corporal Lynch reporting as ordered, sir."

My staff sergeant looked up from mounds of paperwork, and held one sheet in his hand. "Your enlistment is running short, so you'll be minding the store."

"Sir?"

"No sense in sending short timers, mister."

"I got till the end of February."

"Unless you want to up for another year, you stay."

I had nothing.

"Get back to your crew. You'll have new orders soon enough. Go."

Back on the crew, word was already spreading that some men had won the lottery. I kept my mouth shut and went about my work. But I could feel the prying eyes upon me.

"What did Nickels want, Joe?" It was Digger O'Dell, his head a full foot above the others.

"Just told me I'm doing a fine job."

"Ha! Yeah, he's good like that."

Everyone was spent when we finally got back to quarters that evening. The silence, brought on by tiredness, sore bones, and thoughts of an uncertain future filled my ears like water balloons. The guys were peeling sweaty shirts from aching bodies, and tossing balled up socks on the floor beside bunks. I wondered what it'd be like for them. They were a tough group, but even tough guys get knocked down. I opened my footlocker, where I'd already been tossing the things I'd need for the next week or so, and spotted the bundled cards. After pulling the rubber band, I examined the faces by sliding cards aside with my left thumb. The numbers and suits meant nothing. Red and black was all that registered.

I caught Stanley watching. "I'm happy for you, Joe."

I now realized that the rest of the guys were watching me. Maybe they had been the whole time—I didn't know. The nearly-forgotten funk of the Gowanus Canal wafted up around me. "Thanks, Stan."

"You just get home to that pretty girl, kid." He nodded to the picture of Barbara that was lying on my nightstand.

Patrick Parrish dropped his undershirt onto his bunk. "Any one of us would stay behind if we could. Count yourself lucky." Mumbles of agreement followed his lie.

The raft floated down Lavender Lake. As a lone drop formed at the corner of one eye, I turned to my nightstand and blinked it into submission along with visions of the raft. I found the discarded cards in the drawer, and shuffled them into the deck.

"Jesus Christmas. You guys are so full of shit." I continued to shuffle.

Stanley looked at me like I was an idiot. "What the hell are you doing, Joe?"

"How 'bout a game of Gin Rummy?" I asked.

"That's your countdown, you lug."

"Yeah." I looked at the deck, and then back at the boys. "Solitaire is for civilians."

I'm not going to feed you any lines like, *I wanted to go to war because that's why I became a Marine.* I knew why I'd become a Marine, and, by this time, so did most of the guys in my crew: to get away from my father. I'd trusted my brother Marines at Pendleton with the knowledge of my real age and never doubted the faith I'd put in them. If Stan, or Digger, or any of the others thought that I hadn't been man enough to go to war beside them, it'd take one word to have me back in Brooklyn inside of a week. They trusted me with their lives, and I trusted them with mine. I'd do my duty as a Marine—there was no way I was going to stay here to make busy work and play one-handed cards for thirty-five weeks.

With that choice, I would also make my mother furious. She'd understood duty. And she'd been proud of my brothers when their time had come. But to extend my enlistment in order to make my deployment *possible* had been the ultimate in arrogance—or stupidity—to her.

"What the hell are you thinking?"

"I have to do this, Ma."

"They said you don't."

"Ma, you want the men to think I'm a coward?"

"Yes. No. They won't think that. You go tell that sergeant you changed your mind."

"I can't tell him that, Ma. It's too late. I want to go. "

"You just wish your friends well, and get home when you're supposed to."

And that's the way that went.

It'd turned out to be the right choice, even beyond the notions of patriotism, honor, brotherhood, and duty. Shortly after we'd embarked for our first stop in Kobe, Japan, Truman announced that all military personnel would be extended for a period of one year. So I'd beat him to the punch. Now, all those guys who'd opted out of the opportunity to extend would be going anyway. They'd ship out later, with different units. There is nothing I could have imagined worse than having to go to war with a bunch of strangers. To deploy without the likes of Stanley Zabodyn, Digger O'Dell, Patrick Parrish, Paul Kreiger, and all the other men from Able Battery would have been the loneliest feeling since Adam—before God took one of his ribs. I knew everything I'd needed to know about my gun crew, and there could be no others whom I'd want to have my back. I promised my mother that I would come back, and these were the guys who would see to it that it hadn't been a lie. And I don't think it's a stretch to say that they were glad to have me with them. We'd been trained as a team, and—together—we'd serve as such.

I'd learned two other important lessons. First, spending three days out on the USS Henrico had been all the time I'd needed to understand that the Navy recruiter's shiny, black size-ten had saved me from years of misery. And second, dropping out of Merchant Marine studies at Met High had been a decision made in Heaven. From the first rolling wave out of San Diego Harbor—on the morning of July 14th—I'd been sick as a pig on a roller coaster.

I'd thought I was alone on the top deck of the Henrico when I puked over the rail. A warrant officer screamed at me—scared the crap out of me. He made me stand at attention in front of him while he chewed me out over a little blowback that had dirtied his shoes. Embarrassed beyond measure, I tried my best to apologize, but (instead) emptied the remaining contents of my stomach down the front of his uniform. *Oh, God.* There'd been no holding it back. We were each more mortified than the other. He steamed off without a word. He probably hated my guts—I'm sure they smelled awful.

Every time I'd ever been on a ship, it had been the same story. On a later passage, somebody had thought it would be a great idea for me to help out in the galley. I'd thought it a slap, what with me being a corporal and having to serve up the slop to privates and such. But the Marines had been taking care of their own since we'd left San Diego, and my number had finally come due. I sucked it up, played the good Marine, and did my share of the work scooping Jell-O alongside creamed beef on the already-loaded plates. Green Jell-O to match the color of my face. *Why'd it have to be green?* I covered two large tins of jiggling, shiny, lime-green gelatin with everything I'd eaten earlier in the day. The other men in the serving line jumped back as vomit splashed to nearby trays. Disgusted Marines on the other side of the counter left their heaped dishes and walked away. From then on, I'd been branded. I was never invited back to serve my fellow Marines in the slop line, and—in fact—lucky to even be offered food on any ship ever again. I'd spent the remainder of that trip in my bunk eating crackers, just trying to stay alive.

CHAPTER 9

Fire Brigade

I HAVE AN OFF-COLOR JOKE that I like to tell in certain company. Forgive me for telling it here:

A guy asked me once, "Where's the first place you took a crap when you got to Korea?" I told him, "In my pants!" Ha ha!

This is obviously not a true story. Who on earth would ask a question like that? The rest comes pretty close to the truth, though.

The USS Henrico coughed into the Port of Pusan on a rudder and a *Thank you-God,* due to a series of mechanical problems that had dogged us ever since leaving port in San Diego. We'd been separated from the fleet during an unexpected side trip to Oakland, CA before our sail to Japan. When we'd made it out of the Oakland Navy yard on July 15, after a day of kicking the rudders and applying Band-Aids, we'd been a full day behind the fleet—alone on the high seas.

Denny Flom cracked, "I hope the torpedoes don't get us."

Great. Every Marine on the ship is sick, we're out here on our own, and now I got this to worry about. I didn't even know if the Koreans had torpedoes.

The entire fleet's side trip to Japan had later been cancelled due to the grave conditions in which the Army had found themselves in Korea, and all were directed to Pusan without delay. On August 2, 1950, the Happy Hank (as she was lovingly known—although Hank had been in a lousy mood the entire voyage) loaded with three firing batteries of the 1st Battalion, 11th Marines, chugged and belched her way into the port only an hour behind the George Clymer (Greasy George) and the Pickaway. We were all now part of the 1st Provisional Marine Brigade, a temporary brigade set up for the occasion. The Marines had landed.

Our welcome party consisted of the brigade commander, Brigadier General Edward Craig, the Marine guards of the displaced Embassy staff from Seoul, Army personnel, as well as a hodgepodge of local Looky Loos. Everyone shuffled about the pier around and between two long, triple-peaked, wooden warehouses of dubious repair that would hold in reserve any unneeded supplies, including our seabags. We stood at the rail in surreal wonder at the sights. Mist—maybe smoke—did its best to obscure our view of mountains that were not far beyond the port. Distant artillery fire nudged its way to our consciousness—a hint that the surreal would become real soon enough. In the calmer waters of the Pusan harbor and the hedged excitement of our arrival, my stomach had finally settled down, only to reverberate with the bass vibrations of explosions that carried much better than the sound. This was my nineteenth birthday, and I'd never imagined that I would visit a far-away, exotic port, at the hairy edge of war, on such an occasion. It proved a bizarre kick off to the start of my twentieth year.

Everybody loves a parade, and the South Koreans were no different. After the Henrico tied up, the dignitaries lined the pier. Then a Korean band, led by a Republic of Korea (ROK) Army color guard that carried the South Korean, United Nations, and United States flags, rounded the harbor end of the nearest warehouse building, and struck up the Marine Corps Hymn. Despite the unfortunate effort of the band, it was a proud, albeit humorous, moment. Sharp salutes and rowdy cheers alike swept through the decks of the Henrico. The locals below us appeared confused.

Stanley nudged me with an elbow. "Maybe they'll play Happy Birthday next."

They didn't, although I'd thought it would have been a nice gesture.

Festivities behind us, we shrugged our packs onto our backs, donned our camouflage helmets, and slung M1 Garands and Browning Automatic Rifles

(BAR) over our shoulders before we swaggered down the gangplank. We'd salted our spirit with a confidence born of hard training and a commitment to a long Marine Corps tradition, though it had surely been peppered with a trepidation for the unknown. We then worked through the night unloading supplies—glory would just have to wait.

The next morning, we marched off to hurry up and wait. Hours passed at the Pusan rail station while we waited in subdued camaraderie to be moved to the front lines of what they'd called the Pusan Perimeter. The North Korean People's Army (NKPA) had rushed across the border at the 38th parallel, stormed through the South in a rampage that overtook the ROK and US Armies, and pushed them back to the southeastern-most corner of the peninsular, which contained the city of Pusan. After only a month of fighting, the war was about to be lost, and the local citizenry knew it. Every face we saw was solemn at the least and terrified at the other extreme. Their excitement at the arrival of the heretofore-unbeatable Marines had been darkened by their fear, not of the unknown, but of certain death should we fail. The one hundred-forty mile perimeter had been set up to prevent that total defeat and the fall of Pusan. But it had been a losing battle, and—almost by the day—the perimeter had shrunk. We'd been informed that the 1st Provisional Marines would act as a fire brigade, and that we'd be placed in the hot-spots of gravest concern in order to stop the offensive—or be driven back to the sea and annihilated. *Oorah.*

Some of the boys took advantage of this last opportunity to tell jokes or funny stories in order to occupy our minds with tension-breaking humor. We all laughed at the right spots. Cigarettes were going to be in short supply because most of the smokers sucked them down like soda pop through a straw, and the ground was littered with their dead, unfiltered soldiers. Paul Kreiger, God love him, rolled an imaginary marijuana cigarette (someone finally filled me in) and worked his magic:

"Got a rosebush full of diamonds,
Got six Cadillacs,
Don't bother opening the door, man,
I'll just float through the keyhole."

Just the ticket. Paul was now the funniest man in Korea. A Jeep ambled by, and a Navy chaplain nodded to us from the passenger seat. It stopped on a short rise adjacent to the rail platform. This prompted a little discussion between some of the men.

"I'll go talk to him," I volunteered.

I approached the chaplain and his driver who both stood by the Jeep chatting.

"Excuse me, sir." I saluted the chaplain, who bore the rank of lieutenant commander.

"What's your name, Corporal?"

"Joe Lynch, sir."

He extended a hand. "Father Sporrer—Otto Sporrer."

I was nervous, but he seemed nice enough.

"What can I do for you, son?"

"Father, some of the men would like their confessions heard. Do you think you could do that?"

I felt like I was outside Katie's, asking that beautiful young lady to the movies.

"Oh, yes. Absolutely. I'd be happy to."

"Thank you, Father. I'll go tell the others." I spun around and got three steps into a trot.

"Wait. Stay. I'll do you first. No sense in running down and back again."

I glanced around for what might make a nice make-do confessional. Nothing presented itself.

"Right here, Father?"

"Ha. Right here, Joe."

Oh, brother. Face-to-face confession. I looked back at the guys who'd been watching closely. Father Sporrer's driver wandered off and I got down on my knees. He sat beside me in the Jeep.

"Go ahead, Joe. Just like at home."

"If I remember."

"What's that?"

"Uh, nothing Father."

"Humph. That's okay. Just like riding a bike, son."

Well, at least I'd *seen* bicycles before. I positioned my hands for prayer, and looked at the front tire beyond his feet.

"Bless me, Father, for I have sinned."

Within a few minutes I'd been absolved of all my sins, and was deemed free to enter Heaven should the unthinkable and unimaginable—which now seemed very thinkable and imaginable—happen.

"Thank you, Father."

I stood, extended my hand to shake his, yanked it back to a salute, and then clasped his hand when it was offered with a chuckle.

"That wasn't so bad."

"No, it wasn't," he said.

"Uh, sorry. Meant to say that to myself."

"Your friends are waiting, Joe. God be with you." His smile was genuine and comforting.

I spun about to get the others, only to find them lined up, beginning about twenty feet back. John Gruber was first in line. He'd been an acquaintance back at Pendleton, but we'd get to know each other a lot better in the days and weeks ahead. He swatted my shoulder when I passed.

"Thanks, Joe."

"Nothing to it."

After a half-day of sweating in the August sun at the Pusan train station, we moved out. Some had departed ahead of us by a truck convoy that had been borrowed from the Army. We rode the train, an old wooden-coach relic of the Japanese occupation of the peninsular. The train lumbered at little more than a walking pace through an unnoticed countryside, as Marines sat near open windows that carried a hot and dusty breeze through the cars. Frequent, unexplained stops in remote areas gave us pause. We occupied the time by cleaning our weapons, and preparing mentally for what lay ahead. If the train had been moving faster, we wouldn't have seemed much different than Monday-morning commuters riding into Manhattan, exclusive of the lives we'd take—and perhaps forfeit—once we arrived at the office.

Our destination was a town called Changwon, near the port of Masan, which was maybe thirty miles to the west of Pusan. Changwon was used as a staging area, where we'd regrouped, prepared equipment, and even did some last-minute training. The Marines loved training—giving and receiving. We were within ten miles of the North Korean invaders, and it had been reported that the enemy had eyes on us. The NKPA scouts, knowing the terrain, had disappeared into the hills when they'd been discovered. It had made for a tense first night during which jumpy, itchy-fingered PFCs shot at shadows in the near-total darkness. One, two, three, and then a crescendo of aimless shots filled the night to manifest the peaked anxiety that filled the ranks. Silence—and the miracle of no friendly-fire injuries—followed the pissed-off screams of non-commissioned officers (NCOs). The persistent tension could be cut with a bayonet, though, and so too could another Marine if he hadn't been careful. Every man slept in shifts with his rifle held tight, and a 1.9-pound finger on a two-pound trigger. What we'd needed most was to just meet a real enemy, so we would not kill each other.

On August 7th, we got our wish. It had been lost on no man, that the Marines would launch its first offensive of the Korean War on the eighth anniversary of the landing at Guadalcanal. The mission, which was obvious even to the grunts, was to restore 8th Army lines that had been taken by the NKPA. During our training in Changwon, we'd gotten one last bit of good news from the brass before that training put us to work: *Do not retreat.* Period. End of story.

We'd been informed that General Craig had been very clear: "It has been necessary for troops now fighting in Korea to pull back at times, but I am stating now that no unit of this brigade will retreat except on orders from an authority higher than the 1st Marine Brigade. You will *never* receive an order to retreat from me. All I ask is that you fight as Marines have always fought."

And our battery commander, Capt. James D. Jordan, made the directive even more simple for us to digest: "If I order you to retreat, feel free to move to the back of your foxhole."

We'd assembled in Chindong-ni on the 6th, and by early morning of the 7th, the 11th Marines were at war. *The real thing.* No training prepares you for the real thing. The big difference between this and the merciless bombardment of the hillsides at Pendleton was the presence of people in the target zones. Of course, we now occupied their target zones. Shells fell all around us. That had never happened at Pendleton, and it shook us bad. One Howitzer of Baker Battery took a direct hit. I mumbled confession to myself as a quick update to God of any bad-thought infractions—the only new sins time had allowed since leaving Pusan—I'd committed. When word got to our gun position in Able Battery, the news was unthinkable: Porter and Pittillo were dead, and an additional eight others were wounded. I loaded the gun and prayed for them. Then I thanked God for the sergeants in attendance, who had all seen action during World War Two. Master, Gunnery, Staff, it didn't matter—they each knew what to expect, and the coolness of their heads soon found it's way to us. *Stick to the training. Gun loaded.* Those sergeants had been our guides, our angels, our saviors. *Hands over ears.* We'd thought we knew it all, but when the shooting began, we understood just how ignorant we were. *Fire for effect.* We were scared. *I was scared.* Men I'd trained alongside were already dead.

Through fire control, we received coordinates from our forward observers, and then pockmarked hillsides with the Howitzer, as we fired upon targets unseen to us from up to four miles out. I thanked God for the anonymity of the death I rained down on invisible souls—if they even had souls. I wondered if *they* were relieved not to see Pittillo and Porter shredded by their hand—not to witness the eight men hurriedly evacuated from the battlefield, and be forced to wonder if they'd survive.

Hours passed, and I prepared round after round for the hungry gun. We set the charges for high explosive, with fuses set to explode the ordinance very near or on the target. We didn't want to just kill men, but to also take out their guns, equipment, and supplies with them. When ordered to advance our positions, we coupled guns to trucks (Prime Movers), pulled them to new locations, and were then back in action within ten minutes. *Training.* There'd been no fooling around. Asses were on the line now. Soldiers and Marines ahead of us had their objectives, but the bottom line is they were each fighting for their own ass. *Stay alive* is foremost in a guy's head. And we needed to react instantaneously to help them do just that. It was the same all the time: prep the gun once it had been moved into freshly dug pits, point in the enemy's general direction, and shoot. The gun would jump. Nothing you could do about it. Then we'd get the orders from the Fire Direction Control Center, and we could concentrate on precise aiming with the now-stable gun. We'd entered the zone. Our movements were fluid, because we'd done it a thousand times before we'd ever heard of Korea. As darkness fell that first day, it'd felt as though we'd done it a thousand more. And we had only just begun.

KATUSAs (Korean Augmentation to The United States Army) helped move rounds from trucks to the guns and prep them for loading. Sungyong Park had been a police officer in another life—the life he'd lived up until five or six weeks prior to our meeting. He didn't speak a lick of English, but he watched with the intensity of a hungry great white egret eying a fish, and he learned. He'd called me *Joe* when we met, which was perfect; He'd called everyone *Joe*, which was weird. Sungyong had the motivation to learn. It was not his ass that he was determined to keep safe, but that of his country. As I became close to him, I felt his anguish. If the Marines failed in the days ahead, we might all go home in bags, but there'd be a home to which we could return. The purple mountains and amber waves wouldn't even miss us. Sungyong Park was fighting for his very home.

I'd met him at Changwon when he'd joined us for training. Having been a well-trained and experienced police officer—and previously attached to a unit of the 8th Army—he'd already been comfortable around the gun and easily jelled to our routine. When sleeping arrangements had been made in the camp, many of the other Marines held back, so I offered him a spot in my pup tent. That had been the start of a bond that equaled that of any Marine Corps brothers in combat. In my mind, Sungyong Park *was* a Marine, and the reluctance to accept him as such by some of the other men in the battery soon faded. Marines and KATUSAs became one. They learned our names and we learned theirs. And in spite of the language barrier, they responded to orders with seamless efficiency.

One day, we advanced the dirt roads through valleys in The Perimeter and encountered a sight that I knew would stay with all of us to the grave: US soldiers, dead, face down on the road. Their wrists had been bound behind their backs with barbed wire, and they'd been shot in the back of their heads. Executed. Anger swept through the Marines, and KATUSAs needed no language to convey their thoughts. Guilt at the knowledge that these men had been murdered in the name of justice for their country had been written across their ashen faces. I put a hand on my friend's shoulder in silent acknowledgment of his sorrow. We Marines made a vow on that very spot to never be captured. If we were to die anyway, those savages would not have the satisfaction of killing a Marine who was not fighting for his life. We'd take a few with us.

In less stressful times, Sungyong and I had done our best to communicate and bond. Beginning in Changwon, and continuing on the battlefield, we'd enlisted the one language that transcends all others: music. We'd had no radio with which to tune in Bing Crosby, and no phonograph to spin Hank Williams records upon, so we'd been left to our own devices.

I taught Sungyong the only song I thought he could easily learn, and the one song that filled me with thoughts of home: *God Bless America*. There'd been no way for him to understand the words, but he surely gleaned the spirit in those foreign lyrics. He struggled to mimic the sounds, while the melody flowed from his heart. He seemed to understand the spirit behind the phrase *God Bless America*, and sung it with boisterous pride. His grasp of the encapsulated meaning of the song—if not the definition of its individual words—flushed me with pride, joy, and homesickness. At times, we'd catch him singing *God Bless America* as we loaded the Howitzer, and fired certain death to an enemy who did not wish God's, or any other deity's, blessings on the country that threatened their—until now—pre-destined victory. Stanley, Digger, and a few others allowed appreciative chuckles for Sungyong's heartfelt rendition, as they'd continued their jobs with sharp focus.

But Sungyong hadn't allowed my beautiful voice to go wasted on only the tried and true patriotic music. In the tradition of giving as well as receiving, he taught me one of the most beautiful songs I have, to this day, ever heard:

Arirang. It is a Korean folk song that, over time, has become the unofficial national anthem of South Korea. I'd thought I would sprain my tongue in a clumsy attempt to recreate the sounds. But once I let go, its soft melody squelched my voice's demanding ego, and the words slid out as naturally as a Ka-Bar through SPAM.

Translated:

> *Look on me! Look on me! Look on me!*
> *In midwinter, when you see a flower, please think of me!*
> *Chorus: Ari-arirang! Ssuri-Ssurirang! Arariga nanne!*
> *O'er Arirang Hill I long to cross today.*
> *Moonkyung weak Bird has too many curves*
> *Winding up, winding down, in tears I go.*
> *Carry me, carry me, carry me and go!*
> *When flowers bloom in Hanyang, carry me and go.*

With Sungyong and the other KATUSAs at our side, Able Battery—a tiny yet integral force of the full strength of the 1st Provisional Marines—continued on a rampage to equal that of the NKPA's drive through South Korea in the days and weeks before. Thoughts of the men who had been lost in the few days since the offensive had begun, hung over us as a heavy reminder of the now-certain cost of protecting freedom. We'd fought on and off around the clock, displacing, setting, and firing the guns by flashlight at times, while the North Koreans shelled us with 105 and 155mm artillery, shot from the Howitzers they'd taken from the US Army in the weeks before. Sleep, when we could steal it, was difficult. Eventually, we'd learn how to get our rest with all the chaos that spiraled around us. But for now, however, it was catch as much shuteye as we could before either the next round exploded near us or the succeeding cannon bellowed it's unforgiving reply. Waking hours throughout the night became dreamlike. Near-sleep hours turned nightmarish.

The daytime heat scorched and parched us. Water supplies had run low from the start, and been difficult to replenish. Empty canteens teased us as we prayed for airdrops of water and other supplies. Daytime temperatures reached 114 degrees and, at times, we fired the Howitzer wearing nothing more than our helmet, boots and undershorts. It seems comical today, but at the time, no one laughed. Our hands burned on sun-scorched shells, and fear of a premature explosion loomed as overworked Howitzers became overheated.

At one point, I set the charge on a round, and then woke up to see a Navy corpsman soaking me down with alcohol. My mind had lost whatever happened in between. Time and space had collapsed, and I'd been left with no reference for the minutes or hours that had passed. I hadn't, of course, been the first to succumb—heat prostration had continually taken scores of men from the fight beginning on the first day. Infantry who stormed enemy positions in the hills had dropped in greater numbers than NKPA bullets could ever hope to accomplish. At times, the battlefield was littered with fighting men who needed nothing more than hydration. Dust filled our lungs and ran down our sweaty bodies. Our clothing rotted. But still we continued.

Without rest, the infantry of the 5th Marines stormed hill after hill behind the shellfire from our Howitzers, and the air support from Marine fighters. Their efforts had often been reduced to small-arms fire and hand-to-hand combat. They had the toughest job, and—now more than ever—I was thankful that some wiseass had put me into artillery when I'd requested my transfer out of Parris Island. But, even as I prayed for them, the craters that formed around us and the dust that enveloped us served as stark reminders of our lost brothers of Baker Battery as well as of our own mortality.

Hills. Everywhere hills. All of them had been cleverly named for their height in feet. By August 9—exactly one week after we'd arrived in Korea aboard Happy Hank—we had already become battle-tested Marines. On that day, the three firing batteries of 1st Battalion hammered Hill 255 in order to take the high ground from the NKPA, and clear the way to Chinju through Kosong. The enemy got its first taste of an opponent with the manpower, training, weaponry, and will to take and hold ground, no matter the cost. They also got their first taste of napalm, which Marine Corsairs rained down as follow-up to our relentless artillery barrage. Fire erupted in vast swaths across hillsides, and smoke billowed above. *Oh my God.* I'd done my best not to think about the horror. But it had all made relatively easy work for Infantry Marines to capture the high ground that had previously been lost by the Army. Then, on the 11th of August, we had Kosong in our sights. We blanketed the town with 105mm Howitzer fire, and sent the enemy's 83rd Motorcycle Regiment into retreat.

Beyond Kosong, Hill 88 had been held by the NKPA, where they blocked our way to Sachon. My gun sergeant and I moved out in front of the guns to scout a new position. The roar of a plane approached from behind, and we turned to see the craft swoop in low, and then drop something in a line directly toward our position.

Sergeant McAbee shouted, "Napalm!"

With full knowledge that no escape existed—when the napalm hit, it would spread, and everything within a hundred yards (including us) would be incinerated—we ran full out in the direction of our gun. Certain death had been a moment away, yet it never came. The Marine Corsair lifted and turned away, its ejected, empty, auxiliary fuel tank lay smashed on the ground thirty yards away. Presumably, the pilot was unaware of the condition of my shorts. *Shit.* McAbee and I returned (me on shaky legs) to the guns that were already coupled to the Prime Movers. The laughs of our fellow gunners were more in the name of stress relief than humor. Nobody thought it was funny. Quick work was made of taking Hill 88.

August 12th brought an unexpected, if short, respite. Father Otto Sporrer visited with us behind the lines near Sachon. About the time I'd given up on school, I had also walked away from the Catholic Church. It hadn't been so much a lack of belief, as a faltering of faith—I'd no longer seen the point of it. Ma, on the other hand, had been a staunch believer in the Church, and saw to it that we attend every Sunday. But what had it gotten her? She was still dirt poor, and living with a drunk who offered her no hope for a better future.

Even with all my prayers, God had never blocked a single punch from the old man, and hadn't made fitting in at school any easier. My father's love had never manifested, and neither did God's. Any faith that *He* was listening, that *He* would protect me and show me the way, had dwindled to the point of no return. Then I went to war. And, *oh brother,* there is nothing like war to make a man *want* to believe in the Divine Omniscient, Omnipresent, and Omnipotent, like war. I'd mumbled more prayers in my first six days of battle than my mother had uttered during her entire life. And I'll tell you something else: When you get sent home—alive, with all your parts, and all five and a half quarts of blood you'd arrived with—your religious faith is strong enough to last a lifetime. And mine has.

When the chaplain arrived and offered mass, fourteen filthy men in need of a bath, a shave, and fresh-from-the-clothesline uniforms jumped at the opportunity to attend. This wasn't a *Would you rather clean the latrine or go to church?* kind of thing. More to the point, it'd been *We could actually die out here, and I could use a talk with God.* When you know that you're going to war, you understand—on an intellectual level—the risks, and you accept those risks as part of your duty. But even though we all may have strong beliefs about death, to conceptualize it is impossible without experiencing it ourselves. That right there is a problem, because concepts die with us. So, the closest we can get to this abstraction is to see it first hand, know that it is all around us, and acknowledge that we are exposed in such a way that our own death may come at any moment. It becomes as real as any notion can. That acceptance hits hard and fast, and we'd been conscious of it at all times. Losing two guys in Baker on the first day had helped.

We gathered in a grassy clearing between spindly evergreens, up on a hill that overlooked our temporary camp at a middle school. I couldn't say for sure if all the guys in attendance were members of my battery, but I do remember that John Gruber was there. He knelt behind me as Father Sporrer offered prayer and comfort from the makeshift altar that had been hastily erected with a cot. As a field wireman, John had a tough job. Every time we'd moved the guns, the field wiremen had to run wire between the forward observers, fire control and all the gun positions. If the wire got cut or damaged—which happened all the time—they'd have to repair or replace it. They covered a lot of ground, often while being shot at. So, John had been anxious to attend mass. Sergeant Buckles, a World War Two man, was on his knees with folded hands two spots to my left. He'd landed in Korea knowing exactly what he was getting himself into, and had probably been looking for this opportunity long before the shooting started. I'm sure the other men were there for similar reasons. Amid chaos, fear, and tragedy, Father Sporrer had been a calming presence. I would have four more opportunities to attend mass and receive communion with him during my time in Korea, and I am thankful for that.

Lieutenant Commander Otto Sporrer was more than a spiritual leader. This Navy chaplain—serving with the 1st Battalion—had been in Chindong-ni days before when we'd lost those two men in Baker Battery. Under relentless enemy fire, he'd administered first aid, and evacuated the wounded. His life-saving heroics that day, earned him a Bronze Star as well as the unwavering respect of every Marine who knew him. When he'd come to us in Sachon, the chaplain had already proved to be a man I'd trust with my life—in addition to my soul. A week after that mass, on August 18, he would display his courage once again during the Battle of Obong-ni Ridge, and this time he'd be awarded the Silver Star. Many years later, in 1984, I drove from San Diego to Laguna Hills to visit Father Sporrer at the Catholic Church he had founded after his retirement from the Navy. I'd been fifty-three years old at the time, and still felt the call to thank him for the life-saving faith he'd helped set in my heart. That rekindled faith filled me with the strength to persevere for another eight months in Korea. And although it would be tested at times, it had also gotten me to that mid-century point in life, where I'd faced even greater odds than the war had provided.

CHAPTER 10

Obong-ni Ridge

It takes a while, but eventually you calm down. It's a gradual change, but if I were going to identify a turning point for me, I'd have to give serious consideration to that field mass near Sachon. I'd left that hill, and the makeshift altar, with the ability to accept the struggle that had been thrust upon us. The transformation must have begun before that day and continued beyond it, but I finally understood that I was not alone. Father Sporrer had reminded us that every Marine was there for each other, and that God, too, was with us at all times. None of this is to say that fear ever left me. Anyone who says he wasn't scared is a liar. Even the heavy, steel shield that wrapped around the barrel of the Howitzer became an enemy weapon in my mind whenever I imagined it breaking apart and severing my body—which was the very fate that Billy Porter had suffered on our first day of battle.

There were times that I'd jumped in my foxhole with dirt and rock—from a newly-formed crater that was only yards from our position—following me, and wished I could dig deeper, then sideways below the surface, and finish up with a right angle where not even the light of day could reach me. One time, I lay on my back in my foxhole, and rested my legs on the ground above, just as if I were fully reclined in a La-Z-Boy. In a prolonged state of anxiety, I waited for a bullet or shell fragment to penetrate my calf, or ankle, or foot and send me home with the Purple Heart of heroes. But after a four-second eternity, good sense seized my lower extremities and yanked them to safety. Determination propelled my desire to not part with an ounce of blood or a shred of flesh. I would give my life in the fight before I'd surrender so much as a toe on Korean soil.

Fear lurked around and within us, but cowardice kept an agreeable distance. The closest glimpse I'd had of it had been there in The Perimeter. A lieutenant in my battery—who'd been with a forward observer team—had come back from his post with so-called *stomach problems*. The consensus around the guns was that the real problem with his stomach had simply been a lack of guts. Useless to an artillery battery, he'd been sent back from the front lines. I don't know where or how far back he'd gone, but we never did see him again, so I'm sure his stomach hadn't merely suffered from bad C-rations.

Timeless jokes around the military have centered on lieutenants who are poor leaders, are in need of a gunnery sergeant to make decisions for him and cover his ass, or are just flat-out cowards. We'd finally met the man who lived up to the mostly-unwarranted ridicule. I could certainly understand the fear. I could even *imagine* fear so great that it might render a man incapacitated. And let me tell you—without a doubt—forward observers have the worst job. In order to observe, these men often leave themselves exposed to observation by the enemy. Out of necessity, the observation posts are generally on or near the front lines. This means that their positions are often targeted for enemy artillery and machine-gun fire. Essentially, these men are always sticking their heads up and those heads make great targets. For sure, that lieutenant must have felt the heat of bullets as they passed his head. Civilians are under the impression that a bullet will bounce off a helmet, but I've seen clean holes through helmets. Who could blame the man for being scared? Not one Marine would. But, when a man leaves his post *due to that fear*, he is essentially saying, *Let someone else take the bullet.* I'd lost all respect for him, and so had every other man in the battery—maybe even the battalion. Somebody else would die doing the job he'd chosen to avoid. There had been times during the war (few, thankfully) when a forward observer team—their post about to be overrun—actually called in artillery on their own coordinates. You think fire control or the guys at the gun didn't know what was happening? That's real courage—all the way down the line.

I look back now, though, and wonder if it hadn't been for the better. A Marine's most powerful weapon—his greatest chance for survival—is the man next to him. Unless, of course, that man happens to be a coward. Over the course of my tour in Korea, I'd had two buddies killed at that post. That's in addition to the guys I hadn't known very well or at all. I eventually stopped blaming Lieutenant Stomach Problems, because I had plenty of North Koreans and—later—Chinese to blame.

Despite screams of terror, sobs of despair, and heartbeats of sorrow, no other Marine I'd encountered would ever display anything less than gallant service. I'll leave it to them to pass judgment about my service.

On the 14th of August, we'd finally gotten our first baths—in the river—as well as fresh uniforms to replace our rotted and torn old ones, a hot meal, and even cold (*coldish*) beer. To me, a fresh pair of socks on clean feet—even with my open sores—felt like a miracle. For others, the hot food had been their answered prayer. But, for the vast majority of the boys, the cold, sweaty can, the point of openers piercing the tops, the whoosh of released gas, and the first taste of fermented barley and hops awakened images of neighborhood bars and living-room easy chairs. Weary smiles replaced puckered lips to cans of Schlitz. I helped myself to a couple, and handed the beverages—for which I'd never developed a taste—to the first two sets of thirsty eyes that cut me with their lasers. Stanley stuffed one in his pack, while Paul rolled his between his hands.

"Number three. I'm off through the keyhole, boys."

A good-night's sleep followed—another first.

The next day, short of our objective of Chinju, we'd been pulled out of the theater, because the *Fire Brigade* had a new emergency. It was seventy-five miles to the north on the Naktong River at Obong-ni Ridge, and would eventually become known as the First Naktong Counteroffensive. The NKPA's 4th Division had crossed the river in stealth, taken the six main hills that made up the ridge, and were now poised to disrupt US supply lines that, if lost, would end the war with a US retreat from Korea. With no knowledge of—and little care for—what lay ahead, the opportunity to climb in the back of the truck and distance ourselves from explosions and gun fire had seemed like a welcome reprieve. Of course, we all felt that we'd left a job unfinished, and knew that we'd be back in action soon enough, but, at times during the twenty-six hour drive, it'd been easy enough to reflect back on that trip from Pendleton to Elliott in Southern California. The dusty road—with its ass-pounding bumps—had been a welcome escape back to a carefree time filled with new adventures for youthful Marines who'd not been shot at during their training.

There'd been little conversation on the road as each man reflected on his own experience thus far and, perhaps, on his own mortality. Paul Kreiger—minus the usual soliloquy—savored his imaginary marijuana cigarette in silence. Quiet chuckles drifted among guys who weren't so clear about how to be entertained anymore. I imagined Paul speaking the words in his mind—*Got a rosebush full of diamonds*—choosing to entertain only himself as he greedily inhaled more. *Got six Cadillacs*. Then he erupted into a coughing fit—just as I'd seen a few cigarette smokers do in the past—right on cue after taking an imaginary deep hit. Now, all of the guys in the back of the open-bed, two-and-a-half-ton truck (deuce-and-a-half) laughed hard. It turned out that Paul Kreiger was the funniest guy, even when he wasn't trying. The same convoy-stirred dust that had triggered his cough, filled our lungs as well and set off a gagging and laughing fit that fed off itself and built to a crescendo that mixed with thunderous booms of distant shellfire, which signaled the coming of our next battle and more lives lost. Once again, quiet filled the truck, if not the wretched front lines of the Pusan Perimeter.

Twenty-six hours after abandoning Sachon, we arrived in Miryang, and were placed under operational control of the Army's 24th Infantry Division. There'd been little difference seen by us boots on the ground, however. Just as we had thrown back the NKPA attackers to the south in their first defeat of the war, the central western front of the Pusan Perimeter would be the next battleground upon which we'd take orders directly from fellow Marines and, either save the day, or suffer our first stinging defeat. Those orders were to move *one way,* and push the enemy back across the Naktong River. The North Korean command had other plans, and believed that they would become the first army in history to defeat the mighty US Marine Corps.

With merciless bombardment of air support and our artillery, the 1st Battalion moved quickly, albeit with great losses. Our lungs were caked with dirt and dust from the long drive—as well as our previous engagement in the south—but we fired an endless artillery assault into enemy positions along the ridge. Edward *Denny* Flom, coughed up bits of dirt, yet continued to prepare rounds with an, as-yet, sturdy heart. The day wore on, and our eyes remained shielded from the realities of Marines losing their lives on the hills beyond us—even though our hearts saw it all in stark detail.

When Denny was relieved to get some much-needed rest, he said, "I'm okay,"

"Catch your breath," had been the order.

He found a comfortable patch of dirt behind Patrick Parrish's truck, and a corpsman checked him out. Denny was soon back in the fight, but he wasn't looking so good.

Day turned to night, and turned back to day. From our various gun positions, little changed, although one by one, the hills of Obong-ni Ridge came back under control of US Forces. But the price paid had been heavy for the Marines, and devastating for the North Koreans. On the morning of August 18, while Denny Flom was moved to an aid station, we continued to receive orders from fire control. We slammed shells into Howitzers and, subsequently, into a weakening enemy. Although we had not seen it, by 12:30 that afternoon, a flood of NKPA soldiers had made their way from various positions on and near Hill 207, in a haphazard retreat toward the Naktong River. Our artillery followed them in an onslaught that brought madness along with death, and filled the river with bodies. And so, without rest, the Marines now looked at Hill 311 for the final offensive of the battle, which would be completed the next morning.

The First Naktong Counteroffensive would go into the books with no men of the three artillery batteries of the 1st Battalion, 11th Marines killed, and only a few injured. Once again, the Army took up positions along Obong-ni

Ridge, and relieved the men of the 1st Provisional Marine Brigade—who had seen scores of their own killed, hundreds wounded, and one go missing in action. The NKPA's 4th Division had been destroyed. Among the hoards of equipment captured by the Marines, were five 105mm Howitzers, which had previously been lost to them by the Army—guns that had been turned against their rightful owners.

By August 19, Denny Flom was blowing mud out his nose where there should only have been snot. The sleeves of his shirt were spotted and smeared with it. He coughed up mud, complained of chest pains, and ran a high fever. Then, on August 20, as the Fire Brigade had been detached from the 24th Division and fell under the 8th Army's reserve, the coughing stopped. Not a gun could be heard, and no cannons fired. No man ran for the safety of foxholes or for the replenishment of mortars. The frantic pace of day-and-night battle had ceased and so, too, had the incessant cough. In the two weeks of past fighting, Marines had died all around us, yet I'd not seen my first dead Marine until this day. There was no blood or gore, only Edward Allen *Denny* Flom lying on his back with mud running from his nose. *Mud!* The official cause of death had been dust pneumonia. *Dust pneumonia?* I hadn't even known there was such a thing. If I'd paid attention on the front lines of my abbreviated Brooklyn public education, I might have learned that this very real disease had taken many lives during the dust bowl of the 1930s. But this wasn't the Great Plains. This was Korea, we were at war, and one of my closest friends was lying there dead because he breathed goddamned dirt. I wanted to pound his chest, and tell him to get the hell up and wait for a freaking bullet. No. I just wanted him to get up. I wanted him back. I didn't know how to stop the tears from running down my filthy face where they formed their own rivulets of mud. And then I didn't care a lick about either the tears or who saw them.

Denny would never know that—only a couple of weeks later—we would turn around and go back for the Second Naktong Counteroffensive. That's right. Denny breathed his last breath of dirt in order to give the ridge back to the Army who turned around and let the North Korean Army sneak back across the river. This time, they came in the form of the 9th Division, and they cap-tured the ridge a second time. But worst of all, we would now have to go and take it back again.

As we returned to the scene of the first battle at Obong-ni Ridge, angry Marines spit harsh words at their Army counterparts. Frustration on both parts ruled the day. Even Father Sporrer allowed a few unkind re-marks to pass his otherwise forgiving lips. Thus would begin a disrespect for the Army that would over time—with further shortcomings (not the word he would have chosen) witnessed by the priest—fester into hatred within a man who had dedicated his entire life to the love of all God's creatures. I would not want to have been the priests to whom he must have confessed the Korean-born contempt in his heart. Father Sporrer's eventual outspoken criticism of the Army would create discomfort within the Corps, and it led to his removal from the theater. The boots of the brigade, however (myself included), as well as many officers, would forever hold him in our highest esteem.

I will admit to a degree of disrespect, if not outright enmity, for the Army when I learned of their retreat—two retreats—as well as those that had happened before we'd arrived. For men who'd been vigorously trained on the importance of standing their ground, it had been difficult to fathom US Forces running away and leaving weapons—and in some cases, wounded comrades—behind. I hadn't been there, though, so who the Hell am I to judge? But I like to think that I would have given my life, even if the protec-tion of others and myself had been futile. And it's easy to imagine any Marine doing the same thing.

The truth is, I pitied the Army their circumstances at the beginning of the war. When the conflict had begun, they'd been pulled from their cushy posts in the occupation of Japan and thrust—undertrained, under equipped, and undermanned—into hopeless battles like bait dogs in a ring of vicious pit bulls. They'd been out maneuvered and overrun—brutally murdered when captured—in a strategy meant only to slow down the NKPA advance on Pusan while they'd waited for reinforcements. In essence, the first Army arrivals had been the sand-filled, plastic barrels on today's freeways that are designed to absorb the brunt of the blow between auto and bridge abutment beyond. No one envied their position.

The Marines, on the other hand, had arrived with recent, rigorous training—even if we were short of manpower and equipment. Every job we did, we'd lunged into with one or more elements of the Army beside us, where they had previously been left to their own devices. I didn't know it at the time, but one day I'd be in the Army—so I'm glad I hadn't judged them too harshly.

The Marines did recapture Obong-ni Ridge. But this time, the Army had been told in plain language: *You come down from that ridge again, and* we're *gonna shoot you.*

All of that happened after we'd learned that every bit of ground we'd gained in the Sachon Offensive had been given back to the North Koreans. So, we'd been sent back to Chindong-ni, the place where it had all begun for the 11th Marines. This was where Pittillo and Porter had died on our very first day of combat. We'd driven the NKPA twenty-six miles to the west, and after we'd left for Miryang, they'd taken it all back. Every shitty town, dirt road, and boot-rotting rice patty. It was not the way I'd envisioned the war progressing. Frankly, I'd figured we'd all either be dead, or we'd have sent the Red bastards back to the north where they belonged. I'd certainly not foreseen running up and down the western perimeter like the short kid in a game of monkey in the middle.

The Fire Brigade had one thing going for us, though: yellow leggings.

The Marines wore leggings over our shins that we tucked our pants into, and that came down over our boots and then strapped beneath them. By the time the Second Naktong Counteroffensive had begun, the NKPA had already been wise to *The Yellow Leggings*, as they referred to us. They'd been anxious to stand up to, and charge against, the Army, because they'd had great success against them. But—as a captured NKPA major had admitted—they feared the might and will of *The Yellow Leggings*. None of this is to say that his 9th Division handed the ridge back to the Marines when we'd arrived, but at the onset of hostilities, panic is always a preferred condition for one's enemy.

The brigade, this time attached to the Army's 2nd Infantry Division, fought gruesome battles from September 3 through 5. In regaining Obong-ni

Ridge in the Second Naktong Counteroffensive, we'd lost over thirty more Marines and almost 100 had been wounded.

When the deed had been accomplished, we coupled the Howitzers to the Prime Movers and set off for the Port of Pusan. Our final destination was unknown to us. A somber thirty-plus hour convoy had provided the necessary time to mourn the lost and digest the destructive nature of our own actions. The enemy had suffered close to 10,000 total casualties at the hands of The Fire Brigade in the Pusan Perimeter.

Now, General MacArthur had other plans for the brigade. If the Army lost Obong-ni Ridge again—unimaginable to us—they'd have to deal with it themselves. In a couple of days, we'd learn that Mac's plan was to break the back of the NKPA at The Perimeter from its flank. The trucks bounced and squealed into the port city of Pusan. LSTs (Landing Ship, Tank) loomed in the distance, there to greet the still-undefeated and reigning-champion United States Marines, and sail us off to a new front for the defense of our title. As I said "Good-bye" to Sungyong Park, I wondered how long it would take for me to puke on my second ship. I walked down the pier with the beautiful words and melody of *God Bless America* in chase. Sungyong's Korean accent had made it all the better.

CHAPTER 11

Back Breaking

DARKNESS FADED TO REVEAL TWO hundred and thirty warships—a United Nations armada—that dotted Korea Bay and Flying Fish Channel. The fiery glow of gunfire from destroyers spread through the early morning mist; its thunderous resonance manifest in every direction. The target of the allied ire had been Wolmi-Do—translated Moon Tip—an island on the northwestern coast of South Korea. It was only one hundred miles south of the 38th Parallel, which—at the time—had been the dividing line between North and South. The lovely and romantic name, *Moon Tip,* seemed misplaced among the smoke- and fire-ravaged island playground of the capital city, twenty-six miles inland. *Blood Soaked* or *Funeral Pyre* would have been much more appropriate.

Our previous month in the Pusan Perimeter, during which we'd experienced battles—the likes of which great tales of bravery, hardship, and strategic prowess would eventually be told and then largely forgotten—had not prepared us for the epic firepower and colossal effort staged in order to deliver MacArthur's newly formed X (Tenth) Corps—of which we were now part—to the shores of Inchon.

From the moment I'd trudged aboard the LST—which hadn't afforded nearly the luxuries of the old grease trap we'd called Happy Hank—in Pusan, the oily smell of diesel had filled my nostrils and infuriated my stomach. The fumes crept through my sinuses, and even seemed to coat the back of my eyes. In spite of the impending sleepless night—during which I'd fully expected to lie in my own vomit—and the lack of amenities aboard the utilitarian ship, I'd allowed myself thoughts of a leisurely cruise of a month or more. Once underway, though, we'd been assembled for a briefing, during which congratulations for our hard-fought, yet decisive victories had been offered up with the kind of pride only a Marine gets to experience. It was nice. Then the communal back pat turned to new objectives: the repatriation of Inchon and the capital city of Seoul—both of which had fallen to the North Koreans during the first days of the invasion. Apparently, I'd booked a short vacation.

The strategic plan was to starve the NKPA front of supplies and reinforcements at the Pusan Perimeter by severing its lifeline from the north. The Marines would launch the kind of assault that brings to mind the great landings of Corps lore. History would one day allow the names *Iwo Jima* and *Inchon* to be spoken in the same breath, if not with the same reverence. For those of us aboard the LST, all selfish thoughts of taking a break turned to anticipation of the fight ahead. But first, I needed to find someplace where I could be sick in private.

The Land Of The Morning Calm, as Korea is known, saw pre-dawn chaos on September 15. That's when tranquility gave way to the horrific pummeling of Wolmi-Do—a continuation of the assault that had begun two days before we'd arrived. We watched the show of force, and followed Navy destroyers through shallow Flying Fish Channel, which cut through widespread mud flats, for an amphibious landing on the triangular island in Inchon Harbor. Upon its capture in the opening days of the war, the North Koreans had fortified the island in order to protect their greedy hold on the city. Once the Marines seized it, Wolmi-Do would become the command post for the second-stage landing at the mainland city of Inchon.

Navy and Marine Corsairs swooped low through light rain, and delivered bombs to remaining hillside fortifications of the North Koreans. Deafening explosions of loosed bombs that had found their targets, the whine of seventeen landing crafts that carried men of 3rd Battalion, 5th Marines, and the thunder-evoking shells from destroyers, combined in a cacophony of ear-splitting and stomach-churning madness. From our perspective, return fire had not been evident. The LCVPs (Landing Craft, Vehicle, Personnel), crammed full of Marines, raced on the incoming thirty-two-foot tide toward Wolmi-Do. At 6:33 am, boots covered by yellow leggings scurried onto Green Beach at the northwest corner of the island, and fanned out in several directions. Three LSVs (Landing Ship Vehicle) followed them to the shoreline with a cargo of nine M26 Pershing tanks from A Company, 1st Tank Battalion. With continued air support from the F4U Corsairs, our fellow Marines had secured the Island by 7:50 that morning.

As Able Battery prepared DUKWs—landing craft referred to as *ducks*—for our approach, the tide rolled out. This left Wolmi-Do unapproachable in a sea of mud, and for the time being, the 3rd Battalion was left stranded on the island. The next high tide peaked at about 7:30 in the evening, and we struggled into Green Beach at 8:45. The ducks—loaded with Howitzers—had painfully inadequate engines, and they labored through the extraordinarily rapid currents of Inchon's outer harbor. It was a miracle that we all made it to shore, given that the powerful tide had pushed many of the ducks perilously astray.

The distinctive smell of gunpowder plus the thick odor of burnt out buildings and forest made its way to the beach as tires of the six-wheel amphibious vehicles splashed onto the small island and crunched through sand, rock, and debris. One hundred thirty-six North Korean prisoners had been placed in the swimming pool of the island's resort. As luck would have it for them, there was no water in the pool. The remainder of the enemy's forces on the island was either dead or sealed into various caves from which they'd refused to surrender. By 9:45 that evening we fired support into Inchon for the main landing force, which had already breached the city's beaches and seawalls under heavy fire. Darkness, a heavy blanket of smoke, and a lack of substantial targets all combined to give us a much-welcomed easy night that would be followed by days of grueling hard-fought battle all the way through to the capital city.

At noon the next day, with Howitzers coupled to Prime Movers, we made our way across the causeway—which was then exposed because of the low tide—and on through the coastal city. We left Wolmi-Do behind as a smoldering ruin with an American flag marking its 335-foot peak, and advanced on a northerly route from Inchon toward Seoul in support of the 5th Marine Regiment. While the advance was swift, there had been little relief from both constant displacements and a sustained barrage leveled upon the enemy as we pushed them—in a fighting retreat—toward their stronghold in and around Seoul. By the evening of the 17th, we'd made it to the perimeter of Kimpo Airfield, part of which was then captured by elements of the 5th.

In the middle of that night—the early morning of the 18th—I'd been relieved of the watch in a preplanned rotation by Stephen *Smiley* Grzesick. Exhausted, I crawled under the muzzle of the Howitzer, and curled up on top of several empty ammo boxes. The relentless pace of the prior two days had left me weary beyond reason, and—despite the rumbles of distant engagements—I fell into deep and immediate sleep. During one of many small counterattacks sometime in the following hours, an artillery shell fell on our position. It was so close to the gun that I should have awakened and scrambled into a foxhole. The truth is, I should have been asleep in the damned foxhole to begin with. But there I'd been, under the gun, and I hadn't even stirred. Finally, dawn's soft light snuck up over the distant airfield and filtered through my eyelids. I awoke to discover that Smiley had been evacuated during the night, because shortly after relieving me, he'd been severely wounded in that isolated attack on our position.

The chatter that morning within Able Battery about the nighttime attack swirled around me like spirits in a B-grade ghost story. I was left speechless at the thought of tragedy striking so close. I never felt as though the offending shell had been intended for me—and that Smiley had suffered my fate—because our change of watch had been predetermined. He had been exactly where he was supposed to be when misfortune had found its mark. I, however, understood that if the attack had taken place just a little earlier, I'd have been that mark. Moreover, I knew that, in spite of my own good fortune, I had let my guard down. Weeks of robotic action in battle, combined with a measure of luck in the form of few casualties for the battery, had not diminished the fear in any of us. Still, a degree of complacency had seeped through our ranks unnoticed. Whereas even short naps had been fitful at best in the opening days of the Pusan Perimeter, it was now possible to sleep deeply right through chaos. The relative safety of the foxhole gave way to thoughts of comfort. Its a hell of a thing to wake up floating in your foxhole because of torrential downpours during the night, and sometimes that was reason enough to take a sloppily-calculated risk beyond my personal place of refuge. In that night's case, the simple lure of neatly placed wooden crates as a makeshift bed had been enough to seduce me.

I'd dropped my defenses, and could just as easily been headed to a MASH unit with life-threatening injuries as my friend Smiley had been. I'd never learn of his fate. It seems reasonable that, if he'd later died of his wounds, word would have come back to us. I hope that today he is sharing that ever-present smile with his great grandchildren—just as I am fortunate enough to do with mine.

The truth is, though, with all the battle we'd seen, I really hadn't ever known how fortunate I'd been. The luckiest day in my life had been when someone up the chain had decided that I was—in response to my request for the Fleet Marine Force—well suited to Artillery. I still believe that was my "punishment" for wanting off the rifle range at Parris Island. As I've said, The Marine Corps is funny that way. I excelled with my rifle, but even though it was at my side continuously, I'd rarely fired it. The infantry is my vision—it's every Marine's perception—of what makes a man a Marine. *Rifleman first.* Yet every day, I'd rest my M1 Garand—along with the others—against ammo crates, trees, or backpacks in the vicinity of the big gun. Meanwhile, the infantry stormed up hills to enemy positions in close combat where rifles, and the brave men who wielded them, ruled the day. Grenades and bayonets had both saved and taken lives, as we'd fired support from relatively safe distances. I knew the truth, but from my personal battle cocoon, I was not forced to *see* it. Our sense of the war popped, clanged, and boomed all around us, and—like the space between the artillery and the infantry—it shielded our view of the everyday hardship and horror they endured. It may not seem like much, but even getting from one battle to the next had been a blessing for us that we rarely acknowledged. We'd covered hundreds of miles in the Pusan Perimeter on the backs of Deuce-And-A-Halves, while the majority of the infantry had trudged it on foot or, at best, rotated on and off various available vehicles. The transportation-inflicted piles that had tortured my ass were merely a physiological manifestation of my good fortune.

And now, with the all-important capture of Kimpo completed on the morning after Smiley's injuries, we advanced toward Seoul. The Marines left the airfield in good hands for much-appreciated air-support operations that could now be based closer to the city. It was there, at the doors to the city, where we met an impassioned NKPA that was determined to defend the city. Once again, the infantry would lift small arms beyond the reach of our sanitized view and, eventually, our mighty cannons. We crossed the Han River and faced three intensely-fortified hills of opposition northwest of the city.

For the next three days—September 22 through 25—we fired hundreds of rounds of high-explosive artillery throughout hills 105A, 105B, and 298. To me, it was just another sea of hills that, for all the punishment they received, I'd half expected to crumble before our eyes and reveal the once-great, ancient city of Seoul. But return fire continued to bedevil our positions from those high and mighty strongholds. Just as in every previous battle, boots would storm these hills, and the inhabitants of those boots would either die or conquer for the greater good. Even though their advances were made possible by the unforgiving guns at our hands, every advance, each conquest, and hill after hill captured, was accomplished through the grit and fortitude of foot Marines who knew only one direction—forward. The final hill, 105B, was secured on the evening of the 25th. Hundreds of Marines had died taking the lives of thousands of North Koreans. I was merely dirty and tired.

The frenetic pace had shielded me from an empty feeling that I would not fully grasp until a couple months later, when I, too, would walk the walk of the infantry. For now, I continued to lay fire for men who laid down their lives. Late on the 25th, we turned our guns toward the city. Without respite, the best-trained fighting force in the world entered the city on foot behind M-26 tanks to clear all enemy positions within its crumbling walls. The arduous and menacing process of clearing every house, office, storefront, and street had already begun. We leveled our artillery in order to clear roadblocks as well as any pockets of resistance. Marines made slow progress along dark, quiet, and seemingly deserted streets that could be identified at night. Then, from three miles out, the unmistakable cracks of automatic-weapon fire rushed to us from the city. Opposing tanks bellowed their disdain for the enemy on each side, and we added our occasional, well placed rounds to the mix as the death chorus sang throughout the night. People were surely dying down there; we just didn't know what uniforms they wore.

For the next two days, we tracked the progress of Marines in the city by the coordinates of our fire. From so far away, only the slightest adjustment of the gun could mean a full two city-block advance. With the passing hours, we watched our rounds erupt deeper and deeper into the city. Our fire—always precise—was intensive at times, and measured at others. We knew that no good would come from creating more destruction in the city, which might provide better opportunities for concealment of gun placements and a fervent enemy.

Behind every pile of rubble and every splintered door, the Marines met fanatical NKPA soldiers who would cause great casualties in their futile attempt to hold the city. House-to house combat saw Seoul littered with casualties from both sides. So, as the 5th Marines came face-to face with enemy combatants, and they walked into well-placed traps, and snipers picked off men left exposed in dusty streets, we reflected on the lucky favor bestowed upon us. We'd enjoyed an accidental blessing that was akin to a child who happens to be born into a wealthy family. We performed our long-straw duties with urgency, yet—at times like these—we didn't necessarily feel good about the infantry's short straw.

On September 29—with sporadic fighting still sprinkled about the city— Republic of Korea troops marched in a parade, while Marines provided security, and General Douglas MacArthur turned over the city of Seoul to President Syngman Rhee. It is certainly true that the Marines had savaged the NKPA and, at this point, Seoul was repatriated with a thankful nation that only a few short weeks ago had been on the brink of extinction. But it seemed disrespectful to indulge in ceremonial pomp and circumstance when Marines were still ducking bullets mere blocks away. There was—and is—little doubt regarding the greatness of the military mind that was cradled beneath MacArthur's helmet. The bold and successful amphibious landing at Inchon, which many military minds had feared would prove epic in its failure, the speedy advance across the twenty-six miles from Inchon to Seoul (during which the NKPA had been rolled over, plowed through, and chased in scampered retreat), as well as the crushing defeat of a hell-bent, fanatical opponent within the capital city, had all proved—beyond question—the general's superior skills as commander, and fed proportional measures of ego beneath that already snug head cover.

At the end of the day, I guess it's okay. You and I don't think the way men of MacArthur's stature do, and I doubt many would want to. He'd moved his chess pieces with dauntless dexterity and cunning. Despite the assemblage of hundreds of ships off the coast of Inchon, he'd managed a surprise attack upon a city that had been considered unassailable from the sea. If self-aggrandizement and showmanship were his only valued rewards, let him have them.

When the liberation of both Inchon and Seoul was complete, and security of the city rested with the 8th Army—who then chased the North Koreans across the 38th Parallel—X Corps made way its back to the coast. We took with us a measured understanding that history had been fashioned beneath our weary bones, before our crushing guns, and on the very backs of hard-charging Marines. Less than two-and-a-half months after the start of the war, the battered and beaten aggressors scurried back across the border. The entire offensive would be remembered as one of the toughest battles in Marine Corps history, with far too many killed and wounded. Little solace could be found in the staggering number of enemy losses: nearly 14,000 casualties and 4,800 prisoners. Many of us had the sense that the three-week operation had all but sealed a soon-to-follow total victory. With dwindling supplies and no reinforcements, the NKPA front around Pusan had crumbled and those soldiers were cut off in their retreat to the north. The 1st provisional Marines—the Fire Brigade—had trampled the enemy in the Pusan Perimeter, and MacArthur's X Corps had broken the back and paralyzed the Red Giant from the north. The Korean War was destined to be the shortest conflict in modern US warfare.

Or so we thought.

CHAPTER 12

Duck Soup

WE FLOATED ALL NIGHT. THE engine of the DUKW struggled as we entered the still waters of Wonsan Harbor, and we fell behind the landing party. Then, with a sputter, the engine fell silent. The rest of the 1st Battalion had already disappeared in the dark night, and presumably gone ashore without us. Behind us, silhouettes of LSTs sat quiet at immeasurable distances. We didn't have a radio, and—to our dismay—none of us aboard the duck knew Morse Code. But everyone knows the dots and dashes of S.O.S. *Or is that dashes and dots?* It didn't matter. Sergeant Buckles spun the signal lamp toward the flotilla, and flashed a convincing series of light pulses back to the ships. Coherent message or not, they'd at least know we were out there. In short time, a one-sided conversation began by way of flashing lights. *S.O.S.* from us, and gibberish from the LST. We followed with another *S.O.S.*, and then the ship returned more gibberish. Aboard the duck, it had been anybody's guess whether the second string of nonsensical flashes was a new message or the same as the first. So we settled back and awaited assistance.

It didn't come.

Buckles allowed ample time for a LCVP to be launched and deployed to our position. The sound of the approaching craft would be evident long before a sighting. Total silence. After an hour of waiting, the sergeant lifted the lamp and sent another S.O.S. When the return illumination of blather reached us, it became apparent to all of us that we were far off our earlier coordinates from the mother ship. Additionally, we had little clue where the landing area was in relation to our position, or how far away from shore we had now floated. The LST went dark. Buckles didn't know if he should respond again. Then the signal lamp pierced the darkness, and reflected off the black, rippled surface of the great harbor. We scoffed and moaned at the meaningless light show.

With irritation, Buckles flashed his own incoherent signal back to the useless Navy vessel, and said, "Just come get us, assholes."

With the rising sun, came the drone of a slow-moving craft. It was going to take an eternity for these clowns to reach us. I surveyed our position a full 360 degrees, and—even in the soft morning light—could not determine where the landing zone was. That had never been my responsibility, anyway, so I didn't dwell.

"What the fuck?" Said an exasperated Sergeant Buckles to the sailors in the approaching landing craft.

The guy on the bow tossed a line. "Sorry for the wait, boys."

Two other sailors were scanning the surface of the water, and the fourth steered the vessel with a soft touch.

"We're gonna do our best to get back out of here in one piece."

"Whadda ya talking about?" Buckles's head snapped back and forth—his eyes surveyed the surface of the water.

"Mines, buddy. We're in the thick of it. We signaled that you were approaching the field."

"Oh, shit."

"You guys don't know Morse Code, do ya?"

"Shit."

"Ha! We figured as much when you flashed all dots—the universal code for frustration. We'd just informed you that you'd entered the mine field and that we'd see you in the morning—Godspeed and all that."

I was never so happy to *not* know the code behind the blinking lights developed by Samuel Morse. The late news of our predicament had been met with gladness for my earlier ignorance. The sailors made slow and careful work of towing us back into the previously-cleared channel from which we had strayed. Sixteen eyes in the disabled craft—and eight in the towboat—studied every shadow, sparkle, and splash in the water.

We'd reached Wonsan Harbor five days before, but could not attempt the landing. Unlike Wolmi-Do and Inchon, the Rockets Red Glare did not precede us—not that we'd seen, anyway. The city had already been taken by the now feisty and reequipped ROK Army. All we'd had to do was get men and equipment onto the unprotected beach. A major supply port in North Korea, Wonsan Harbor had been littered with Russian-made mines long before the aggressors had attacked across the 38th Parallel. By the time we reached the theater, the clearing operation—which was yet completed—had been well underway. For five days, we'd steamed to and fro like an expectant father pacing the maternity ward waiting room. Others had dubbed our back-and-forth delay "Operation Yo-Yo."

The Army's 7th Division and Marine Air maintenance crews had arrived ahead of us. And so had Bob Hope. On the evening of October 26, Hope and Marilyn Maxwell had entertained while we *yoed*—or maybe we'd been *yoing*; I couldn't tell the difference. When we'd made it ashore, we learned of Hope's visit, but he was already long gone.

I said, "Jeez, we missed a show."

I never did get to see a single USO show during my deployment.

On shore, the flyboys waved us in, and repeated the entertainer's jokes that had been leveled at our expense. Apparently, everyone had found it funny that the Marines had been engaged in Operation Yo-Yo while the rest of them yucked it up. And it had been especially amusing to them that one duckling had gone astray of the flock and had floated into a crowded mine field. Laughter eluded me. Whatever. Marines don't depend on entertainment. We didn't give a crap one way or the other. That's the truth. We had a job to do, and we were going to do it. Leave the laughter to the Army. *But we would have gone to the show if we'd been there on time. Ha ha!*

With our delayed arrival, we were now in place for the Home By Christmas Offensive. The North Korean People's Army had fled to the only place they'd ever had a right to be—North Korea. This wasn't good enough for MacArthur, however, and he'd received Truman's blessings to chase them down and destroy them. We would neither corner the NKPA, nor incapacitate them. We would not demand their unconditional surrender. Where there was now an army still capable of doing harm, in the end, there would be none. And that end would be swift. Home by Christmas was the battle cry of troops who would—within the following month—lay waste to the invaders who had overrun and terrorized the South. We would reunify the severed peninsular into one democratic country of Korea. Then, by December 25, we'd cozy up with eggnog, light the Yule log, and sing carols around the tree.

CHAPTER 13

Frozen

CHRISTMAS IS FOR KIDS. IT'S magic to them. Santa, the tree, lights, decorations, music, toys, treats, parties, vacation from school—it's the stuff that developing imaginations run away with. As a child, I'd been no different. Although the holiday brought less of everything on the list than many of the kids in my neighborhood experienced, it had been my favorite holiday from the start. The whole family went to church together, and the place was packed. Ma would make a special dinner—sometimes turkey—and a couple sides more than the usual potatoes and cabbage. She'd pull out the small box of decorations that she kept in a closet, and she'd make our drab apartment sparkle. Sometimes there'd even be a tree. But, tree or not, it was always a special day. My Christmas-morning, mama-bear hug would be followed by a fifty-cent piece placed in my palm by her gentle hand. A fortune! I used to anticipate that gleaming coin as much as the kids up by the park anticipated their shiny new Schwinns. By the time I'd reached my teens, I'd slip the coveted currency back in her change purse next to a couple of lonely dimes and pennies that held much less luster. It was my gift to her.

"You're a good boy, Joey," she'd say later—her way to let me know she was on to me.

Later in life, when Barbara and I had made a family of our own, Christmas would always see a seven-foot tree in the far corner of our living room. The size left just enough room for the tree stand below and the silver star atop, which fit right under the eight-foot ceiling. Gifts for nine children would line the two walls that led to the tree and they'd meet at an ark of more gifts neatly piled around the base of the tree. Slight of hand and well-managed mirror tricks made the lot seem more than it was, and—gratefully—our children never felt slighted. Barbara and I would set out to shop for gifts armed with the few dollars we'd managed to stash away in the Christmas club at the bank, as well as the uniform allowance that the police department coughed up every December. Half the gifts had always been things the children actually needed, and we had to buy anyway—like clothes. Plus, each of them got at least one toy that they'd had their heart set on. And each year, a couple of them would get one extra-special item—a bicycle, a sled, or some other gift that held special meaning and cost us extra money. We'd keep careful track of who got what when, and we'd rotate costly gifts among them through the years. The rest of the presents were rounded out with less expensive yet fun items. All nine children had always been excited and grateful.

We'd run through the Christmas-gift money like a dog through a turkey sandwich, so there was usually only a pittance left to buy gifts for each other. One year, I tore through the wrapping paper of Barbara's gift to me and found a very serviceable pair of pajama pants.

"Oh, these are beautiful," I said. "Thank you."

Then I opened the gift she'd gotten for the children to present to me and found the matching shirt.

"Aha ha ha! It's like you guys knew exactly what the other had gotten me!"

Christmas with our kids was always fun and filled with love.

But in November of 1950, I hadn't yet held those fond memories that were still decades in the future. I did, however, cling to thoughts of the Christmas that was just over a month away. *Could it be true?* I hadn't had a Christmas at home since I'd joined the Marines, and I prayed that this year would be the one. But the tunnel through which I saw the ever-more dubious light at the end came to me in the form of rising mountains, deepening valleys, and a deteriorating dirt road that led north through enemy territory. Rather than the end of our trek, it now looked more like the beginning of a new and ominous odyssey. Powerful winds that buffeted our faces pushed the temperature down and stung our bodies through the lightweight dungarees and field jackets we'd been issued in the south during warmer days. Cold-weather gear had failed to arrive in time for the early winter incursion that filtered down from Siberia and assaulted us.

First, the motor march took us through Hamhung, and then to an agricultural station where we laid low for some days while the 7th Marines prepared to launch the attack through to the Chosin Reservoir. With the 1st Battalion, 11th Marines, I would soon follow in the footsteps of the 5th Marines, who would sustain the attack that the 7th had initiated. As we moved forward, we encountered villages that the 7th had left in shambles. Whispers of *Chinese* filtered their way to the enlisted men in trucks and on foot. Nobody verbalized the question that was apparent in every set of eyes. *What, exactly, does that mean?*

By the time we'd reached Chinhung-ni, the dirt road climbed steeply, and the Deuce-And-A-Halves labored with the weight of the 105 Howitzers through narrow switchbacks on the edge of terrifying drops.

The 11th's convoy was a day behind the 5th's when we reached the gatehouse at Funchilin Pass. The scene here, with its soaring, snow-covered cliffs, and plunging valleys of steep, ragged terrain, was one of majesty and mystery. I had not, in all my time in Korea, felt so far from home, and so completely isolated. The flat bridge at the gatehouse crossed over four enormous pipes that—in perfect symmetry—zigzagged down the mountain in order to carry water from the Chosin Reservoir to a power plant in the valley. It was an impossible feat of engineering. From the back of our truck, I watched the bridge pass beneath the Howitzer, and the realization that this was the only way out rolled through my head with the steady crunch of the tires.

Winter gear, and Thanksgiving, caught up to us at the plateau village of Koto-ri, a few miles north of the gatehouse. Cumbersome, knee-length parkas covered layers of clothes that included two pair of pants over long underwear, a long undershirt, two heavy shirts, sweater and field jacket. With thick, warm gloves, we unhitched the Howitzers while our bulldozers dug gun pits in the frozen, rugged earth. The smell of diesel and exhaust from the heavy equipment was crisp in the frigid air. More dozers scraped the finishing touches of a rough airstrip even as planes landed with supplies and brass. On

Thanksgiving, November 23, a melt-in-your-mouth meal, with all the traditional trimmings, made its way to our positions. It *had* to melt in our mouths, because by the time it reached our hands, it had been frozen solid. Braced against the wind and snow, we hunched over behind the prime movers and chipped away at the delicacies. Bricks of mince pie dumbfounded us.

As we reached Hagaru-ri, at the southern edge of the reservoir, the temperature dipped to zero. By this time, even the grunts had been made aware of the Chinese Communist Forces (CCF) that were massing to the north. We knew the time was about to come when the now relatively-clear way that the 7th Marines had provided us would vanish. Hard fighting was only days away, but—based on past experience—we were all confident in our ability to crush the opposition. Most of us were now seasoned combat veterans, and we could lead the replacements to victory, just as the Second World War veterans had done for us in the Pusan Perimeter.

By the 27th, we'd dug in the guns in the Yudam-ni valley at the western edge of the reservoir. It was here that we would make a stand and cover the 5th Marines for their assault on the CCF troops massed on the reverse slopes of the mountains to our north and west. The guns of 1st Battalion took the west. By midnight, the Siberian winds had made a joke of our parkas, with the temperature dropping to twenty or more degrees below zero. The blare of bugles carried with the wind, green and white phosphorous flares filled the sky, mortars exploded throughout the valley, and machine-gun fire erupted in a continuous stream. Every position was under attack. Tracers ricocheted around us as we loaded and fired with machine-like efficiency. Guns of the entire regiment pocked the mountaintops with fiery explosions as the onslaught of Chinese soldiers mounted their campaign. My repeated prayer as I prepared round after round for the Howitzer had been, *Just stay alive.* I said it for myself, as well as for every other Marine in the valley.

The battle had raged without a break until dawn, when the CCF retreated to regroup. There'd been a fair amount of regrouping to do for the Marines, as well, since lines had been penetrated and casualties had mounted. That day, additional aid tents had been erected, and a steady stream of choppers evacuated the worst-case injured. Only occasional mortar rounds exploded that day, as warning to the Marines to stay back. We got what sleep we could in the harsh cold that had not let up at all, not even at midday. I suffered from what had become known as *Korean Back.* The freezing cold penetrated my body, and caused the muscles of my back to cramp in unbearable pain. It'd been bad enough when I worked at the gun—moving constantly and generating some body heat. But to lie down in a bag on the frozen ground, it had been impossible to find a position that would calm my back. Sleep, if it arrived at all, came in winks.

At midnight, distant bugles once again sent chills through our already-frozen bodies. The fiery battle eruption repeated itself and followed the same routine as the previous night. Mortar explosions on both sides blended into one continuous heart-thumping drumbeat of devastation, and machine-gun fire syncopated the morose melody. The mountains glowed with explosions, fire, flares, and tracers. Nostrils and lungs burned with the smoke that whipped through the valley floor on the frigid wind. Morning would find air support with bombs and napalm that would drive the Chinese back, but the long hours until then required the men on the ground to go it alone. I could not imagine the toll we'd taken on the enemy forces or how they could sustain the battle, but they did—and at great cost to the Marines. The knowledge that they'd suffered ten, twenty, or even a hundred times more dead then we was of little consolation. The basis of that multiplier had been the number of our dead Marines. Each one of them had been a heavy burden to every single surviving Marine out there.

By dawn, word had reached the battery that, although we'd sent the Chinese scrambling for cover once again, our Main Supply Route (MSR) had been cut. We'd walked into a trap unlike any the Marine Corps had ever encountered before, and we'd been surrounded by elements of six or more Chinese divisions. The feelings of isolation and dread that I'd experienced the previous week at Funchilin Pass had jelled into the painful reality of the present. The new plan was to join the forces of all the regiments and stage a breakout to Hagaru-ri, which was fourteen miles to the south. It was obvious that the Chinese plan was for the utter destruction of the 1st Marine Division. I avoided making any mental wagers on the outcome.

On the 29th of November, the 7th Marines once again took the lead in an attempt to drive the Chinese out of Toktong Pass to our south—the only route out. Heavy fighting and mounting losses forced the 7th to pass the load to the 5th, and retreat into reserve. Late that night, our convoy inched from the valley toward the pass. Trucks were now loaded with the dead and wounded. All unnecessary gear and materials had been destroyed in the valley to create the space needed in order to carry them out.

As we made our way through the pass, the Chinese sniped in a constant barrage from strongholds on the hillsides to either side. Frequent pauses in our advance had been required to systematically drive them off. As we lifted rifles or loaded mortar shells to fire at point-blank range, *Korean Back* played havoc throughout the ranks. Wind whistled through the pass, and into our weakening bodies. Examination of Chinese casualties found many men dressed in dungarees, light jackets, and—in many cases—only sneakers on their already frozen feet. Perhaps the cold would kill the rest of them before we'd have to.

Dawn of November 30th found heavy snowfall whipped up by swirling winds. Visibility had been nearly as low as our chances of survival. I couldn't see anything beyond the second truck in front of me, and the eerie feeling of being enclosed by an unseen enemy crept over me as surely as the Chinese did the convoy. Our Battalion advanced to the front of the line in order to set up a battery to cover those at our rear, as well as for the infantry ahead. With guns dug in and pointed in every direction, we waited for the snow to subside so that targets could be identified. But the only target that materialized had been for the enemy. A forward observer from my battery, Donald Gerald Miles, rode the rest of the way out in the back of one of the trucks as part of a pile of frozen bodies. My buddy, Bryan Simmons, volunteered to take his place on the front line that encircled us.

"Bryan. Are you sure about this?" I asked.

"Yeah, I'm sure. Somebody's gotta go, and I've got more experience than the rest of you clowns."

It was a good use of humor to hide the nerves.

"I'm proud of you." I gave him a hug. "You got anything you want me to hold on to?"

He looked to the south—the direction he was about to move with one of the captains—then back to me. "I got 300 bucks on me."

"300 bucks? What are you doing with that kind of money?" The majority of my money had been sent home to Ma.

"Ha! No place to spend it, slick."

"I'll hold it for you, if you want. When you get back, I'll give it to you."

"What if I don't come back?"

"Don't even say that."

"Yeah." He rocked his M-1 on its butt, which rested on the ground. "But what if?"

"I'll send the money to your parents in Pennsylvania. Every dollar. Promise."

"Humph. You think I don't trust you? I don't want anything going to my parents."

He pulled off his gloves, and made work of tugging his wallet free. Then he huffed steaming breath across cupped hands and recovered them.

"Send it to *your* parents."

"You'll get it back in Hagaru or Koto-ri or Hungnam. I'm proud of you."

When Bryan left with the captain, I went to Digger's truck and stuffed the wallet in the bottom of my pack—with no certainty at all that Bryan would ever collect it. Two days later, on December 2, I said a prayer that the bullet that had entered Bryan's head had killed him before he'd frozen to death. Bryan Simmons's body joined countless others in the back of one of the countless trucks.

When word of his death reached the battery, I was devastated. He'd had a good friend, Bill Araujo, in Baker Battery. They'd served together in China before reaching Camp Pendleton. I didn't know Bill very well, but felt he should know. My CO assured me that Bill was already taking the news about Bryan hard. I wished that I could go see him, but there was a war to fight.

CHAPTER 14
Ambush

WHEN IT COMES TO WAR, there is a big picture that most people—especially those who peer in through the television news or local newspapers—readily see and understand. Nations' armies moving en mass—gaining or losing ground, routing an enemy force or retreating from a relentless assault, and raising flags in battles victorious or licking the collective wounds of stinging defeats—stir our emotions and pride.

But the boot—the foot soldier, the grunt—rarely gets this panoramic view that sums up the events of days and weeks of battle and troop movement. His is a small, albeit seemingly never-ending war. It is measured in anguished moments that string themselves together in a connect-the-dots drawing of survival. It is not seen in casualty numbers strewn across a foreign land, but in knowing that the man to his right, and the man to his left are still alive. *Or not.* That he himself is still alive, even though he is not truly sure what being *alive* feels like anymore.

As the generals and commanders—a safe distance from the smell of battle—move paperweights over a large map on a table in order to visualize the advance of battalions, the grunt futilely shakes the cold from his feet, rolls from his position behind a berm, and prays that the next gunshot he hears will not be his last. He knows nothing of the generals' plans for advancing thousands of Marines over hills, through valleys, or across rivers, only of his lieutenant's last order. He will know his next move when that superior shares it with him. In his microcosm of the war, there is no need to know the why, what, where, or when. He doesn't ask. He isn't told. Survival is foremost on his mind—for himself and for the man in the foxhole next to him. *Kill or be killed* is his mantra when gunfire shatters the still night.

It's personal. I don't know if the family who peeked in on us at the Chosin Reservoir, through the evening news—their stomachs filled with pot roast and mashed potatoes—understood that. At times, I felt that someone was trying to kill me—like a drive-by shooting on a city street, rather than like an enemy army that was trying to win a war or a battle. In war, every battle is staged through smaller battles—platoon against platoon, man against man, and it is very personal. Every day, every moment, we knew that the next fight was coming, but we rarely knew when. Battles aren't scheduled like a lunch-hour fistfight in the schoolyard. A timekeeper's bell doesn't sound as opponents circle each other and rock from foot to foot in considered appraisal of each other. When we were lucky, our signal to commence hostilities came in the form of a shell exploding to our flank or the sound of rapid gunfire that—while it moves close—provides an instant to dive for cover. Often, we were not so lucky.

The infantry losses continued to mount, and replacements flowed from the artillery batteries to the rifle-in-hand ranks. I was on a still-active Howitzer team, and I didn't think I would have to volunteer. Of course, I was theirs to use as they pleased. But we had all been taught from the start that Marines are riflemen first. Everything else is secondary. So I volunteered. I don't remember how many other guys volunteered with me, but it was a lot. The way I saw it was that somebody had to do it, and it might as well be me. I'm sure the others felt the same way. I'm not going to say that I—or any of those other guys wanted to go. There's something to be said about firing 105mm shells at an enemy we didn't even see, because he is three or four miles away. Those days were over, though. We didn't know what we were getting ourselves into, but we all believed in the call of duty, and nobody wanted to be called a coward. Nobody. So we volunteered.

What might have been on my first day with Item Company, 3rd Battalion, 7th Marines, I reported to Lieutenant Buckley. I was later assigned to a squad of thirteen men and sent out on a nighttime patrol. We had no idea what the objective was, although I'm sure the sergeant with us—my friend Buckles—did. The rest of us found out soon enough: find and clear any traps that had been set before the convoy chugged through.

We spread out in single file, and walked south down the left side of the road. The rumble of the M-26 Pershing tank that lead the way provided a semblance of comfort. I was the last man in the line, while another corporal—Sanchez—had the front, about ten yards behind the tank. The darkness was close to complete, and I followed along by the sound of footsteps ahead of me as much as by sight. Someone screamed a warning from up front and the road ahead erupted in flames. Sanchez would later explain that a Korean local had crossed the road carrying what appeared to be a bundle of firewood or rice plants secured to an A-frame on his back. When the man had dropped the bundle, it burst into flames, and he disappeared into the night. The bright light blinded us. From the enemy gun positions up the hill to our left, there may as well have been a bank of spotlights on us. This, of course, was their intention.

Machine-gun fire flared up with the flames and swept to the right. It started with the second man in line and ended with the twelfth. The quick reaction time to dive for cover on the slight grade off the right side of the road was fruitless. There were no trees, no rocks, and no walls to hide behind—just frozen, rocky earth that sloped down away from the road. Every one of the eleven men between Sanchez and me was hit. I made myself as flat as possible and tried to gather my thoughts. *Tonight's the night I die* was all I had.

I would receive the Bronze Star with Valor for the things I did next. *Valor.* I was nineteen years old, a product of sewage-basin Brooklyn, and a runaway from my father's heavy hand. What did I know about *valor?* For what it's worth, here is what the secretary of the Navy had to say about it:

The President of the United States takes pleasure in presenting the BRONZE STAR MEDAL to

CORPORAL JOSEPH A. LYNCH,
UNITED STATES MARINE CORPS,

For service as set forth in the following

For heroic achievement while serving as a Squad Leader in a Provisional Platoon consisting of components from an Infantry Unit and an Artillery Unit of the First Battalion, Eleventh Marines, First Marine Division (Reinforced), in action against enemy aggressor forces in Korea on 8 December 1950. When an outnumbering enemy force attacked his platoon's position, Corporal Lynch repeatedly exposed himself to the blistering shellfire to assist in evacuating casualties and, when both his platoon commander and platoon sergeant were wounded, unhesitatingly assumed command. Effecting a prompt and skillful reorganization, he boldly led his men in a brilliantly executed assault to rout the over-whelming force and wipe out several enemy positions. By his daring initiative, forceful leadership and courageous actions in the face of grave peril, Corporal Lynch served as an inspiration to all who observed him and upheld the highest traditions of the United States Naval Services.

Corporal Lynch is authorized to wear the Combat "V."

For the President,
F. P. Matthews
Secretary of the Navy.

I'll say this: Whoever writes these citations must be paid well, because when I received mine, even I was impressed. I'm sure these writers must have found lucrative jobs after the war reporting the news, providing descriptive prose for catalog companies, or writing greeting-card tearjerkers.

Tonight's the night I die. I had no time to deal with this thought or the reality I found in it. Machine-gun fire continued over my head. I didn't know how many of the other men had already died. The tank was gone. Apparently unaware of the situation behind them, the tankers had continued churning up the frozen road to the south. I accepted the truth that I and whoever else was still alive would be wiped out on the side of this road. But I was not going to just lie there and wait for death.

I'd seen some men run, stumble, or roll off the road with me. Someone slithered down right beside me. Curses and moans made their way through clenched teeth of the wounded and to the shallow ditch where I held my position. "I'm hit." "I'm hit." The echoed exclamation of pain and confusion came from several voices. Screams from the road pierced my heart. Someone was still out there, and despite the dying flames, his calls for help kept our position pinpointed for the enemy attackers. If he didn't die from the wounds he had already suffered, more would soon follow to finish the deed. The Marine screamed, "Help me. Help me." I felt a chill that had nothing to do with the temperature.

Someone else called, just loudly enough for me to hear—it was Corporal Sanchez. He let his position be known to anyone who was still with us. Other than stifled cries and the screams from the road, he and I were the only ones who checked in. We each now knew that it was just the two of us. I could make out the shape of someone lying on the road. I looked to my right toward the barely-glowing embers of the fading fire. If Sanchez, who was closer to the fallen Marine, moved to the road, I'd be able to see him. He did not. So the Marine on the road was mine.

I stayed as low as I could and ran out to the screaming Marine. *Is this when it happens?* When I reached him—it was Ben Perry—I did what I could to quiet him.

I whispered, "You have to stay quiet, Ben."

He was badly hurt, but he cooperated. He understood.

I said, "I'm gonna pull you to the side of the road. Okay?"

He said, "Yeah. Yeah." and nodded.

I got hold of him under his arms and pulled. The scream he let out stopped the blood in my veins. I thought I would shit myself. Bullets scattered the ice about us, and pieces stung my face. I dropped down and waited to be hit. I thought we were dead. It turned out that the bullet he'd taken had gone in the back of his left shoulder, through the top of his back, and had come to rest in his right shoulder. I could not have chosen a more painful way to move him. He whimpered in pain, and I shook all over. We both buzzed with adrenaline-laced terror.

I said, "Okay, okay, okay, can you move your feet?"

He said, "Yeah."

"Do you think you can get up on your knees? I'll help you."

He said, "I'll try."

I knew that when a Marine says, "I'll try," he's damn sure going to do it. I got under his chest and rolled him up, and he got to his knees.

I held him steady and asked, "Can you get up on your feet now? I'll help you."

He nodded. Even in the darkness, I could see the pain in his face. He was really toughing it out. I didn't want to touch his back, so I helped him from the front, and he was able to get up on his feet.

I said, "Okay? Let's go. Move as fast as you can." And I hurried him over to the side.

I had lost all sense of time. I didn't know if five minutes or an hour had passed since the enemy had opened fire. At life or death intersections, time is irrelevant. But I did know that we had a long haul before daybreak would bring relative safety. I had Corporal Sanchez help me move all the dead and wounded together for warmth. Sergeant Buckles had been hit in the groin and could not be moved, so we dragged and pushed and carried the others close to him and then piled them all together. The enemy was shooting into the dark now, and could only hit us with lucky shots. But some of the wounds were bad, and the possibility of losing more men to the subzero and subhuman temperature was real. Sanchez's and my warmth would come from movement.

It had not been so long before this night that nobody had known the Korean War was about to come. The other guys at Pendleton and I had never even thought about war. We just did what we were told, and we did it as well as we could. It makes me proud to have been a Marine, because they trained me for what was to come on that frozen road during that terrifying night, whether they knew that war was coming or not. By the time I made the decision to get that Marine off the road, I knew that the training I'd received at Pendleton had kicked in. When Sanchez and I hurried to gather the dead and wounded together, even while the enemy sprayed the roadside with bullets, the thinking came easier.

Buckles assured me, "You can do this."

By this point, it no longer felt like thinking. I merely reacted to the situation the way the Marine Corps had taught me to. Sanchez and I would spend the rest of the night alternating between moving and firing, with periodic checks on the fallen. They had to stay warm, and they had to be encouraged to last the night. I hurried into a position about thirty yards to the left, and sprayed the hillside with gunfire. As soon as I stopped, Sanchez fired a salvo from far off to the right of the wounded men's position, while I made haste to find another spot closer to the enemy. When I fired, Sanchez moved. We continued this routine in an effort to keep the Chinese confused about our positions and numbers. Their fire always came from the same positions, so at least we knew where to shoot. The strategy worked. I didn't know if we'd inflicted casualties on them, or if they merely tired of us, but eventually—about an eternity and a half later—all of their gunfire ceased.

Sanchez and I took turns staying with the wounded, while the other kept watch. At first light, the unmistakable rattle of diesel engines began to tease us from the north. I stopped the first truck to reach us, and reported the night's events to the commanding officer. Survival is always the first priority, while getting our wounded and dead out is the second. As far back as Parris Island, it was always washed into us: *Don't leave your dead behind. If there is any way they can be evacuated, you take them out.* We had no desire to leave them. If I had been killed, I didn't want to be left, and none of the others did either. Each of us wanted the dignity of being sent home to our families, and we wanted that for each other, as well.

I explained that we had eleven wounded and dead, and with the help of men in the convoy, we loaded all of them into that first truck—frozen dead, and near-frozen wounded alike. The dead were difficult to handle and gut wrenching to see. A PFC lying on his back, reached for the sky with his frozen arm. Another froze in a fetal position. I knew they were dead and that there was nothing we could do for them, but my heart ached to see their bodies in such a sorry state. I would have felt a lot worse if we had left them behind, though. I'd have stopped every vehicle on the road if that first truck had passed us by. The only way to straighten them out was to break the offending limb or limbs—an often-necessary evil at the Chosin Reservoir. We didn't do it there, but I imagine that when they were eventually transferred from our charge, it would become a necessity. Some of these corpses couldn't even be put into body bags because of the positions in which they had fallen. The breaking of frozen limbs was not a job for me, however, and I am thankful I was never called upon to perform such a gruesome task. I feel sorry for those who were.

Soon, we moved off again, Corporal Sanchez and I on foot, with hundreds of other men in the convoy. We eventually made a supply stop, and I found Lieutenant Buckley. I filled him in on the details of the ambush.

"What patrol?" That's what he said to me. "What patrol?"

This crazy son of a bitch did not even remember that he'd sent us on the patrol, only the night before.

I had just moved to the infantry the previous day. *Right? Right.* I pushed through it in my mind. *They asked for volunteers, and I moved to the infantry. Me and my rifle.* Time slipped and twisted. *Yesterday. What about the day before? Doesn't matter.* I looked for Sanchez. *Buckley must be shell-shocked. How do you not remember sending thirteen guys and a tank on a reconnaissance patrol ahead of the convoy? What about the day before yesterday? Able Battery. What did*

I do? Blood rose to my face. I felt the warmest I'd been in a month. *What about the day before that? Doesn't matter.*

I spotted Sanchez. "Let's go."

"Where?"

"Out of here. I don't work for Buckley anymore."

"What? Why?"

I pointed with a stiff arm behind us. "He doesn't even remember sending us on the patrol."

"He's the one who sent us?"

"Yes, he's the goddamned one who sent us."

I walked away, and Sanchez followed. I thought to ask him about the day prior, but decided not to. Didn't seem like a good question to ask.

"We'll fall in with another unit."

I searched my mind for a solid reference to time and place. I backtracked to the patrol, and then I fell into a soup of confusion. *Able Battery. That's where I was before. So, that was yesterday.* But it seemed so long ago now. *Why does it matter?* I told myself it didn't. I just needed to be away from the crazy lieutenant who'd sent thirteen men into an ambush—*a goddamned massacre*—and didn't even remember. I'd spent the scariest night of my short life, thirty-plus below zero conditions, with Marines dying at my feet—feet that had no feeling left in them—and that shithead says, "What patrol?"

I wanted to rip his throat out. I didn't really give a crap where I'd been since I left Able Battery—a day, a year, a month. I only cared where I'd be going. We sidled up to another infantry unit, and made ourselves at home.

"Just look like you belong," I told Sanchez.

He didn't seem entirely comfortable, but he went along with my plan. And really, what difference did it make? The entire operation had gone to shit when we'd reached Yudam-ni. Men were dead, wounded, missing, and scattered. I could be with Able Battery, Item Company, or the cast of *Oklahoma*, and it wasn't gonna make a shit of difference anymore. From here on, we'd keep moving south and kill every Chinaman who got in the way. It didn't matter what company patch was on the uniform of the guy next to me.

We came upon the patch that did have meaning to me only a few days later. We'd walked south with the convoy, and the fighting began to taper. Although it had been noticeable, I wouldn't allow myself to think that it might be over. Sanchez stayed at my side. We didn't talk about anything that had taken place over the past few days—or week. I fell back into thoughts about the recent timeline, but didn't trouble him with my questions. And neither of us brought up the ambush. I didn't ask why he'd stayed down on the side of the road and hadn't helped me get Ben to safety. I didn't want to know. The last thing I needed now was to have bad feelings about someone else. *He did what he did, and I did what I did. That's it. We made it. Leave it alone.*

And then I saw the patch.

3rd Infantry. The guy wearing it was standing guard. I was so happy to see that guy—that patch. And he had not a single care in the world. I could have kissed him. Trucks moved from the single-file convoy as they were waved toward various staging areas in the port city of Hungnam. The leaden anvils I'd had strapped to my shoulders vaporized. Beyond the guards, a group of reporters looked for any first-hand nuggets about our harrowing ordeal they could chip off the frozen Marines.

"Hey boys," one of them called. "You got a minute for the folks at home?"

"Hell yeah, I'll talk to you."

I told them what I could. Then one of them asked about the Marine Corps *retreat* from the Reservoir.

My cheeks flushed, and I pursed my lips tight. I had to take a moment to compose myself, so I wouldn't jump down the ass's throat.

"Don't call this a retreat," I said—my tongue sharp. "We killed Chinese coming and going. I don't know how to explain it to you, but this was not a retreat."

The remainder of their questions didn't piss me off so much, and I was able to walk off on friendly terms.

"I gotta find my unit."

The reporter who'd asked the retreat question called after me. "Hey, is there anything I can do for you boys?"

I didn't think long. I walked back over to him.

"Yes, as a matter of fact, there is. You can notify my mother that I'm okay. She must be beside herself."

"Huh. That's an easy one, Joe. We'll get word to her right away."

I really had no way of knowing if he would or could, but I believed he was going to make it happen. This day kept getting better. As I'd learn months later, a reporter from the *Brooklyn Mirror* visited our apartment that same day, took pictures, and ran a story the following morning that included my quote about the retreat business. Stand up guy.

Hungnam bustled with ant-farm activity. Warming tents provided comfort and hot food sustenance. I ate until I puked, and then I had a snack. Trucks, cranes, bulldozers, military equipment, and supplies covered every open space. It all looked like enough material to take over the world. People swarmed to and fro throughout the port—Marines, soldiers, sailors, and refugees. Yeah, refugees. We were in North Korea, and tens of thousands of refugees had poured into the port—some on our own heels—in hopes of securing safe passage out. Their own country didn't give a damn about these people. The only thing North Korea cared about was their Army, and even then, only to the extent that they were the means to the government's dirty ends.

And then there were ships. I'd never been so happy to see a ship. The harbor was filled to capacity, and still more arrived in a steady stream. Every tank, Jeep, mortar shell, bullet, man, and woman—including nearly 100,000 refugees—would be removed from this port by December 24, during the now-legendary Hungnam Evacuation. Even though I had no involvement with the hordes of newly-homeless people who were desperate for a new life, it made me proud to know what was being done for them. When the last of the ships made way, thirteen days after I'd arrived in Hungnam, the waterfront had been destroyed. The North Koreans and Chinese had been left with a seventy-five mile trail covered with blood and 30,000 scattered bodies that started in Yudam-ni and ended in rubble and a windswept spaghetti bowl of tire tracks in Hungnam. It was our reminder to them that the United States Marines had staged the greatest breakout from an aggressor trap that, by any account, should have ended in a crippling defeat for America and the U.N. Forces.

The 11th Marines were among the first out of Hungnam, on the 12th of December. Our numbers were seriously depleted due to death, wounds, frostbite, and a few missing in action. Aboard ship, I'd learned that Staff Sergeant Donald Foster, a wire chief for the battery, had been killed on the 5th. Corporal Ralph Engtsrom from Headquarters Battery had been declared missing on the 10th—only a day before he would have reached the evacuation point. The ship drifted from shore, and I looked back to the distant mountains with the painful realization that men had been left behind—a fate unfathomable. I swallowed the hard pill, and descended below deck.

With the port a day behind, I searched for rest on a bunk aboard the LST. Images of places never seen, battles never fought, and people never encountered peppered my dreams. During waking moments, ghosts of men with no faces flashed before me and in their wake, I experienced a feeling of dread that rolled through my stomach and mixed with the bile of sour seasickness. The ambush was only five days gone. Beyond that there was only battle, cold, hunger, and fear.

The Chosin Reservoir Campaign was—in terms of objectives—a rousing failure. Yet—in terms of grit, passion, courage, and *esprit de corps*—its legacy would live on as one of the greatest tests of Marine Corps fortitude and resourcefulness passed in our glorious history. We weren't just lucky to have gotten out—we *made* the luck that got us out. I was out. I was whole. And I was glad. I pushed aside questions of time, place, and circumstances. I ignored unexplained, whispered visions. Whenever those thoughts invaded my consciousness, I repeated my mantra: *I made it. It doesn't matter. I made it.*

CHAPTER 15

Stars And Stripes

Stars and stripes. On New Year Day, 1951, I received one of each.

From Hungnam, we'd sailed to Pusan, despite hopes that Japan and the end of the war for the 11th Marines would be our destination. I was not alone in my belief that we'd done enough. The harrowing experience in the Chosin— The Home By Christmas Offensive—had left the regiment and the rest of the 1st Marine Division in shambles. Friends had been lost, equipment destroyed, and the will to continue eviscerated. With the severe depletion of both our ranks and our weapons, we were a division in name only. To a man, we were prepared to go home, heads hung low, and leave the sorting-out process to a replacement division. The Marine Corps, however, had better faith in us.

From Pusan, we'd moved directly back to Masan. This was the port city where it had all begun for the 11th Marines in the Pusan Perimeter where we'd set camp in what we called The Bean Patch. The days were cold and wet, and yet—so soon after the Chosin—it felt like a Hawaiian vacation. Christmas dinner lasted for days. We ate and ate, and then we ate some more. Warm showers and clean clothes had been our salvation. Beer, for those who wanted it, was rationed, but never in short supply. Cigars had been passed around, but after choking on the first drag, I handed mine off to one of the other men. Thanks to Father Sporrer, who went back to Pusan to retrieve the necessary gear from storage, basketball (which I was terrible at), football, baseball, volleyball, and every other form of recreation was provided and encouraged. Men who had hidden their wounds and severe frostbite during the battles of the frozen north—so they wouldn't be evacuated from the fight—were weeded out here, and treated. Some were sent home. Those of us who had frostbite that hadn't manifested in blackened legs, just kept our mouths shut. I, for one, was too ignorant to even know I had frostbite. I just knew that my feet weren't right—they tingled and hurt, and I figured the discomfort would diminish over time. Someplace on the peninsula, a war was being fought. The 1st Marine Division was needed. But, at the time, rebuilding and rejuvenating was more important to the Division, and the remainder of the UN forces would have to go it alone for a time. We regrouped and trained. Over time, reinforcements, new gear, and equipment arrived.

On January 1, 1951, while morale and physical energy still lagged, I was presented with sergeant stripes and a Bronze Star with the "V" attachment for Valor. The presentation, which came during our formation that morning, mimicked the mood of the battalion—low key. Only the day before—New Year's Eve—the Communists had taken the capital city of Seoul for the second time. In The Bean Patch, there was no pomp and circumstance, no reading of proclamations or citations, and no pinning of medals on proud chests. As with the other men who received an award or promotion, our C.O. simply handed me the Bronze Star in its closed box, along with sergeant stripes as if he were issuing me a new pair of socks. I hadn't expected the promotion, so it was a swell surprise. I had anticipated a *Silver* Star, since that is what I'd been nominated for, so that bit had been a let down. I'd learn later that Colonel Chesty Puller, one of the most decorated and—arguably—the greatest Marine in Corps history, had been equally disappointed to receive a Bronze when he'd expected a Silver. Of course, about the time I received my spiffy new stripe, he'd gotten his first general's star, and shortly thereafter, received command of the entire 1st Division. He got over the whole Bronze/Silver thing. Besides, there were already enough precious and semi-precious metals hanging from the guy's chest to sink a DUKW. I got over the medal thing, as well. No matter the color of the star, it felt good to be recognized for doing the things they'd trained me to do, and for having done them well. Months later, when I got home, I found a nice drawer in which to tuck it away—right next to my socks.

After the formation, PFC Ben Perry found me at my replacement gun.

"What the hell are you doing back?" I asked.

He pulled a bullet attached to a chain from under his coat and dangled it for me to see.

"Turns out it didn't hit anything important."

"Jesus Christmas. I figured you would've spent the holidays at a stateside hospital."

"Ha! No such luck. Just wanted to thank you for helping me out back there."

There'd been no talk of life saving—neither of us saw it that way.

"Yeah. No problem. How you feeling?"

He flexed his shoulders and drew up his face.

"Can still tell it was in there, but I'm okay. So, anyway, we both got a nice, new piece of jewelry out of the deal," he laughed and pointed at the box that held my Bronze Star.

"Yeah. Let's try not to collect anymore."

Like Ben, the division and 11th Regiment recovered more quickly than I or the others might have imagined. The recreation, training, and ample chow lifted spirits and restored both our pride and eagerness. But when the orders to prepare to move out came on January 9th, it was still a blow. The painful truth was that the United Nations forces, led by the United States, were losing the war. The situation at this time closely resembled what the 1st Provisional Marines had found in the Pusan Perimeter, with the obvious exception of the 8th Army as a now well-trained and willing partner. The 1st Marine Division—under 8th Army operational command—was either going to help turn things around or provide cover while the rest of the U.N. forces evacuated through Pusan. If that turned out to be the case, we'd be the ones shutting the lights on the way out. On the next day, January 10th, we began the sixty-five-mile trek northeast to Pohang-dong on the east coast of Korea.

The operation was tagged the Pohang Guerrilla Hunt, because the NKPA 10th Division—short on necessary supplies and equipment to execute an all-out assault—staged hit-and-run attacks and ambushes throughout the region with startling success. Quiet, still, and invisible during the day, they'd spring surprise raids at night to devastating effect. Despite their limited resources, the estimated 6,000 men of the NKPA division caused greater casualties than any other North Korean division during the war. The 5th Marines, with the 1st Battalion, 11th Marines in tow, patrolled the thirty-mile coastal region between Pohang-dong and Yongdok to the North. Rugged, snow-capped mountains and hills, intertwined with treacherous valleys in which the enemy hid and that the 5th Marines continually sought to clear, covered our western flank. I wished somebody could grab the wrinkled-blanket terrain of this country at its corners and snap it flat.

Whenever the infantry found enemy emplacements, our batteries were expected to respond instantaneously. At times, firing orders arrived in rapid succession, and our Howitzers would simultaneously crush the hills north, west, and south. The pace was relentless and our vigilance at peak, even when we were not engaged.

On February 1, more reserve replacements arrived from San Diego with an old friend from Able Battery at Pendleton, Angelo *Angie* De Stefano, among them. Angie was a Los Angeles, Italian tough guy full of bravado. Everybody liked the guy, and I was glad to see my friend—chrome-plated revolver and all.

He held that gun up and said, "Here's one Guinea them gooks ain't gonna fuck with."

"Careful, Angie," I said. "They may not know you're Italian."

Two days later on February 3, Angie was dead—a bullet to the head. I was stunned. Though I'd been there for six months, I'd suffered only heat stroke, frostbite, hemorrhoids, a few blisters, and a cough. That's it. Everybody's favorite *Guinea* was there for two days, and he's already dead. Even though we'd been engaged continually for a couple weeks, the reality of what was taking place around me—the danger we were in—rushed over me just as it had when Porter and Pittillo had been killed on our first full day of battle in the Pusan

Perimeter. I felt just as I had when Flom died from freaking dust pneumonia two weeks after that: lost.

But what really got me was the unfairness of it all. They'd brought in reserves to replace the guys who hadn't made it, and they were already dying. Maybe I should have been dead, and Angie should have gotten his six months before having to give his life. I didn't want to see any more reserves. No more old pals from Pendleton. *Just let us do the fighting until they kill us all. Then bring in the new guys. Or better yet, just stay out of it after we're gone. Go home. Leave it alone.* The crazy thing is that the Pohang Guerrilla Hunt was finally winding down. We'd done so much damage to the NKPA 10th Division that they were retreating to the west. The job was done, and we'd be moving on soon. But Angelo De Stefano would go home in a bag.

Then, in Mid-February, I found out that I was going home, as well. That was it—game over. Digger O'Dell would go home also, but only because he'd stopped his truck on a landmine. The delayed explosion had allowed Digger only enough time to set the brake, open the door, and extend his foot onto the running board. Then the mine exploded, and the door slammed completely shut on his leg and broke through the bones below his knee. During the ensuing rescue operation, his fragile leg had been broken again above the knee. So, as thirty officers and another 594 grunts headed back to Pusan to await transport, my friend, Digger, was flown to Japan and, unbeknownst to me, was later delivered to Oakland, California.

In Pusan, The USS General J.C. Breckenridge arrived with over seventeen hundred fresh replacements for the division. We silently watched them disembark with all the esprit de corps we'd brought to Pusan seven months earlier. Most of them were completely ignorant about what they were getting into. Well, I'm sure they'd been reading the news, so they must have had some idea. But war is never real until it's actually real.

While our cargo of fallen Marines was loaded, we'd boarded the General Breckenridge in a daze. A young Marine, private first class, greeted us at the top of the ramp with the vigor of a freshly commissioned officer. He's wearing crisp blues like he's God's gift. *Dress blues!* And he's barking orders at us.

"Get up that ladder. This way. That way. Move along." In return, he was greeted with cold stares. When we got out to sea, he was still breaking balls. He'd picked the wrong Marines to mess with. A small group dragged his ass to the fantail and hung him over by his legs. He looked down at the churning water below and, I'm sure, pissed in his fancy blues.

"You son of a bitch. You bother anyone on this ship again—you open your mouth to any Marine—you are dead."

They pulled him back up, and that was the last anyone ever saw him.

They would have done it. After what we'd been through? Everyone knew at least a handful of guys who were lying dead below deck—cargo. De Stefano was down there. And this clown who never saw any action wants to play Marine tough guy with us? Yeah, they'd have dropped him straight onto the propeller and then gone and had some lunch. Nobody would have ever known what happened to the Marine, PFC in his Dress Blues. Pusan, Inchon, Seoul, Wonsan, Chosin—those Marines weren't taking any shit from some badass PFC in his dress blues. *Son of a bitch. Dress Blues!*

CHAPTER 16

April Fools

THE LAST TIME I'D BEEN an instructor at Parris Island, I'd been way too young for the job. Too worried about how the recruits saw me. Too concerned about the level of experience some of those men had over me. This time I didn't give a crap. I had something to offer, and they'd damned sure better be receptive to it.

I received my orders as soon as we landed in Oakland from Korea, and I wasn't a bit happy with them. I didn't want to work at Parris Island when I'd completed boot camp, and I didn't want to work there now—even though, as drill instructor, there was no fear that anyone would question my authority this time.

Then there was the guilt.

How do I describe the feeling of being told I am finally going home? Of knowing that I'd made it through eight months filled with the belief that my life would end in a strange land far from home? How could I sort out the flood of emotions whenever I flexed my fingers, or stomped my feet and realized that everything was where it should be, and not a drop of blood had been left behind in Korea. I knew that visions of my mother's reaction to the dreaded—but merely imagined—telegram that could have been sent home would eventually fade from my consciousness. During those eight fearful months, too many boys—*men*—I'd served with had lost their lives. Parents of my Marine Corps brothers had endured those all-too-real telegrams. Countless other Marines—Digger among them— had gone home short of whole.

When I got on the ship, I left behind so many others to continue the gruesome work of war—to endure the fear, and to live the nightmare. Oh, I can assure you that I'd wanted to go home. But part of me would never leave the battlefield as long as either the 1st Marine Division continued to storm the ever-present hills, or the Cannon Cockers of Able Battery fired in support of the greatest Marines to ever hit a beach. Generous portions of both my heart and mind remained in Korea, and feelings of guilt and remorse—to this day—still fill the void.

The two matters—the orders for Parris Island and my guilt at leaving Korea (and my covert happiness about it) left me with a sick stomach, and an angry disposition. Then, before going back to Brooklyn for a thirty-day leave, the men I traveled stateside with and I received a terse "talking to," in which we were admonished to never speak publicly about either President Truman or anything in relation to the Army in Korea. The first I didn't care about. The second set my mind to thoughts of Otto Sporrer. I wondered what the chaplain would think about what he'd surely been told. Apparently, history would be recorded at the pleasure of the first subject of our rebuke. It didn't matter much, though, as I had little expectation of the press ever knocking at my lowly door.

Expectations are a lot like car salesmen… you just can't trust them.

When I returned to Brooklyn on March 31, Ma answered the door and smothered me with flesh, housedress, and tears. Over her shoulder, I could see glimpses of the surreal peek at me from the living room.

"Is that a Christmas tree, Ma?"

"C'mon inside, Joey."

The apartment had been festooned in Christmas decorations, including a borrowed fake tree, garlands of spruce and hemlock, and a string of cutout letters that spelled out Happy New Year. I couldn't remember the place ever looking so festive on the Catholic Church's most joyful holiday. Ma knew how much it had pained me to miss the last three Yuletides. I'd written her just before we'd gone up into North Korea to let her know that MacArthur said we might be home by Christmas and, I guess, to warn her that the going would be rough.

I'm going with a bunch of swell fellows, I had written. *But a bunch of them won't be coming back.*

That had turned out to be an understatement of grand proportion. I was so grateful to the *Brooklyn Mirror* reporter who had visited my mother to let her know that I'd made it out in one piece. With her following the news so closely, I knew that she'd already understood that "Home for Christmas" had been a pipe dream for her Boy Marine.

I stood in awe at the sight. "This all for me, Ma?"

"I told you that no matter when you got home, we'd have Christmas for you, Joey. Everyone's gonna be here tomorrow, Christmas Day."

"April 1st? No fooling?"

"No fooling, Joey."

The next morning, she showed me the Sunday paper.

Today's Xmas Day For Sarge Lynch!

Page one. I was stunned.

"That same reporter did the story. You're a celebrity, Joey."

Then she showed me a newspaper article the guy had written after I talked to the reporter in Hungnam. It was accompanied by a picture of my mother and father holding up a framed photo of me in my dress blues. I allowed myself to feel like a big shot for a few moments, and thought, *What a swell guy that reporter is. Sure would like to meet him someday.* Then, after allowing my head to shrink back to its normal size, I did what all good Catholics do on Christmas morning—I went to church and received communion.

Barbara and I went over to St. James Pro-Cathedral on Jay Street and received the sacrament together. I couldn't think of a better way to do it—with my best girl. We had a nice breakfast together at the Hotel St. George, and then stopped at our own parish church, St. Mary's Star of the Sea, for another prayer on the way home. By this time, prayer had become a deeply-ingrained habit for me. I believed that prayer was the only thing that had saved me from the Red Trap at the reservoir. I'd prayed that I would come home in one piece, and my family had prayed for me, too. Those countless prayers had been answered, and, now, I'd had an extra prayer granted—I was able to spend Christmas at home with my family.

"Merry Christmas!"

Flash.

The roar of Yule tidings filled the little apartment, and a simultaneous camera flash punctuated the festive cry. A newspaper photographer popped a spent bulb from the big silver bowl atop his camera and pushed a new one in. A reporter from the *Brooklyn Mirror* stood next to him.

The reporter said, "Merry Christmas, Sarge. So, whadda ya think?"

"Gee whiz, I don't know what to say."

Ma, my father, the reporter, and about twenty others laughed. The remaining air space around and between all the visitors in the tight space was filled with the unmistakable aroma of roasting turkey. The photographer used up another precious bulb.

Flash.

"Your mom was real disappointed you didn't make it home for Christmas, so here it is."

Orbs of red floated across my eyes, compliments of the momentary white out caused by the camera flash.

"Gosh, Ma."

"Joey, Mr. Hanscom is the reporter who came here to tell us that you'd made it out of that awful place in North Korea. We invited him and Mr. Carson for Christmas dinner."

"Thank you for doing that, Mr. Hanscom."

"Call me Les, Joey. And my photographer is Tom."

"Joe," I corrected him.

Flash.

"Sure. Joe. Your mom invited us for dinner—not work—but I figured this was a great story. Hope you don't mind."

Flash.

I didn't. This guy had been nice enough to get word to my family for me, so let them have their story. I was still a bit stunned. The small apartment was stuffed with about 25 friends and family. There was my sister, Eileen, and all five brothers, each of whom bombarded me with hugs and kisses and handshakes. Wally and Bobby (in the Navy) and Jimmy (in the Marine Corps) had all scored weekend passes for the occasion. Yeah, Jimmy was now a Marine. While he was a Navy CB in Okinawa, he'd been working with the Marines. He'd liked the Marines so much that he'd enlisted in the reserves when he finished up with the Navy. Then the whole Korea mess had started, and they called him to active duty. Ha! I don't think he'd expected that. So, here we were—my former hero and I—a couple of buck sergeants in the Marine Corps.

Jimmy waved cigarette smoke from his face, and held a half-full can of Schaefer in salute.

"Semper Fi, kid."

Then he downed the beer and went in search of its replacement. Well, as the ads said, it is "The one beer to have, when you're having more than one"—or eight. Whatever. I was just so happy to see him. My older brothers, whom I had so adored and idolized because of their service to our country, now beamed over me for mine. And eleven-year-old Raymond looked at me with movie-star adoration.

Flash.

I helped Ma carve the turkey while Tom Carson snapped photos to capture every moment. The feast, which also included roast pork, homemade bread, and every trimming I'd ever imagined the folks up by Prospect Park might lay out on Christmas day, was served to the guests promptly at noon. Throughout that unimaginably luxurious meal, my eyes were split between Barbara, at my side, and the enormous, oblong cake that was covered in white cream, circled in strawberries, and festooned with *Merry Christmas Joseph* and *Welcome Home*. It had to be a huge cake to get all that writing on top. My folks must have saved ever since I entered boot camp in order to pay for it all.

Directly across the table from me, Leslie—Les—stuffed a wad of sweet potato in his chops and, then after a few chews, carved off a chunk of pork before he asked, "So, what about that Bronze Star, Sarge? What happened there?"

I first glanced at Barbara—who smiled sweetly—and then back to Les.

"Yeah, what'd ya do to those commies, Joe?" Wally, with two fat cigars poking from his breast pocket, sat at Les's side. He dragged some turkey through his gravy. "Heard you Devils gave 'em some hell."

"Hey, ya know, there was a lot going on. We were just glad to get out."

I nodded toward Ma, who was at my left, and shook my head a little for my inquisitors. Les caught my meaning.

"You boys did real good, Joe. Happy for the chance to meet you." He seemed like a straight egg.

Wally, on the other hand, was a lug sometimes.

"C'mon, squirt, ya musta done—" He sized up Les, who was still pulling his elbow from Wally's ribs.

"Oh, sorry about that, Wally." Then he asked, "So what are your plans for your leave, Joe?"

"I'm just gonna do some loafing—take it easy. Before I go to Parris Island, I'm going to stop and give a pint of blood for the boys back in Korea. I got away with all of mine—a lot of guys didn't."

A few solemn moments passed, during which Barbara gently rubbed my back. Jimmy tilted away from his half-finished plate and lit a Lucky Strike.

"Maybe the vampires can wait till we've had some of that cake." He took another slug of his beer.

To my relief, the moment had passed. Jimmy knew what he was doing, and I appreciated it. I didn't want to talk about that stuff within earshot of either my mother or Barbara. They didn't need to hear it. The other truth was that I really didn't want to talk about it at all—to anyone. This was such a happy occasion for me, and I had no desire to spend even one single moment of it back in that godforsaken place. The fiery flash of light on that dark road, the explosion of automatic gunfire, the agonizing screams that filled my head, the feel of my heart pounding in my ears, stomach, and feet, and especially the smell of my own fear were all things that I cared not to relive merely for the sake of a newspaper article or a casual "remember when" conversation.

Once the dishes had been cleared away, we moved on to everyone's favorite part of Christmas—the gifts. I felt a little self-conscious because so many gifts were for me, but it was grand nonetheless. Everybody brought something. Tom Carson made sure to get a great shot of Ma presenting me with a gold wristwatch, as my father and Barbara looked on. The photo, which looked like an ad for Bulova, made the paper the next day. There were also some handkerchiefs, ties, shirts, and even a new suit. I sat there looking at a sizable chunk of the money I'd sent home since I joined the Marines—money meant for Ma. Pools formed at the bottom of my eyes. It'd turned out that my father had another considerable share of that mailed-home money in his mouth. Ma would never buy a thing for herself, but she made sure to get a new set of teeth for the old man. I felt bad that I wasn't particularly happy to have provided the means for this gap-tooth-induced necessity, but I let it go. Like him or not, he was, after all, my father. I took care of Ma by picking up a few nice things in Japan: music boxes, silk pajamas, and scarves. I even got the old man a new lighter. What the hell. You show respect even when you don't feel it.

That April-Fools Christmas Day was one of the happiest days of my entire life. I prized each of my brothers, adored my sister, and cherished my mother. The strange thing, though, was that, while each of them—as well as every other person who was there—had elevated me to hero status, a hollow feeling permeated my core. Under the love, the laughter, and the exuberance, a part of me remained out of body and lost. At no time did I feel that I deserved the hero's welcome. Does a hero stand center of attention while Marines are still dying in a world that already seems unreal? A month or so earlier, I'd hated everything that surrounded me. Fear and anguish filled my days, but my life was filled with a clear purpose every waking moment. I'd been closer to the boys in Korea—the guys I'd trained so feverishly with at Pendleton—but at this convincingly-contrived Christmas celebration, the people I loved most in the world, almost seemed like strangers.

I caught my oldest brother, John, eye me a couple times. Finally, through the smiling faces and the laughter, our eyes locked, and at that moment, I felt that he'd actually been studying me. The gaze lingered an eternal second or so, and then—with no particular expression—he nodded. In the bottom of my hurting heart, I knew that he understood. For that brief moment, John— who, in another time had brought the vegetable scraps home for supper, who'd compassionately disciplined my younger self in order to save me from my father's wrath, and whom I'd wished to someday be—and I were the only ones in that crowded apartment. And he'd understood.

Later, when the party winded down, John approached me.

"They don't get it, Joe."

I didn't know what to say in response, so I kept my mouth shut. He looked around the living room.

"Maybe Wally and Jimmy have an idea, but not really."

My eyes welled. All the sound in the room, except my brother's voice, faded away.

"Maybe even me, kid, but don't count on it. In some ways it's the same for all of us, but mostly it's different. You're their hero, and it's okay to enjoy it. But don't expect them to ever understand—they don't have to. And don't ever feel like you need to make 'em understand, or that you have to talk to that reporter. He means well, just like the rest of 'em. You ever want to talk, I'm here. If not, that's okay, too."

He gave me the kind of hug that you feel in your soul, and then he pulled away. Distant laughter floated into my consciousness until it surrounded me once again. I became aware of friends and relatives saying goodbyes, sharing hugs, handshakes, and pats on the back. John took a few steps toward his wife, Mary, and then he turned back to me.

"You're *my* hero, too, kid."

And then, like an angel who had delivered his blessing on behalf of the Almighty, he was gone in a wisp. A degree of sadness remained in his wake, but a palpable blanket of comfort fell over me. My brother, John—*my angel.*

Barbara was at my side. I had no idea how long she'd been standing there. Maybe she had just approached. She gently brushed a tear from the corner of my eye.

"It's good to be home, huh?"

"Yeah, it's great to be home."

It wasn't until sometime after I'd left the Marine Corps that I had that talk with John. It's funny, but I don't even know what I told him. I'm not sure I even knew what I said as the words spilled from my mouth. And during our conversation, he shared a bit of his experiences from his war in Europe—I guess just enough to make me feel comfortable with the whole process.

CHAPTER 17

Drill Instructor

I REPORTED TO PARRIS ISLAND in May of 1951, and my first recruit platoon stepped off the bus a few days later. There was no drill instructor school to get me ready. No two-week training period with current DIs before these first shitbirds sauntered in. All I had to get me started were faded three-year-old memories of Sergeants Dean and Nethery, and the lead of my head DI, Staff Sergeant William E. Rappold. Corporal Nick Capuano and I would pay attention and follow along. Actually, I was fine with that. I was ready.

I looked over the recruits, and half of them looked like they should still be in elementary school. *Jesus Christmas.* Memories of my tender age during boot camp and the doctored up birth certificate that had secured my passage through the gate trotted through my head. *I hope none of these kids have an older sister named Eileen.* Let's face it, most of these kids were going to war sooner rather than later. There would be no two-and-a-half year cooling-off period, as I'd had, to get cozy with the idea. Even as I studied these faces, men were dying in Korea, and replacements were desperately needed. I didn't know who, or where, or for how long, but the majority of these guys would draw the short saber and ship out with little time to kiss their mamas goodbye.

Most of them were my age—nineteen—or a year younger. The former servicemen of the lot had been easier to spot than I would have guessed. They all had that *been-there, done-that* look about them. Well, guess what? They hadn't been to Parris Island before, and they sure as hell hadn't done what I was going to have them do. And without calling them out personally, I told them just that.

"Forget what you know, because you don't know nothing. You think you seen training? Now you see Marine Corps training. I got you for twelve weeks and I'm either going to make you a Marine, or I'm going to send you crying home to Mama."

I thought it was an act when I'd been a boot—a macho show to scare us into submission. At times, the over-the-top theatrics had cracked me up. Well, it's no act. Those DIs trained us for the *eventuality* of war, and I was training my platoon for the *certainty* of a war to which many of them would eventually go—little difference in the end, with the distinct exception of the absolute knowledge of a war we were already fighting. I'd been there. I'd seen its brutality. I understood fear. And I'd known men who had frozen to death before their blood had the opportunity to drain from their bodies. I feared most that some of these men would not return home to their loved ones, but I went to sleep each night knowing that it would not be for lack of rigorous training. These men would learn to respect my authority, they would jump when I gave them an order, and they would learn to act like a Marine. My job was to give them their best possible odds of survival.

When you're a boot, you sometimes have the mistaken impression that the DIs hate you. Why not? You're just a shitbird, after all. Nothing is further from the truth. I loved my recruits, just as I loved the men I served with. When I barked at them that I'd be their mama for the next twelve weeks, there was truth in my words. These men were mine to nourish and mold. *Tough love* wasn't an expression back then, but how fitting it seems now. They might despise me for the next twelve weeks, but I'd been willing to bear that hatred for their sake, just as Nethery and Dean had done for me. I'd held those men in high esteem when I graduated—deviated septum and all—and I knew that what they'd done for me had made it possible to be here for these guys now. I worried when I saw recruits who had trouble keeping up. Would Private Philip Walsh need to march into the Chosin with temperatures reaching forty below as I had done on the way out? *He'll freeze to death.* What about this Frank Irwin character? Is he going to make it through the night with eleven of thirteen dead and dying at his feet? *I hope so.* I dogged these guys, and had the others stand or run at their sides to fill them with encouragement.

I wasn't about to break anybody's nose, but they'd understand respect, and I would receive it from them. And I didn't give a rat's tail end if they'd carried the same rank as me during their former lives as soldiers, sailors, or airmen.

Come June, the thick soup of South Carolina, Lowcountry humidity drenched their bodies in the form of hard-earned sweat. Now, *my* sand fleas hovered, swarmed, crawled, and snacked, as I watched boys learn self-control and discipline. When I'd been in those boots, it hadn't occurred to me that the fleas did not discriminate between recruit and instructor. My only advantage over these recruits in the swamp was movement. Those little bastards were in my hair, up my nose, and crawling under my collar, so I moved a lot. But those boys never saw a sign of discomfort in their heartless DI.

Sometimes we were downright mean to them. "Smoke 'em if you got 'em," was one of the first things these boys had heard when we met. Two weeks later, when I got in Private Benson's face during drills, I flared my nostrils and sniffed loud. The look in his eyes would have given him away, had the smell of cigarette smoke not already done so. Benson had shown a deficit of discipline at best, and a lack of respect at worst. Neither was acceptable. I didn't ask how he'd procured the cigarettes, or where he'd hid them.

"Go get me a full pack, and be back here in thirty seconds."

He was back in twenty-eight.

"Good boy. Hang on to those."

We stood him up in a locker, shut the door, and spun the lock.

"Let me know when you're done."

For the next thirty minutes, smoke poured from the small vents near the top of the gray steel door. About ten minutes into his lesson, coughs and gags followed the bluish stream. At the twenty-three minute mark, it sounded as though he'd puked. A minute or so later, the stench from the locker confirmed the last. A half hour after he'd stepped in, a banging came from within.

"Who is it?"

"Sir, Private Benson, sir!"

"What can I do for you?"

"Sir, I'm finished, sir."

"If I open the door, will I find twenty butts on the floor?"

"Sir, yes, sir."

"No halvsies?"

"Sir, no, sir!"

"Ready to come out?"

"Sir, yes, sir!"

"If I find any halvsies, you're gonna lick all of them off the floor."

"Sir, yes, sir." By the weakness in his voice, I could tell that Private Benson was fading.

I opened the door, and Benson stumbled out onto the floor. A cloud of cigarette smoke billowed from the locker and drifted through the room. He heaved like a cat with a ten-pound hairball, and then splashed vomit all over the floor. The floor of the locker was covered with cigarette butts, ashes, and puke. Disgusting. I didn't bother asking if he'd be sneaking around back of the barracks to smoke anymore. And I didn't care if he had any more cigarettes squirreled away. The thought that other recruits might have a stash had occurred to me, but I would have bet dollars to donuts that several cartons of cigarettes would be disposed of by day's end. Private Benson would not be a problem anymore.

"Jesus, Mary, and Joseph. Clean this mess up, and get out of my sight. You're a disgrace."

Sometimes discipline had been as simple as placing a galvanized-steel bucket over a recruit's head and banging it with drumsticks. I couldn't carry a beat, yet they always seemed to understand my tune. But on the morning of graduation, I treated them with the respect they'd earned. These guys would wear the Eagle, Globe, and Anchor for the first time that day, and they knew their DIs were proud. They'd never forget the harsh treatment, but they'd wear those memories with the same pride as the Marine Corps emblem that would grace their uniform. All may not be forgiven right away, but when they took to the parade field, they would be Marines, and they'd know what that meant. And from that moment, they'd begin to appreciate what their drill instructors had done for them. *That guy was a bastard on wheels, but he was a good man,* is typical of the description most Marines have of their former DIs. These guys would be no different.

My third and final recruit platoon was designated C-1—Conscientious Objectors. *What the hell?* At the time, the Marine Corps was 176 years old, and this had been the very first platoon of objectors in its long and glorious history. Today, the Corps is 242 years old and, to my knowledge, there still has not been a C-2. I had the dubious distinction of being one of the three drill instructors—me, Corporal Jackson, and Sergeant McClain—to ever train a platoon of conscientious objectors. *What the hell are we supposed to do with these guys?* I couldn't imagine for the life of me what good these guys would ever be to a Marine.

Forty-two young men had been drafted into service against their wishes and religious sensibilities, and then given to the Marine Corps for God knows what. During their abbreviated training regiment, they would neither carry a weapon nor visit the rifle range. Now, by this time in my life, I considered myself a religious man, and I certainly had a deep disdain for war. But first among my strong moral beliefs was honor. War is ugly, distasteful, scary, humbling, and in every other way, awful. Unfortunately, it is also, at times, a necessary evil. And when the need arises, a Marine will—without question—lift arms. He will kill and maim. He will bloody and be bloodied in the name of justice. He will face death for those who cannot or will not. And he will offer up his own life for his fellow man. These men stated clearly, and without shame, that they would do none of the above. This is not to say—although some certainly did—that they were cowards. To my great irritation, some demonstrated their courage from the get go.

On their first day of physical training, I called formation in front of the barracks. Some recruits remained inside where they prayed. I stormed into the barracks and found five recruits sitting on two bunks.

"Get your asses outside."

The lead pain in the ass was easy to spot when the other four looked to him for guidance. Chisholm.

"We will stay right here."

I didn't know what to do, so I did what any good DI would do: I yelled louder. "Get your asses outside."

Nothing.

"Harrison, get off that bunk."

Harrison jumped to his feet, but looked at Chisholm again.

"Get outside with the others," I said.

In contrast to Harrison's nervous countenance, Chisholm remained calm. "You must remain here, brother. We will continue our prayer."

James Chisholm was what I supposed to be a Holy Roller. In the name of God, he would test me at every turn, and if I were ever to get control of this platoon, I would first have to gain sway over him. I had no idea, however, where to start, so I settled for the tug of war over *Brother* Harrison, who now had beads of sweat on his brow.

"I don't care what you believe, what God you worship, or how you pray to him. When I give you an order, you will do as I say. Now, GET OUTSIDE."

Harrison leaned into a step toward the door, but froze when Chisholm spoke again.

"If you falter and acquiesce to this false God, brother, the Lord will come down and strike you upon the face. The Lord will break your nose."

Oh, brother! I could hardly believe what I was hearing. Harrison looked like he was ready to burst into tears. His eyes pleaded with me, and my heart ached for him. But I was in a power struggle that I could little afford to lose.

My right hand balled into a fist at my side. "As God is my witness, if you don't get outside right now, I will do the Lord's work for him."

Harrison took one last furtive glance at Chisholm and then bolted through the door. I locked eyes with my Holy Instigator for a moment. Then I removed myself without a word. One down. I accepted this win with the knowledge that the battle would be a systematic one. Outside, I brought the recruits to attention. Harrison screamed and covered his face with his hands. *Shit.*

I stormed over and bellowed, "What the Hell is it now?"

Harrison wiped under his nose with the back of his fingers and came back with blood. When I pulled his hand away, I didn't see the kind of gusher I'd experienced in my days as a recruit, but a steady stream did run over his lips. The boy shook uncontrollably. My mind raced for an explanation, but came up empty. I never did believe that Jesus Christ visited that boy to administer corporal punishment, but I did consider that the power of suggestion, combined with his strong beliefs, had caused the nosebleed. Or maybe he'd shoved a pencil in there when I wasn't looking.

I said the only thing I could think of, "Go back inside. We'll talk later."

"God bless you, Sergeant."

He ran back inside.

Later, we had the talk. I reminded all of them of their terms of service—that in light of their devout beliefs, they would not receive the same training as the other recruits. They'd never have to touch a weapon, or cause harm to anyone. They would learn the history of the Marine Corps, which God should not have a problem with. They'd probably end up being stretcher-bearers, or work with the wounded. They'd be given an opportunity to do God's work among the chaos. They'd receive physical training, which would benefit them and the bodies God had graced them with. In return for proper behavior, they would be given ample time for prayer and fellowship. In the end, we came to an understanding that, over time, developed into mutual respect. I grew to appreciate their situation and refrained from the normal harassment shown to the typical recruit. They showed me every day that they were genuinely good people, and I learned to love them for who they were.

"God bless you, Sergeant."

I heard those words, in some form, several times a day. Break formation: "God bless you, Sergeant Lynch." Send them for chow: "Thank you, Sergeant Lynch. God bless you." Lights out: "Good night, Sergeant Lynch. God bless you."

At first it annoyed me. We had our difficulties, and I often felt as if they were goading me. But they were not. It took me some time to understand that they truly wished God's blessings upon me, no matter that I was the vehicle for the work of—as they saw it—a police state.

"Good night, Sergeant Lynch. God bless you."

"Thank you. Good night."

My "Thank you" was always sincere, but I never said "God bless you" back. I should have, but I guess it just didn't seem very Marine Corps. I sometimes wish I could go back and do what I now believe to be the right thing. What I knew at the time to be right. *Good night, Harrison. Good night, Chisholm. Good night, men. God bless you.*

Over the six-week period of their training, my opinion of these guys changed one hundred percent. Bitterness had been replaced by love—apathy by pride. I was very proud to see them graduate. I'd never had any doubt about my first two platoons; graduation for them had been a given. Graduation day for Platoon C-1 was one of my happiest as a Marine. And these men truly seemed proud. I felt that it was a great accomplishment for all of us. Over the years, I've often wondered what had become of them. I knew that many had gotten good duty stations, but, of course, I did not follow their careers. Why would I? These days, as nostalgia more and more often fills my heart, I think of them frequently. Recently, I managed to catch up with James Chisholm in Ohio. I was sorry to learn that my old nemesis's Marine Corps experience had almost immediately taken a turn for the worse. He'd been assigned to easy duty at the post office on a base down in Georgia, which should have been to everyone's liking, except that his commanding officer insisted that he wear a sidearm. Chisholm refused. The CO, in the spirit of compromise, told him the gun could remain unloaded, but, as a Marine, he must wear it. Chisholm would not agree, and requested a transfer to the Army, where he understood that he could work unarmed at a hospital. The CO refused.

Two years later, the FBI caught up with James Chisholm in a small town in Pennsylvania, where he had managed to build a new life as a fugitive. His days had been filled with anxiety.

In a phone conversation, he said to me, "I never so much as spit on the sidewalk, for fear of being noticed. I'll tell you, if everyone was a fugitive, we wouldn't need any police."

His statement struck me as funny, even while a feeling of melancholy over his long-ago plight seized me. The Marine Corps had welshed on the deal, and Chisholm had acted on his last resort.

The charge against him had been desertion. Chisholm was placed in a Navy brig until his trial. There, he was harassed and threatened with beatings and death by men who called him coward, traitor, and fag. In the end, a sympathetic judge ruled in his favor, stating essentially that the military had reneged on their contract with him. James was set free, only to have the charge follow him from job to job—if and when he could even secure a job. I am happy to say that he eventually put the whole affair behind him, and was able to create a successful engineering career for himself. I am glad for that. At the age of eighty-five, he admitted that he didn't specifically remember *me* from Parris Island. As a period in his life that held no meaning to him, he'd put all those memories behind him long ago. Perhaps, if I'd been the sergeant who had said, "Good night, Chisholm. God bless you," he'd have better reason to remember.

Three months after graduating Platoon C-1, I stared down my reenlistment papers. Staff sergeant stripes sat on my CO's desk awaiting my decision.

"I want a transfer."

"You'll stay right here."

I had no intention of working at Parris Island another day.

"What if I go someplace else and reenlist?"

"You'll be sent back here."

The stripes called my name and my eyes caressed every embroidered stitch. I took a deep breath.

"Then, I guess we're done here."

CHAPTER 18

The Other Team

I FELT LOST. EVERYTHING WAS familiar, yet it had a dreamlike quality. I knew every street in the neighborhood, recognized every building, and was acquainted with every mom and pop business owner. I could climb on a bus, or descend to the subway, and be anywhere in the largest city in the country without giving it a second thought. I knew this place—these were my streets and rails and alleys. I recognized everything by sense—these were my sights and sounds and odors. Yet it all seemed foreign. The rumble and clatter of the elevated train in which I rode, once a comfort, assaulted my nerves and shook my bones. The view from behind the scratched and smudged windows—red bricks, painted signs, roof-top ventilators, clothes hung to dry between four-story walk-ups, kids playing stickball—reminded me of the Pusan Express. The old wooden-carriage train that had brought us to our first battles in The Perimeter another lifetime ago offered no such views, though. I longed to clean my rifle. I wanted to hold it close. That comfort eluded me.

The other passengers on the train did what they have always done. They read the news. Held a child. Avoided eye contact. They looked out the window, yet they saw nothing. *They don't know I'm here. Ignorance.* A war raged, but it did not affect them. *Life goes on.* They had no clue that a few months ago I had been killing people and watching others die. *Why can't they see that?* They'd cursed their furnace as ice crystals formed in my feet and sucked the moisture from dying, dehydrated cells—frostbite. They didn't know that I was flexing my toes in my shoes—a useless attempt to relieve the discomfort that dogs me today, or that the VA hospital here in Brooklyn had already told me it was not service connected.

"Whadda ya mean it's not service connected? I got it in Korea. I didn't go to Korea voluntarily to stand around in the cold. I got frostbite."

"You'll have to go to your own doctor."

Great.

I had no doctor, no money, and no insurance. I told myself that a doctor probably couldn't do anything for me anyway, so I dealt with it.

These people on the train had moaned about everyday inconveniences and had gone home to hot meals while I'd sucked on frozen bits of Tootsie Rolls that I'd crushed with the butt of my rifle. It had been the only sustenance that the Marine Corps could get to us in the Chosin, sometimes for days at a time. They'd huffed their discomfort and rolled over on a cheap mattress, while I lay on the side of a road, my hugged M-1 to my chest, and listened to a severely wounded Marine scream for help as bullets sprayed so close that I could hear them whistle past my head. *Tonight's the night I die.* I want to ask them, *Don't you know who I am? Don't you know what I've done?* It didn't matter. Life goes on. It wasn't their fault.

I was so happy to be home. I loved that place. *I hate this place. Where is the order? How do people live without order?* Everything used to be so perfect—streamlined. Everybody knew where he was going, how to get there, which bus transfer or subway platform got him to his destination. Trains showed up when they were supposed to and delivered you where and when they'd promised. Cops waved cars and trucks through busy intersections and past busses and cable cars in an urban street ballet. Horns and whistles and shouts and steel wheels grinding on rails formed the melody of an energetic city that filled my soul with its music. All I see now are sheep and cattle herded through meaningless chaos. The sites and sounds slipped by with no significance to them. Everybody just went to work, got their paychecks, and returned home. There was no greater good than a pork chop on the table and Jackie Gleason on the little tube in the giant wooden box. And now I'd become one of them, and I didn't even own one of those tubes.

But my mind did have its own image to play just for me. I see the chase over and over:

I'm with a guy who I do not know, and two men I can't identify are chasing us. Their faces are blank. I don't mean that their faces are expressionless; I mean these men have no faces. Their heads are there. Hair peaks from their caps. But they have no faces. They are blurred out—or smoothed over. Maybe they just never had faces. I'm terrified and run as fast as I can. I am filled with an unexplained awareness that if they catch me I will die. They will kill me. I won't let them catch me. My ankles roll with the rocks beneath my feet and with the uneven ground. My shoes continue to find purchase even as they slide in a sandy decline. Another look back at my pursuers, and right foot collides with left calf—*Don't fall.* Green scrub and brown dirt rush up at me, and I extend my hands in order to break the fall. *Stay up.* Sharp pebbles scrape and sting the skin of my left cheek—*Gonna need to clean that out*—as I slide like a backpack tossed from a speeding Jeep. Kicked up dust fills my nostrils and lungs—*dust pneumonia.* The two men are on me before I can finish the thought. I flail and kick and punch and scream.

I bolted upright in bed and struggled for a breath. I could smell the sweat that covered my body. My blanket was twisted in knots. With wide-eyed confusion, I scoured the bedroom in my parent's 3rd Street apartment—I am alone—and threw my feet to the floor. *Dream. Bad dream.* I dropped my head into my hands and pushed sweaty hair back on my head. *Shit. Just a dream.*

But that dream had stuck with me the rest of the day. I kept seeing those featureless faces, hearing their footfalls get closer and my gasps for breath intensify, and feeling my heart leap into my throat as they pounced upon me. I continued to ask the same questions: *Who was the other man with me? Where had he gone when I'd fallen? Why hadn't he helped me?*

The commuters on the train had no idea. If they'd even thought about me, they'd figure I was paying my bills in my head, or planning my next beer, or wondering what Ralph Kramden might be up to. I'm sure they didn't give me a thought. Why the other man hadn't helped me was moot. It had just been a bad dream, and it was over. Like all dreams—good or bad—I knew it would just drift away to Meaningless Dreamland where it would fade, never to be heard from again. For the time being, though, it rattled me. The emotions—fear, anger, and defeat—were real.

My mind drifted to the Chosin. Nothing like fear with a purpose to get your mind off bedtime stories. The ambush had held real fear. I didn't even want to think about it. Then there were The Missing Days. That's what I had come to think of them as—*The Missing Days.* Whatever I'd been doing during the days that led up to that patrol was now gone. Those days had drifted down the path of so many forgotten dreams. At first there'd been pieces—more days of freezing cold and crippling fear—and then only glimpses of emotion. One day Artillery and, a week later, Infantry. Nothing but the ghosts of gut feelings in between, until they, too, were gone. *The Missing Days.* I didn't know for sure when they had left me for good. I was not convinced that *for good* was even the correct characterization. *Surely they will return.* Try as I might, though, I couldn't find them.

I'd had my chance to investigate while I was still in Korea. Maybe Sanchez could've filled in the blanks. I didn't think so. We'd been together for several days after the ambush, and he'd never offered up the slightest suggestion that we'd even been together during those previous days. I didn't ask. After I'd walked away from Lt. Buckley, I had been separated from Item Company and anyone there who might have given me a glimpse into my immediate past. Then, a few days later, I'd reunited with Able Battery in Hungnam. I certainly could have asked around. *Hey, just wondering, when did I actually move to infantry? Hey Digger, did we do anything exciting before I volunteered for infantry?* It just hadn't seemed the place to go. *Lynch has got amnesia. Lynch is off his rocker. Maybe Lynch shouldn't have that gun. We're just gonna have the nice corpsman take a look at you, Lynch.* There seemed to be too many down sides to announcing my lapse to the others, so I'd kept it to myself. And now, four months after returning to Brooklyn, I told myself to forget the forgotten. *It doesn't matter.* Getting a new job to replace the one I just quit held higher priority. I had something lined up, though.

I was only 20 years old, so, occasionally, some things still whizzed by over my head. The irony of saving Junior Sheehan from a life of making tin cans, only to stare down the red-brick edifice of the American Can Company four years later, was not one of those occasions. I stopped on the sidewalk and stared up at the bright white sign with black lettering that was painted directly on the brick at the top of the building and wondered where Junior was. *Probably wearing staff sergeant stripes at Lejeune.*

Shortly after my discharge, Barbara's Uncle Tom had gotten me a job in a factory that manufactured turrets for tanks. Barbara and I were still dating and planned to get married. My mother wanted me to wait until I was twenty-one years old before marrying, and after the whole enlistment mess, I figured I owed her this one. So, we waited. I was living with my parents, and Barbara still lived across the street with hers. Tom Quinn, the brother of Barbara's mother, had talked to some folks on my behalf and got me in. Marine Corps sergeant and drill instructor to low-man factory worker in a matter of weeks. You do what you gotta do. The tin-can job wouldn't pay any better, but at least it was walking distance from the apartment, right on the other side of the canal.

Working in a factory had not been my big plan for the future. Wally had landed on the New York City Police Department the previous year, and was working in the First Precinct over in Manhattan—on the Emergency Service Squad (ESS). The pay there wasn't anything to get too excited about, but it sure beat making tank turrets or the lowly tin can. Plus, it offered a real career—with insurance, vacation, sick pay, and retirement. I had put in an application, and hoped to be wearing the uniform sometime soon. The public wasn't too keen on the department in those days, crying "Brawn over brain." There was probably something to it. Later, when I would get the call, over 30,000 people had taken the test, but only 1,600 passed. The city had been forced to lower the standards in order to qualify enough recruits for the fast-growing force. I still couldn't pass. So, I was off to tin-can alley.

James McCorkle showed me the ropes at American Can. It was all so complicated: pull the sheet of tin from pile A, and feed it into Machine B. That was it. The machine did the rest. I was confident about my abilities, and was anxious to provide the country with all the baked-bean cans they could stand.

"Not so fast."

McCorkle pulled a sheet, and he placed it in front of the feeder.

"Make sure it's snug against this block right here, and then slide it in."

"I can do that."

"Once the rollers grab it, get your hands off it."

"Sure."

"If it goes in crooked, just let it go. If you like those fingers, do not try to straighten it out."

"Okay."

Not okay. My natural inclination was to try to straighten it out. Every time I shoved it to one side or the other, that damned machine would whip it back at me. *Son of a bitch!* As crappy as the pay was, I felt bad each time a sheet went through crooked. *Goddamn it!* I didn't want to be responsible for wasting the company's material. I thought that mental toughness would translate to physical dexterity, and that I could beat the tin-eating monster. I could not. *Jesus Christmas!* By day three, everything within a ten-foot radius was splattered with my blood. *For Christ's sake!* I went to McCorkle's little office and turned in my one-minute notice.

"Why?"

"I've lost more blood here than in Korea."

The fan in the window whirred.

"I didn't lose any blood in Korea."

It probably hadn't helped that I'd had the dream again the night before. Same dream. Same outcome. I lost count of how many times I'd had it. Every detail, with the possible exception of setting, was always the same. The faceless men always run a bit faster than I do, the ground—sometimes the street or sidewalk—consistently rushes at me and scrapes my face, and, each time, I kick and scream when the pursuers land on top of me. And in every case, it stays with me the rest of the next day. Questions about the unidentified man with me in the dream plague me. I knew how it would go, though: You get a bad dream in your head and it stays a while. You occasionally have the dream again, but eventually it goes away. Over time, your mind tires of it and banishes it. You'll remember for a long time that you used to have that terrible dream, but you are relieved it's gone. So, I knew I just needed to tough it out and hope it didn't happen too often. The problem was, however, it seemed to menace my sleep with more frequency rather than less.

I walked out of the building and pondered my options. I needed the work but, at the time, I still had the police department in my back pocket. If Wally could make it, surely I would as well. In the meantime, there were plenty of factories in Brooklyn. Mergenthaler Linotype Company had a sprawling factory—a city within the city, it seemed—on Ryerson Street, between Flushing and Park. About sixty-five years earlier, Ottmar Mergenthaler had revolutionized the publishing business with the invention of his linotype machine. In 1952, his company was still the world's largest linotype machine manufacturer, selling his product to publishing businesses globally. At the start of World War Two, and continuing through the Korean War, the company also manufactured precision optics and other specialized products for the military. So, after a short ride on the El each day, I now fed glass to a machine. My skill set was going nowhere. Geniuses of mechanical engineering designed and built machines that cut the glass to specifications that no human could measure. I watched. At least there'd been no knife-edged metals slicing up my hands.

As I've said, I did take the Police Department exam. When the day finally arrived, I put pencil to the paper that held the promise of a secure future. But I failed—even after the grading curve had been factored in. Apparently, the department required a small measure of brain to go with the brawn that a former Marine Corps sergeant certainly had. In the meantime, two weeks after my twenty-first birthday, Barbara and I married in a small ceremony at St. Mary Star of The Sea. Jimmy was our photographer, and Raymond was my best man. We had a modest party after the ceremony at Barbara's parent's apartment. The next morning we left for our honeymoon and were back that same evening. We had a fun-filled day at Coney Island, but there was no money for a hotel room. Barbara never held it against me. I got lucky with that girl.

A little over ten months later, on May 26, our son Matthew was born. Then I was laid off at Mergenthaler. I'd been peering through the finest optical glass in the world for almost a year, yet I never saw it coming. I told Barbara that I was having a tough time, and that I wanted to support my family right. I then informed her that I was going back into the service. This was not a discussion about what might or might not be the best thing to do. It was apparent that I was not going to find a meaningful job in Brooklyn, and at least the military offered a stable career with health insurance for the family. I told her I was going, and she agreed. What choice did she have?

I was out of the Marine Corps for just over a year now, but was pretty sure they'd have me back. There was still a war going strong in Korea, and I bet they needed more than just a few good men. I prayed I would not have to go back to the fight, although that was a great possibility. Parris Island sounded pretty good about this time.

Private first class.

That was the offer. Four years in the Marines and staff-sergeant stripes left behind on the colonel's desk, and they now offered me PFC—E2.

"Hey, you don't have to do boot camp."

"Thanks."

For nothing. I didn't think about it long. The Army made me the same offer, and I accepted. My ego couldn't handle the first. It made concessions, however, for my lingering feelings about the Army. I'd been a drill instructor at Parris Island. Many of my recruits were now corporals—some might be sergeants. You know where I'm going with this, right? Those guys may have undying respect for their former DI now, but what self-respecting corporal wouldn't want to bark an order—or a hundred—at the man who took him out to the sand-flea pit by the rifle range, or had him smoke a pack of cigarettes in a cramped locker? The Marine Corps is smaller than you think. No, that wasn't going to happen. I'd never take the chance of falling in under one of my recruits. *Army it is.*

And Germany.

"Pack your things."

At least it wasn't Korea. I was afraid they'd send me straight back, and I didn't ever want to see that place again—not in combat, and especially not with the Army.

CHAPTER 19

Army

IF THE TIME I'D SPENT away from Barbara at Camp Pendleton, in Korea, and then at Parris Island had been difficult, shipping to Germany and the 597th Armored Field Artillery without her and Matthew could only be described as sheer torture. It would take one year of that two-year deployment to make good on my promise to send for them. My goals, once I'd arrived at Fliegerhorst Kaserne in Hanau, Germany in June of '53, had been simple: obtain rank and make more money. The first had turned out to be pretty easy. As a gofer in the motor pool—I was not mechanically inclined—I did everything to the highest standard. If the floor needed sweeping, I swept it better than anyone had ever done before. I kept my uniform clean and in place, and treated everyone with respect. I didn't have my lips pressed to any asses, but my eyes did remain squarely affixed to the prize.

One day, the commanding officer—a first lieutenant—came to me and said he needed to replace his clerk who was out on emergency leave.

"I don't know that job, sir."

"We'll teach you."

"I'd be happy to do it, sir. Thank you, sir."

I figured, if I did the job well, it'd be my fast track to corporal. It turned out to be the fast track to making more money, as well. As I moved in, a building full of lieutenants and a couple of sergeants got shifted around in musical-offices fashion that left the first lieutenant and the second lieutenant, who I'd be working under, in the same office. I landed in an office of my own, right outside of theirs. PFC, and I got an office. My shit stopped stinking that very day. *Ha!*

The second lieutenant handled the cash. The enlisted men liked cash, but never had any—except after seeing the second lieu on payday. When they were short—which was at all other times—they'd come to the one guy who didn't spend his own cash on *bier* and *fräuleins*: me. I kept a pocketful for just such occasions.

"Hey, Joe. I need twenty till payday."

"Sure thing."

That twenty got me twenty-five on payday. Forty paid me fifty. Every guy who owed me money had to walk past me to get his cash on payday. When they came back out of the second lieu's office, I'd have my hand out. No payment plans—I needed it all, so I could keep lending. And it's not like I had to break any knees to collect. My boss was never the wiser to the side business—or maybe he was, and just quietly accepted this time-honored and rarely-talked-about military tradition—so I was able to sock some cash away.

Then, on January 1, 1954, I had a bit of emergency leave of my own. Pain, the likes of which no man should ever suffer, sent me to Hutier Kaserne in Hanau for evaluation. Agony, the location of which no soldier should ever have to reveal, sent me from that camp to the 97th General Hospital at Clark Kaserne in Frankfurt for treatment. I was sure that this had something to do with years of bouncing in the beds of those Deuce-and-a-Halves at Pendleton and in Korea.

From the camp, they put me in a Jeep for the one-hour-plus drive to the hospital. I lowered myself onto the furnished pillows and sighed. I'd learned quickly that Jeeps hadn't been built for comfort. As soon as that thing moved, I reached overhead and grabbed hold of a bar to pull myself up. Tears filled my eyes, and my arms felt like rubber by the time we'd reached the hospital.

"We have to cut them out," the doctor said.

"Oh, God."

"But not until they go back in. It will be easier to do and less painful. A couple of days."

When I'd gotten settled in my room, I called my CO. I was up for a promotion, and needed to make sure this wouldn't interfere.

"They're gonna do surgery in a couple of days, sir."

I didn't bother with the full explanation of my condition. The doctor had told me the name for it, and it was something I'd never even heard of. In fact, it sounded so derogatory, I couldn't allow myself to repeat the words to my commanding officer.

"Please don't give my promotion to another man."

"Nobody's getting your stripes, Joe. C'mon back soon."

Over a week had passed with no change in my condition.

"Okay. We push them in."

"Oh, God."

I was given an epidural for pain, and the doctor got to work. My teeth felt as though they would break as he pushed. Then he cut.

"GODDAMN IT!"

"You watch your filthy mouth in my operating room."

"That hurt!"

"I don't care. I'll have no such language."

I wanted to call that effeminate, French doctor a son of a bitch, but I held my tongue and clenched my cheeks because he held the knife.

"You will have to relax so I can do this."

He cut again.

"Son of a—"

He cut out what he could, and they put me back in my room. I spent three weeks in that hospital—on my stomach—afraid to so much as pass wind. When I finally got back to Fliegerhorst, the CO made good on the stripes. Now a corporal, I had a few more bucks each month to set aside along with the proceeds of the lending business.

A year into my rotation, I had saved enough money to book passage for Barbara and Matthew on the SS Nieuw Amsterdam, one of that era's luxury liners that sailed the North Atlantic. It would have been a bit more luxurious for Barbara, had she been booked on the upper deck—first class—but she enjoyed it, nonetheless, and she made fast friends during the journey.

I'd learned to drive in my motor-pool days, so with the money I had left, I bought myself a used car—an Opel Something-Or-Other. Later, when we'd returned to New York, I failed the driving test three times. I couldn't figure why I could drive in Germany but not in New York. Anyway, we rented German housing in Langenselbold, about fifteen minutes from the camp. Nothing fancy, but after two years of marriage, it was our first place together. Everything was *almost* perfect. Matthew—who was now a year old—wouldn't let me hold his mother's hand. He didn't know who I was. At first it was cute. But then it hurt. My son didn't know me. Thankfully, he got over it.

Now that my family was together, I made it a point to find fun things to do during my free time. Soon after Barbara and Matthew arrived in Germany, we climbed in the Opel, and motored the forty-five minutes to the Frankfurt Zoological Gardens. Although, Matthew's excitement over the animals would have been reward enough for that day, the opportunity to stroll hand-in-hand through the gardens with Barbara had been priceless. We were each so in love. I'd spend a lifetime showing that woman my silly side, and that day had been no different. We came upon a statue of a seated young man (seated and naked). In full uniform, I sat on his lap, wrapped one arm around his neck, crossed my legs comfortably over his, and smiled for Barbara who snapped a single photo. The bronze young man stared at me in disbelief. Barbara's sweet embarrassment at the situation when other visitors caught me in the act, made for easy laughter the remainder of the day. Matthew just thought the stranger in the Army uniform was funny. Then we went home for a good night's sleep.

I hurtle down the sidewalk through a picturesque village. *Germany?* A long row of shops housed in tudor-style buildings of various size and adornment whir past me in a blur. Still, I notice the tempting chocolates in one window. *No time.* The other man is with me—ahead of me. He's faster than I am. When he glances back, I know he sees the fear in my eyes. I want him to see it. I want him to help me. The faceless pursuers are gaining on me and I know that, without his help, they will kill me. The sidewalk ends where a small, cobbled side street begins. I chance a look over my shoulder and I trip over a protruding stone in the road. Worn, smooth pavers rise to meet my hands, which are extended in a futile attempt to stop my fall. The hands bounce, the arms buckle, and my left cheek slides on the pavement. At the end of the side street, a small, red-brick and beige-stucco church, with high-pitched, red-clay roof lines and a short, slender steeple stares back at me—the only witness to my fall. The two assailants attack me with abandon. The other man is long gone.

I flail and kick and punch and scream. *Joe! Joe! Joe!* I don't care that they know my name. I don't wonder how they can speak it with no mouths. They grab at me. I throw punches that I know land hard. *Joe! Joe! Joe!*

Then I'm in bed. One of my assailants is right beside me. I jump back—my wild eyes dart about the room in search of the second. I cock my arm for the knockout blow to the one beside me.

"Joe. Oh, God. Joe."

Barbara. She cowered and cried and begged. I jumped out of the bed and pulled at my twisted, sweaty pajamas. *What have I done?*

"It's okay, Barbara. Oh, God. Are you okay? Oh, God, I'm sorry."

When I reached for her she pulled back. I came closer and this time she allowed me. Her arms were wrapped around herself as I embraced her. She sobbed. My wife cried because I had hit her. Because she was terrified.

"It was a dream. A bad dream."

"I tried to wake you."

"I know. I'm so sorry."

So now she knows.

The nightmares had intruded on my sleep for over two years now, and I had not told a soul. I wasn't sure that there was anything to tell—*Everyone has nightmares.* Since I had arrived in Germany, though, the frequency had increased. They now came two to three times a week. And each time I had a nightmare, it was just as terrifying as the last. I no longer had any normal dreams. Fantasy worlds with people I love, or exotic places, or fantastic adventures never flickered upon the big screen of my subconscious cinema. I never woke up with a smile or a warm heart. I dreamt only of terror and impending death. Waking up was always sudden and violent. I am always chased. *We are* always chased. The stranger is always with me—up until the final moment when I fall, that is. He is never there when I need him most. If sleep was not something to be feared, it was at least something to be leery of. When I awoke after a night with no dreams, I was always suspicious.

In the living room, Barbara listened to all of the details. I held nothing back. The description of the dreams—same theme, different locations—shook her. When she learned how often these nightmares have occurred, she delicately dabbed at the tears that leaked from the corners of her eyes. She was both scared and concerned for me. Eventually, she fell asleep in my arms right there on the sofa. I remained wide awake with no desire to sleep. But it was a relief to have confided in her.

The Army didn't know. I hadn't told my CO, nor divulged it to the other men. They might think I'm crazy and get rid of me—fire me. I needed the job. That's what it was, after all. The Marines had been an escape—the Army was a job. In the case of the Marine Corps, I'd found something that had been missing in my life—purpose—moments after stepping off the bus at Parris Island. I loved the Corps from the first day until the last. The Army was where I went to work. It was my office, my factory. It was my ditch to dig, my furnace to repair. I didn't love it or hate it. I did my work, and I got my paycheck just like all those folks on the El in Brooklyn. I brought home the bacon to support my fledgling family and Barbara fried it up. Just the way life was supposed to be. I refused to do anything to compromise that.

I figured it'd be better with Barbara there. Her touch at night, the gentle sound of her breath, the warmth of her body beside mine would surely have a calming effect. And it had seemed to for the first few nights. Then this. I held her close, and her sobs tapered. Physically, she didn't seem to be hurt too badly. I made a promise to her that I could not fully convince myself I'd be able to keep.

"I'll never hurt you again."

I made and broke that same promise for the next five decades. But in the short term, it was my temper that would actually hurt her. I'd never been an angry person. Sure, I'd get peeved with the old man after a good ass kicking.

But that was something worth getting angry about. And I thought that's what was going on with me now—I was confronted more and more with things worth being angry about.

For example, I arrived home from work one day, and discovered that Barbara had smoked cigarettes. I didn't lock her in the closet with a pack, but I got my point across.

"I thought you quit those."

"I did, but it's hard."

"I don't care. I don't want you smoking."

"I'll try harder."

"No, you won't. You'll stop. If I find out you've smoked another cigarette, you're going home. My wife will not smoke."

And I meant it. I can't say that I would have actually sent her home, but I'd been dead serious when I told her I would. She never smoked another cigarette. At least I don't think she did.

In the corporate world back home, when Pauly Paper Pusher gets transferred to the Chicago office, someone else gets a promotion to fill his spot. The Army operated much the same. Within a month of Barbara's arrival, a real clerk rotated into my company, and the arms room sergeant rotated out, so I was offered a new job. I jumped on it, because I saw the third stripe coming. As the job title implies, the position called for a sergeant—middle management. I told the commanding officer that I wanted the stripe.

"Let's see how you do."

Good enough. I threw myself into learning the job and familiarizing myself with all the weapons. It was simple, really: clean, maintain, and keep track of the weapons—check them out, and check them in. Sometimes I'd administer minor repairs even though it was not my responsibility. When the repairs were beyond my skill level (as most were), I'd send them to the armory at Hutier Kaserne. The philosophy there was simple: *if you can't fix it, get a bigger hammer*. Those guys rarely fixed anything. They'd just break it more and then turn it in as *inoperable* in exchange for a new weapon. I could have done that shit. But they were licensed for the repair work. Go figure.

My biggest challenge in the arms room was getting the stink out. I don't know what the last guy did in there, but the place smelled godawful. Body odor, puke, piss? I couldn't pinpoint anything specific, but it reeked of sickness. It made *me* sick, and it pissed me off. I scrubbed the place down and got some paint for the walls. There's nothing like Army-issue, lead-base paint to smother the stench of previous occupants. It made the place livable.

After a couple of months, the CO promoted me to sergeant and administered the raise that went along with the third stripe. I believe the guy appreciated me, because I was motivated. Hey, I had wanted the promotions when I'd been in the Marine Corps, too, and I probably would have made gunnery sergeant if I'd stayed in Korea—if I'd told them I didn't want to leave. I'd have to have been crazy, though. The opportunities here were a bit more user friendly. One just needed to recognize those opportunities and stay focused. I took very little time off, and when something needed to be done, I would do it, and do it properly. I think the guy actually felt obligated to give me the promotion. Good. That's exactly the way I'd wanted him to feel.

I stayed in that arms room for the rest of my two-year enlistment, and then it was time to leave Germany. Barbara was pregnant with our second child. One day, she told me that she was nauseous, and I knew right away. She did not want to have the baby in Germany, and I couldn't blame her, because she wasn't too happy there. Nobody talked to her. Because we were living in a German home, the locals thought she was a German girl who had hooked up with a G.I. They looked down on her and would have nothing to do with her. American soldiers figured her for German, as well, and talked behind our backs. Some wanted a piece of the action. All this without ever even getting to know her. If any of these people had taken the time to hear her utter one word, they'd know she was American, not German. She wanted out, and I wanted her back home as well. If I'd reenlisted, they would have kept me there, so I would allow my enlistment to run dry, and then head home where I would reenlist in due course.

The Army shipped me, Barbara, Matthew, and our T-minus-two-months baby home with another great experience on the high seas. We boarded the USNS General Nelson M. Walker, and that was the last I saw of Barbara and Matthew until we'd reached Brooklyn. I went down below, and they went into a cabin with three other women. As soon as that ship shifted into drive— or whatever it is that ships do—the contents of my stomach churned toward my throat. I wedged my helmet between the bunk and the wall to use as a puke bucket. On the second day, a sailor came to inform me that Barbara was sick, and that I'd need to go take care of Matthew.

"You gotta be kidding me. Look at my goddamned helmet. You want me to go watch my son? You watch him."

"I can't watch him."

"Well, I can't get out of this bunk. Find someone else."

I stayed in that bunk, in a pool of sweat, and smelling like the arms room before I'd cleaned it up. Fortunately, they found someone to watch my little boy.

Upon our arrival in Brooklyn, Barbara and Matthew got a ride home from my brothers Bobby and Raymond. The soldiers were all bussed to a hotel on Flatbush and Fulton. We drove 3rd Avenue toward Fulton and passed 3rd Street. The fondness I felt for my childhood neighborhood had not been strong enough to reveal that home to the others around me. For the first time in my life, I felt something close to shame at where I had come from. Embarrassment at the grungy appearance stifled my personal excitement. It's funny that I'd never really noticed the differences between 3rd Street and Carroll Street, or even 2nd Street. I'd lived on the crappiest street in the neighborhood, and had never even noticed.

We had a girl. Ellen arrived on July 1, 1955, and I couldn't have been happier. Now we were living in Massachusetts and I was working at Fort Devon, wearing staff sergeant stripes. E2 (PFC) to E5 (SSgt) in two years was not bad at all. I figured the fast track was, in part, due to my previous service in the Marine Corps, where I'd already been a sergeant. But I gave myself some of the credit, because my head was in the game. This was the most comfortable I'd been since enlisting in the Army. The touch, the smell, the sound of the 105 Howitzers filled me with the nostalgia I'd experienced driving by 3rd Street, only this time I was willing to talk about it to anyone who would listen. I knew and loved every inch of those guns. We had a range right there on the post, and we used it often. The gun was old-school to me, so I had no problem there, and I got along great with the other guys of the 4th Regimental Combat Team (RCT). Anthony Peretti (the first sergeant to the sergeant major of the regiment) and I became close friends. Some of the others weren't fond of him, but he was okay by me. Years later, we ended up working together again at another camp. Then, I'd find the relationship less endearing.

So, even though Ayers, Massachusetts was more fond of military paychecks than military men, life was pretty good up there. We had two children and a third on the way. We were four years into our marriage and well on our way to our goal of twelve kids. Okay—*my* goal. My mother had eleven, and I'd always wanted to do her one better. At this rate, we shouldn't have any problem.

Barbara was understanding of the nightmares, though they still frightened her terribly. She was an avid reader, and stayed up later and later at night with her books. Of course, it was for the better. She even understood my worsening temper. I didn't know why I took things out on the one person who meant more to me than anyone else, but I did. On good days, I treated her like gold to make up for it, although I am not sure you can ever truly make up for the bad days. Sometimes the days were mixed. Perfect, happy, loving one moment, and explosive and ugly the next. I loved to laugh and be silly, yet a spilled glass of milk could send me over the edge. My reactions to every day foibles caused a downward spiral in self-esteem that lead to more anger and self-loathing. I wanted nothing more than to make my wife and children happy and yet I found ways to make them sad. I was proud of my rapid ascension at work, but felt I could not do enough with the little money I earned.

On May 10, 1956, Barbara's father passed away. Ernest Chattman was a fine man who loved his two daughters and accepted me freely as part of his family. It was a difficult time for Barbara, her younger sister, Beatrice, and her mother, Maisie. I did my best to set my own issues aside in order to support my wife, but the nightmares didn't care about grief and anguish—other than perpetrating their own. I hung in there as best I could. Later that year, while Barbara continued with the lonely feeling of losing a parent, the Army once again pulled me away from my family. My new orders were crushing: Korea.

I didn't want to leave my family, and there was no way I wanted to go back to Korea—ever. It was the end of 1956, so the fighting had stopped three years before, but I didn't want to see a hill, I didn't want to fire a Howitzer in my underwear, I didn't want to deal with the cold, and for the love of God, I did not want to see a peasant with an A-frame on his back. The fact is, the North Koreans had been crazy in 1950, and they were just as crazy in '56. There was an armistice in place, but I couldn't imagine that it meant much to the North. I had little doubt that, at a time of their convenience, they would pour back across the border and take what was not theirs. I prayed that they would not find it to be convenient anytime during my deployment.

As the nightmares increased to three and four times a week, I believed that maybe a change in geography would help. It hadn't before, but I convinced myself that this time it would be different. Yet, a hollow feeling rose from my intestines, through my stomach, and to my chest each time I thought of returning. That morose sensation did not come with any specific thoughts but, rather, with a lack of specific thoughts. Of course, it troubled me that I could not identify the source.

The war had been terrible, but I think I had dealt with the fear and the gruesome battles pretty damn well. I had never backed down. The old man had beat toughness into me at an early age, the Marine Corps had honed it to a fine edge, and I continued to grow stronger every day. If I was going to have the dreams, I was tough enough to deal with them. And I taught myself to block out any unexplained feelings of dread. My life, my terms.

During my second deployment to Korea, we trained the South Korean Army. We trained them to be better soldiers than we had done the first time around. Hell, *our own* Army hadn't even been trained well the first time around. The North Koreans would find a different situation if they came across the demilitarized zone (DMZ) this time. At McDonald Barracks, we treated every day as if the war would start again that very day. And everyday, we felt that it could. Field training on the Howitzers was intensive and strict. Same thing for the Koreans. They kicked ass. It made me proud.

Other than missing my family, it hadn't been so bad. There were times when I was glad to be there. The hills surrounding the camp shuddered with distant cannon fire, even when our current Howitzers lay silent. Shadows of remembered Marine Corps Corsairs rippled across those hillsides in search of enemy targets that no longer existed. Memories of friends filled me with joy for the closeness we'd forged so long ago. Of course, there were also additional moments of sadness over recollections of friends lost. But I was forever reminded of the good we'd done in The Land of The Morning Calm. The North Koreans were now on the other side of the DMZ, and we had a clear determination to keep them there.

Life in Korea was all about the camp. Outside the gates there were only small villages. I know that some of the guys found entertainment opportunities there that they didn't write home about, but not me. There wasn't too much to do on base either. The Enlisted Man's and the NCO Clubs were it. I became friends with a ROK soldier, Beom-Soo Nam. It was a strong friendship unto itself that filled me with fond reminiscences of Sungyong Park, the KATUSA I'd befriended in the Pusan Perimeter. Who would have thought that nostalgia would find its way through the multitude of hills that I'd loathed beyond measure, and take hold of a needy heart?

Then First Sergeant Anthony Peretti transferred in and we reconnected. It was good to see a familiar face, because I was really missing my family. In Korea, he and Beom-Soo were the closest thing I had to family. When Barbara had our third child, Robert, I reenlisted early for another three years in order to negotiate some leave time. The Army was beginning to look like a career, and that was okay by me. They provided everything I needed, short of a stable family life. We'd figure a way to work that out.

I knew I'd been homesick, but it hadn't occurred to me how badly until I arrived back in New York on leave. The Army sent me on another troop ship, so my thirty-day clock didn't start ticking until my stomach stopped churning when I stepped off the ship in Brooklyn. We had an apartment on 3rd Street right next door to my mother, and across the street from Barbara's mother, so that she'd have plenty of help with the three children. I had no way of knowing how important this leave would be to me. After a short reprieve, the dreams had come in perfect schedule during my months in Korea. When I got home, they stopped for the first couple weeks, and only returned a few times after that. I started to indulge fantasies of life without them. *Maybe this difficult part of my life is finally coming to an end.*

I had my new son at home—another person to share my love with, which was important to me. I am a loving person, and I wanted people to share it with. An Army camp in Korea limits one's options in that respect. And connecting with Barbara again gave me the strength to finish out my tour in Korea. It got me through. The whole trip renewed my *ability* to love again—something I hadn't realized had been missing in my life.

Tearful goodbyes aside, I reported to a base in Seattle for the flight back to Korea. The Army was good about getting you back to work faster than they get you home. I boarded a commercial airliner—a four-prop job—that was chartered by the military, and we took off for our first stop in Hawaii. The night flight saw everyone asleep soon after takeoff. At some point, I awoke to a warm glow, and peeled my face from the window. Flames snapped and fluttered through the rushing air around and behind the far engine on the left side of the plane. *Oh crap.* I stared and wondered if I was really seeing this. *Maybe it's a dream.* In the plane, not a soul was aware—they slept in restful ignorance. There was total quiet, except for the drone of engines—three of which I hoped were operating just fine. I looked at my fellow military passengers, and wondered if I should sound the alarm. *What'll they do? What can anybody do?* And then I was envious of their ignorance. Calm faces—some with mouths agape, others with caps pulled down over their eyes—knew nothing of the peril we were in somewhere over the vast Pacific. I wished I didn't either. I thought about Barbara, the kids, and our new baby at home. I closed my eyes and placed my head back against the window. If the plane was going to crash into the ocean, I would not be the only passenger on board to watch us descend in blackness. I didn't want to know any more about our fate than the rest of these guys, so I went back to sleep. Some time later, we all awoke to the announcement that we were landing—in Seattle. It turned out we had already turned around by the time I had seen the flames. When I looked out the window again, there was no fire, and the prop blades of the disabled engine rocked lazily. To me it was a miracle. To modern aviation, it was merely pilots doing their job well, and an airplane whose safety features had worked properly. *Jesus Christmas.* It was still better than getting on another ship.

Then, when I finally got back to McDonald Barracks, I walked straight into a face slap. I'd known that promotions would be coming down soon when I'd left. I'd told Peretti that I wanted mine, but when I come back another guy was wearing the stripes. It was like the fine print in a raffle drawing: *must be present to win.* I made it clear just how pissed off I was.

"You'll have to wait for the next round," is what I was told.

Our friendship would be forever strained.

I made good use of my reborn capacity for love, however. My friendship with Beom-Soo Nam grew to include his wife and their two beautiful children. They had become my family in Korea. On occasion, he would have me over for dinner. I was getting good at eating things with names I could not pronounce and ingredients I could not identify. It was not about food, though. It was about friendship with people I felt true love for. They shared their home, meals, and dreams with me. It may not surprise you to know that I had never once met anyone in Brooklyn who aspired to one day own a pig farm. But that is what Beom-Soo wanted for himself and for his family.

With a wife, three children, and an apartment in Brooklyn, I needed every bit of my staff-sergeant pay to make ends meet, but I still managed to share some pocket change with him as my newly-hired houseboy. I needed a houseboy like I needed an airplane with an engine fire, but when he asked, I agreed. I could appreciate that he was willing to work hard for his family, and I wanted to help. He'd never just take the money from me. Short of my rotation in Korea ending, his enlistment in the Army had run out. So as a gift to his family, I purchased his first two pigs for him. I'll never know how that worked out, but judging by Beom-Soo's character, I would guess well. That's the last time I've ever bought a pig, but sometimes I can't help but think of my old friend when I eat a ham sandwich.

Near the end of my deployment, the guy who'd gotten the promotion that I felt should have been mine, screwed up somehow. I don't recall what he'd done, but he got busted down and the promotion was given to me. I didn't want to get it that way. Every time I came face to face with him, I felt as though he thought I was laughing at him, but I wasn't. In fact, I felt bad for the guy. It was extremely awkward, so I was glad that my time in Korea neared its end.

Early in 1958, eight months after reenlisting and meeting my third child, I brushed off my new stripes—three up and two down—and came home as a sergeant first class. To me, the new rank was a turning point. I was now in a position of true respect. Two pay grades of sergeants now answered to me. Not that I took advantage of that. It just proved what I was able to accomplish, and it convinced me to take advantage of the ready-made career that lay before me for the taking. There was no doubt that—having made sergeant first class in five years—I was limited only by the rarely navigated chasm between enlisted man and officer. Master sergeant and first sergeant within the next five years or so seemed both obtainable and likely. I even indulged in thoughts of the prized sergeant major stripes, a position of respect coveted by every career enlisted man—yet out of reach to most. After twenty years of service, a fella who retires from the Army with master sergeant or first sergeant stripes—three up and three down—has accomplished a great deal and commands respect even from his superiors. Sergeant majors walk on water.

While in Brooklyn, I bought myself a 1946 Chevrolet sedan, an automobile of timeless beauty—which means it was twelve years old, but I loved it. I planned to someday get a driver's license, too, but I'd have to convince more than just the car that I actually knew how to drive. With big plans for the future, I brought the family back to Massachusetts, where I assimilated into the 4th RCT, 76th Field Artillery, at my old proving ground—Fort Devon. I worked on my high school equivalency, since in order to get future recognition in the form of promotions, I assumed I would need to demonstrate that—in addition to a can-do attitude—I had something worthwhile going on upstairs. I had plenty of left over doubts in that department, but I'd never have anyone call me Master Sergeant without it.

We rented a house that we could not really afford in Whalom Park. Located a couple houses up Chase Avenue from Lake Whalom, and across the street from a park, the setting was as near to idyllic as we could ever imagine. Brooklyn would always be my home, but I wasn't too keen on making it my children's home. Days off from my job in the supply room, we'd take the kids to run around the park or down by the lake. The old photos from that time depict a happy family without a care. And we were happy, although there'd been plenty of cares to go around. A married sergeant first class with no kids could manage okay. Three kids made for a balancing act that left us teetering on a high wire. I wouldn't trade the joy they brought us for a safety net, though. I'd learned at an early age how to stretch a penny, and I knew we'd manage somehow.

The supply room job was nice. It kept me out of the bullshit fray. It was my supply room to run, and I didn't have any lieutenants breathing down my neck. Through focused effort, I'd managed to work my way to positions of trust time and again. Now, on the few occasions when I did need to go in the field, it was always with an intelligence person. We'd ride in a van, and do the mapping for the guys who did the dirty work. It was good. I had arrived.

We didn't stay in the house too long. Stretching pennies felt more like ringing rocks. Base housing became available and we moved in. I knew that Barbara—pregnant with number four—was disappointed, but she never complained. And then devastating news arrived. My mother was sick with breast cancer. I couldn't bear the thought of losing her, so for the next few months, we made the trip down to Brooklyn every weekend that we could. It'd been good that we made the housing switch, because the gas for the repeated long drive alone was killing me financially. One Friday, I made the trip by myself, because the weather was so bad. I didn't want my family on the roads. In driving rain, I made it as far as Troy, New York, where the car broke down. My brother Bobby made the trip up from Brooklyn to get me, and then took me back to the base. I had the car towed to a shop in Troy, and that's the last time I ever saw it. With no money to spare for repair costs, I abandoned the car—just left it there. From then on, we made our weekend trips on the train.

My spirits lifted when Marianne was born on my favorite holiday—Christmas. I held this new life dear, as another loved one slipped away. By the time my mother passed on January 26, 1960, the tumor on the right side of her right breast had grown to the size of a grapefruit. At the funeral, the painful lump in my throat had felt just as large. It was the worst time of my life, and I fell inconsolable. I knelt at Ma's side and sobbed uncontrollably.

Then, just when I believed that life could not get any worse, I was called in by the commanding officer. Through him, I learned that the Army Intelligence Service was investigating me for fraud. They were suspicious of all my trips to New York, while I'd claimed that my family was living with me. I now needed to document every home I'd ever lived in, every trip to New York, and all of the details about my mother's illness and death. All of this over forty-seven dollars—the cost of one round-trip fare on the train to take my family to Brooklyn. The investigation went on for months, while I studied for my GED, and grieved the loss of my mother. I was completely torn up over the entire ordeal. *Call me stupid—I may very well be. Tell me I'm an ass—I know I am at times. But don't ever question my honor.* I told the CO that

I'd give the Army forty-seven dollars if they needed it so bad. In the end, I was exonerated, because I had done nothing wrong. But it was, in fact, the end.

I'd given everything I had to the freaking Army—a branch of service I'd had little respect for when I'd arrived. I'd worked harder than anyone, did the jobs no one wanted to do, and showed up every day with a better attitude than most. In return, they'd recognized my willingness, dedication, and selflessness with a steady flow of chevrons and stripes. But then they'd pulled the rug out from under me by saying they didn't trust me. *To Hell with them. They shit on me, and I'll never do another thing for them.*

My disdain for the Army grew in intensity. In 1960, the country hadn't yet made the transition to the new generation of Marines. I'd been what is known today as Old Corps. I was a Marine when it meant you were tough, but you cared. You were unyielding, yet you had integrity. The Army didn't know anything about any of that. Where the Marines were the elite, the Army was the generic. *Once a Marine, always a Marine* meant more to me eight years after leaving the Corps than my Army service had at any time during the last seven. When I got out of the Army, I disavowed them. I was no longer a soldier. For most of my life since then, I avoided mentioning the Army when asked about my military service. "I was in the Marines," had always been my reply. For me, the concept of "Don't ask; Don't tell" had nothing to do with gay people in the military. I would forever be a Marine, and the Army be damned.

At the time, everyone believed that I'd eventually simmer down—swallow my pride—and reenlist. Even when I got out, they continued to believe I'd go back. After all, nobody gives up eleven and a half years (four in the Marine Corps and seven and a half in the Army) and then walks away. Well, they didn't know me as well as they thought they did. As the investigation had unfolded, I'd rekindled my old thoughts of becoming a cop, and had taken—and, this time, passed—the New York City civil service exam again. Then I let my enlistment dribble away like the last trickle of water from a draining sink. The faucet was shut tight, but in my head, I could hear those last few drops leak out to remind me that it was still there—I could always return for another drink or to splash my face. I ignored it, and in July, I put my family on a train for Brooklyn, and never looked back. Now, I merely had to wait for the call from the NYPD.

CHAPTER 20

New York's Finest

UP AND DOWN AND ALL around. That was my weight during seven and a half years as a soldier. It was a constant struggle for me that would last most of my life. Sugar, and more specifically, chocolate, was the enemy I'd loved. I still love it—in almost any form: ice cream, cake, cookies, donuts, candy. I could pack away the mess-hall slop, too, but I was defenseless against chocolate. This may have begun with the c-rations in Pusan. The chocolate bar that came with them was the only thing I'd been guaranteed to eat. And, believe it or not, some people don't fancy chocolate. It's true. I'd found out who those guys were early on, and buddied up with them at chow time. I'd trade my tin of what hardly qualified for spaghetti and meatballs any day, day after day. Then there were the Tootsie Rolls. Dropped from helicopters in the Chosin, they'd be our meals for days at a time. I'd—quite literally—savored them. The dense chocolate treats are hard and chewy on a good day. At the Chosin, they were frozen solid. Rocks. First, we had to break them into bite-sized pieces by smashing them with the butt of a rifle, a shovel, or some other solid object. Then those pieces went one at a time into our mouths, to thaw before we could actually chew them. One Tootsie Roll could last up to an hour before the process would begin all over again. I'd suck chocolate and sugar for hours at a time, much like a rodeo cowboy's dip. The inside of my cheeks would get numb and raw from the sugar that soaked into them.

So, when I'd passed the civil-service exam, there'd been some serious work to do—on me. The newspaper had listed all of the physical requirements that needed to be met in order to get on the New York City Police

Department, so I knew exactly what I was up against. I'd gone softer than chocolate ice cream on a Brooklyn radiator in January, so I developed an exercise routine that I could do in the supply room when there'd been time to spare. I pushed myself until I knew that I could surpass every test of fitness by a New York mile.

Before I left the Army, I'd managed to line up a job with the New York Central Railroad as a security officer in order to make ends meet until the department called.

Sergeant McInerney, a fine man whom I liked immensely, had asked me flat out, "You're not just waiting for the police department, are you?"

I told him I wasn't. Lying isn't something that sits well with me, and I regretted having done so the moment the words rolled from my tongue. I was even more remorseful when I had to tell him that the department had called. That railroad job had, however, been a futile one from the start. A train loaded with cargo would pull into a cut, where it would wait until it could be moved into place for unloading. There was a wall on both sides of it. I'd walk the length of both sides of the train to keep it secure. When I was on one side, the train would be broken into on the other. There was never an opportunity to arrest anyone, because we'd discover the open car long after the burglars had gotten away. The losses were always small, though, as the thieves could only approach on foot and leave with what they could carry in their arms.

At a little after 10:30 in the morning on Friday, December 16, 1960, I'd been huffing through the snow on 6th Avenue to go buy Matthew some new shoes on Flatbush. His had been worn so thin that there were holes in the bottoms. I wanted to have them with me when I collected him from school later, so he could wear them home. The farther I walked up 6th, the more people ran by me in the other direction.

"What's going on?"

One of the hurried pedestrians stopped. "Plane crash on 7th and Sterling!"

It'd been in the area I was headed to. I cut over to 7th Avenue on the next street up—Lincoln Place. I wish I'd either gone home, or straight up 6th to the store. When I turned toward Sterling, the unimaginable lay before me. Flames wrapped and soared above the tail of the United Airlines DC-8 airplane. Debris was everywhere, and most of the buildings on the block—brownstone apartments, a church, and various businesses—were ablaze. I stood frozen, and absorbed horrific sights that would remain with me forever. *Napalm dropped on far-away hills, and flames engulfed an enemy with no place to hide.* First responders had not yet arrived, but men with badges—off-duty police officers and firemen—were running toward the wreckage. I pulled myself away, and went to buy the shoes. I had to get those shoes. Had to.

What became forever known as the Park Slope Plane Crash turned out to be a midair collision with a TWA plane that crashed into a field on Staten Island. All forty-four people on the TWA flight had been killed. And all but one of the eighty-four people on the United flight, as well as six more people on the ground in Brooklyn, had perished that day. Eleven-year-old Stephan Baltz, whose only spoken concern had been his mother waiting for him at Idlewild airport, had been taken to Methodist Hospital on 7th Avenue, a few blocks from our apartment. The one beacon of hope in the nation's worst-ever aviation disaster at the time, passed away the next day with severe fuel burns to his lungs. The collective heart of Brooklyn, New York City, and the country shattered with the news. Everybody had wanted that boy to make it. My heart still breaks at the thought.

As if the city and its fire department hadn't had enough to cope with, three days after the aviation disaster, the USS Constellation—which was under construction at the Brooklyn Navy Yard—suffered a catastrophic fire. My brother, Jimmy, was a sheet metal worker on the nearly completed super carrier. Panic swept through our family as flames and smoke swept through what would one day become America's Flagship. It turned out that Jimmy had taken the day off. The Navy yard didn't know he'd taken the day off, though, so I guess he'd actually played hooky. When he was able to return to the ship, Jimmy discovered his toolbox melted to the Constellation's deck.

His questionable work ethic aside, we'd been glad he hadn't been added to the death toll of fifty workers, or the 330 who had been injured.

The much-awaited call from the police department finally came in February of 1961. I was finally gonna be a cop. At the time, the good news was that the city had raised the pay for rookie cops from $4,400.00 a year to $4,800.00. I can assure you that, even back in 1961, $4,800.00 was not an exciting wage. I'd been making $500.00 a month in the Army. Today, it is unlikely that a sergeant first class would take a pay cut on the NYPD, but it didn't matter too much to me. After all, this was an opportunity for security beyond a paycheck. There would be insurance, retirement, vacation, overtime, regular pay increases, and the prospect of advancement. It was also nice to know what I'd be doing for the next twenty years or so. And outside the Army, it would be easy to work side jobs to make up the difference—a tried-and-true tradition for law enforcement personnel anywhere in the country.

Police Academy classes were held in the First Precinct down near the Battery, and very close to my former high school. Physical training had been in Brooklyn at the armory on Atlantic and Bedford Avenues. My Uncle George had served there for a while during the First World War. I found his name on a plaque on the second floor. That plaque honored him—along with so many others—for having passed away in February of 1919 from gas poisoning sickness he'd contracted in Europe during the war. As I scanned the names, I thought about friends lost in Korea, and wondered about my own inexplicable good fortune. The dream of the previous night, in which two men with no faces chase me through my childhood neighborhood in Brooklyn, invaded my thoughts. I brushed that unpleasantness away, and said a prayer for Uncle George—a man I'd never met yet felt, somehow, I understood. Then I went off to join my class.

Academy graduation took place in July of 1961, one year after my departure from the Army, and eleven years after I'd embarked from San Diego en route to Pusan. Elements of the 1st Marine Division had boarded the USS

Henrico that lifetime ago as the 1st Provisional Marines—the Fire Brigade. In many ways, that experience had foreshadowed my first assignment out of the police academy. The newly formed Tactical Patrol Force (TPF) was a city-wide unit that had no precinct. Like the Fire Brigade of Marine Corps lore, we deployed to hot spots in order to back up the troops already on the ground. In New York, our dispatch came at the request of the commanding officer of the precinct in need. Sometimes we'd be told in advance to report directly to a particular precinct house or location within the precinct. Other times, we'd be bussed or delivered by patrol car. The root of that request might be riots, shootings, protests, or just a bad night in a bad neighborhood.

On September 4th of that year, the root had been a cop shooting in the 32nd Precinct. Patrolman Francis Walsh and his partner had been walking back to the precinct house at the end of their shift. As they approached a Chinese laundry, an armed robber ran out, lifted his gun, and fired. *Pop.* Just like that, Walsh was dead. Neither cop saw it coming, and in a single, surreal moment, a husband, father, brother, was gone. TPF got the call for backup. It was my wake-up call. I'd never once considered the dangers that a cop on the street faces everyday. We'd been trained well at the academy, and the dangers were part of that training. We were taught when we could fire our gun—even when we could pull it out. We had to qualify with a gun, which for me—as an expert marksman in both the Marines and the Army—was not an issue. But personal danger did not seem real. I'd known personal danger in Pusan, in-your-face fear in Seoul, and the expectation of imminent death at the Chosin. These were long-ago passed tests—or good-fortune lottery wins—that the NYPD could never replicate.

In the war, there had been that singular moment when I'd realized that it could happen to me—that the danger was real. That moment came on our first day of battle when Porter and Pittillo of Baker Battery had been killed by a direct hit on their Howitzer. The only thing in my life to compare was being told that my mother had died. The world slows down. Sound diminishes. *Pop. Could've been me.* Then everything is back, but nothing is ever the same. You do your job despite the voice in the back of your head that is always there—quietly whispering at times, and bellowing through a bullhorn at others. *Pop.*

On the NYPD, Walsh's death had been that moment for me. At least in Korea we always expected to be shot at. On the streets, it could happen anywhere, anytime, and for no other reason than walking past the wrong dry cleaner at the wrong time. *Pop.*

Walsh's assailant was apprehended in the subway.

The dreams now tormented me four to five times a week. I spent my days thinking about them, and was additionally stressed from poor sleep. There were varying versions, but the chase was a common theme. The chase was often in a natural setting—a field, dirt road, woods, hills—but sometimes it is on city streets—New York City streets. There is always another man with me. I have never been able to identify him. We have been chased through hotels and office buildings. In the last one, we were in the city someplace, but I'm not sure where—it may have been Manhattan.

> The narrow sidewalk blurs below my feet. I cannot hear my footfalls over the sound of my heavy breathing. Certain death, in the form of two faceless men, keeps pace behind us as we enter a white building. Our pursuers do not follow us in. The stark white walls, floors, doors, and ceilings are nearly indistinguishable in what I sense to be a hospital. There is an inexplicable chill within. Void of people, the silence is total. Even our footfalls are nearly silent, except for a slight, odd, crunching sound with each step. After wandering a few corridors, we settle for a break. Despite the cold, it is a good place to hide and rest. One of us needs to keep the watch, though, so I take the first shift. I search the entire first floor, and find nothing other than more white rooms with white beds, covered in white linens, over white tile floors. In some rooms, white desks and white chairs replace the beds. I move with care for fear of walking into the furniture, which blends so well with the walls. Down a wide corridor I find an elevator and push the white button. The whir of the elevator motor is the first sound I hear

since we entered the building. On the second floor, the white door slides open to reveal a vast white room surrounded on three sides by windows that are whited out by the bright light from outside. Thirty or more men are in the room—their dark silhouettes form a stark and shocking contrast. Their very presence does, as well. I push the button for the first floor and descend.

"Wake up. They're upstairs."

The other man understands who *They* are—the enemy. Although I did not detect any details in the few seconds during which I observed them, *They* are without a doubt the enemy. What enemy, however, is not clear. Together, we take the elevator back up, and the door opens to reveal a row of faces that are obscured by rifles pointed directly at us—a firing squad. I push the button again, and we both drop to the floor. The door closes, and the deafening silence is broken, as the white wooden walls within the elevator splinter under the assault of robust rounds. The elevator door is no match against the deadly onslaught. Powerful and lethal bullets penetrate the barrier above our heads. My face is pressed to the floor, and my hands cover my head. I squeeze my eyes shut and shake and sweat and gasp for air. When my eyelids release their tight grip, I find darkness instead of whiteness. I continue to shake, and sweat, and gasp, but at least I do not kick and punch.

"Are you okay?" Barbara asks.

"I'm fine. Go back to sleep."

I padded down the hall in my pajamas and found the bathroom. After a cold splash of water on my face, I settled on the toilet—with elbows on knees and face in hands—in order to give Barbara some time to fall back asleep. My mind drifted to *what ifs*: *What if* I'd been in Baker Battery rather than Able? *What if* Porter had lived, and the two halves of my body had been sent home to my parents? *What if* I'd gotten dust pneumonia, and Denny Flom were a cop today in his hometown? *What if* I'd been a boisterous Italian with a chrome-plated revolver and a bullet in the head? I thought about Patrick

Parrish, and wondered what existence was like where he ended up. Is everything white? Does it look like a white hospital or a white hotel? Would he trade places with me if given the chance? I missed Patrick terribly, and wished that we could talk. I knew that we would meet again someday, and wondered when that would be. It occurred to me that sooner might be better than later.

My brother Wally had been on the force for ten years before I put on the blue uniform. He lived for it. There was not a thing in the world he'd rather have done, nor another city in which he'd prefer to have done it. Nothing made him happier than putting on the uniform, strapping up his sidearm, firing up a cigar, and piling into his truck. He was the friendliest cop at ESS 1 Truck, in Lower Manhattan, and he had loudest laugh. But people knew not to mess with Wally, because he would point his cigar at them and dare them to. He was always very clear in that regard. The bad guys always backed down, and Wally never flinched. He was a tough S.O.B. And he was that way with other cops, too. They respected him for it. When a sergeant would show up on a job and tell Wally how to do things, he'd pull his cigar from his mouth—the end as grizzled as his attitude—and point it at him.

"This is *my* job. Don't you come down here and tell me how to do my job."

The sergeant always backed down. Wally never flinched. And the job was always done right. Respect. I only knew one other guy on the force who came close to my brother's stature and command of all situations.

Johnny Amandine was one of those guys who got along with everyone. He had a quick, broad smile, as well as a sharp mind. And like Wally, he had a penchant for good cigars. Johnny was what you might think of when you picture the stereotypical friendly yet no-nonsense cop. Most of the guys in TPF loved Johnny—the others didn't know him. He'd been assigned to the unit since its inception during the summer before I'd arrived. When Johnny was on the street, he was always friendly to everyone he met. He'd remove the sizable cigar from his mouth and offer a laugh, or a "How do you do?"

for everyone. He was downright charming. His innate ability to know the good guys from the bad guys at first contact was remarkable, and was surpassed only by his adeptness at conveying to the lesser elements—with no change in his demeanor—that he recognized them. He could cajole a potential troublemaker while making him understand that he would break his arm without ever losing that beautiful smile. These people knew instinctively that Johnny was a cop to be reckoned with and, if there was any trouble, it was not Johnny's day that would be ruined.

From the start, I'd often partnered with Johnny. We'd become easy friends, and he had arranged to get me to and from work without having to take the subway. The guy who drove him to work also picked me up in front of my apartment on 6th Avenue in Brooklyn on the way in. It was nice of Johnny to offer Greg's assistance that way. And, of course, Greg was only too happy to do Johnny the favor.

When I worked with Johnny, I learned from the best. He'd been on the job a few years when he'd volunteered for TPF. This was never meant to be a rookie job. It was manned by veteran cops who knew the job and were smart, tough (heavy on the tough), and willing to get in the middle of the fray when necessary. I was in the first group straight out of the academy to be appointed to the unit—based on prior military service—when it had been expanded. Johnny showed me the ropes.

Johnny drove the green and white squad car on the Belt Parkway. He passed a '58 Chevy and looked back in the mirror. Then he slowed down to let the car get ahead of us again. I looked over at the guy driving and his eyes darted toward us, down to the *TPF* emblazoned on the door, and then to his mirrors.

"What's going on?"

"Betcha five bucks it's stolen." The smile was huge.

"How do you know?"

"Front and rear plates don't match." He pulled in behind the Chevy, and the driver looked at his rearview mirror.

"Know why I checked the front?"

"No."

"Look at that plate."

"What about it?"

"The car is spotless, but the plate is filthy."

"Yeah."

"But you can see where it's been handled around the edges. See the clean spots? That plate was just put on the car."

He turned the cherry light on.

"You calling it in?"

"Let's see what we got first."

The car pulled off on the shoulder and Johnny planted an unlit cigar in his mouth and jumped out. I followed. A young—twenty-two, twenty-three year old—Puerto Rican fella slunk out of the Chevy.

"Hey, que pasa, man?" Johnny's smile lit up the parkway. "License and registration."

"I don't have my wallet, man."

"That so? I forget my wallet sometimes, too. Mind if I check?"

"No, I guess not."

The snap on my holster was already open, and I rested a hand on my gun. In Korea, my weapon would have been in my hands, the unfriendly end pointed straight at this guy's chest, and the trigger covered by a firm finger. This was a different world.

"You got a weapon on you?"

"No, sir."

"Dope?"

"No, sir."

"Okay, let's see."

Johnny frisked the guy and gave the interior of the car a cursory look-see. He spun his cigar through his lips, lit it up with his lighter, and took a long drag. *I'll just float through the keyhole,* drifted through my mind as the smoke meandered into traffic.

"Nice car, man," Johnny said. "Where'd ya get it?"

"Whadda ya mean?"

Johnny took another long drag and allowed the smoke to drift out through a broad, cheeky smile. Nobody moved until the smoke was gone.

Then Johnny looked the vehicle over like he was at his buddy's house checking out the man's new ride. He seemed genuinely happy for the guy.

"You gonna tell me that you didn't lift this car less than ten minutes ago?"

He looked back at the kid like he'd just asked if he could take it for a spin. But Johnny's eyes told the driver everything he needed to know. He remained speechless. Johnny slapped his hand down on the roof.

"It's a nice one, I'll give you that. But why not a Caddy or a Lincoln?"

Johnny didn't wait for an answer.

"I know. The keys were in it, weren't they?"

He pointed at the keys that hung from the ignition.

"Easy pickings. You transfer the plate from the Volkswagon parked behind it and take off, right?"

The kid actually nodded. I was stunned at how easily Johnny got it out of him. *Nice collar,* I thought.

"I bet this is the first time, right? Saw an opportunity and went with it."

"Yes, sir."

Johnny planted a hand on the kid's shoulder and gave him a shove.

"Get out of here. And stay out of trouble."

The kid hesitated, and then walked through the grass toward the neighborhood by Flatbush Avenue.

"Johnny, what are you doing?"

I couldn't believe he was letting this piece of crap go.

"Not worth the trouble, Joe. Go call it in. Tell 'em we got an abandoned car on the parkway with what looks like a stolen plate."

Then he called out to the luckiest car thief in Brooklyn. "Hey. Hold up a sec."

The guy waited and Johnny walked over to him. I went to the squad car and made the call. About the time I finished, Johnny stepped closer to the guy and it looked as though they shook hands. *Maybe,* I thought, *he gave the kid some fatherly advice.* He got back behind the wheel and showed me two five-dollar bills. I stared at the money and my mind went blank. Johnny held up one bill alongside the cigar in his left hand.

"This is the five you owe me for our bet."

He stuffed it in his shirt pocket. My face heated up. Then he held the other one in front of me.

"This one is yours."

Now I could have lit up another cigar for him with my fiery-hot face.

"I don't want that," I said.

"You're a good cop, Joe. You earned this."

His smile was warm and friendly. But his eyes told me everything I needed to know. I didn't give a crap.

"I'm not taking that."

His brow lifted at the harshness of my tone. The smile evaporated, he took a long, thoughtful drag off his cigar, and blew the smoke out the window. Then he dropped the bill on my lap.

With his smile anew, he said, "That's yours, rookie. We'll get a sandwich later."

He pulled out onto the parkway and drove off in silence. The Chevy was someone else's problem, I guess.

After a minute, I picked up the five and placed it in my breast pocket.

"Don't ever do that to me again," I said. He never did. An hour later, we stopped for a sandwich. The mood had gradually lightened, and we got back to easy talking. Then we were laughing. You couldn't stay mad at the guy. Neither of us brought up the money that day or ever again.

The ten bucks hadn't been the only example of what the good guys were capable of. Even before Johnny had shaken down that car thief, I had my first eye-opening experience with two-bit corruption. I walked a neighborhood in Brooklyn late one night and discovered an open door at an electronics store. All the lights were out, and there'd been no sound when I called inside. I figured the owner must've forgotten to lock up, so I called the desk sergeant of the precinct to report it. *Good cop*. I was relieved—although, a bit surprised—when he showed up himself. He got out of the car and opened his trunk.

"Nobody inside?"

"No, sir."

"Okay. Stay here."

He went inside and came back out with his arms loaded with merchandise and then placed it all in the car's trunk. *Bad cop.*

I was scared shitless. Here I was, a fresh rookie on the force, and a sergeant was stealing shit that we had been sworn to protect. My head spun as he made a second and then third trip back inside the store before he closed the trunk.

"Shut that door and get outta here," he said.

"It's still unlocked."

"And that's the way it'll stay. He'll learn to lock up, himself."

I shut the door, and looked at the contact info on it. I ignored it, but knew that this would never happen again. *Next time I find an open door, I'll call the owner. Screw the protocol.*

Another time—this one happened after Johnny had *shown me the ropes*—I made a collar in Harlem. At about two o'clock in the morning—right before my shift was about to end—I witnessed a guy unload boxes from his car onto the sidewalk. Before he realized I was there, he called up to someone on the top floor of the apartment.

"Get down here, and help me with this shit."

My partner for the night caught up with me across the street, and we approached the guy at the car.

"What's going on here?" I asked. "You're making an awful lot of noise for this time of the night."

"My sister is moving and we had to get this stuff out of her place."

There was a television still in the box on the sidewalk.

"This stuff is brand new." I stepped in front of the TV. "What kind of TV is this? Where'd you get it?"

Nothing. His partner came out, and I took him back upstairs while my partner stayed with the first "moving man" at the car. The place was filled with stolen merchandise, ranging from TVs, and stereos, to furs, watches and jewelry—it was like a department store. So I called the precinct for assistance.

"I need a wagon to carry stolen goods."

We got everything to the station where I had to inventory it all. While I did that, the other cops went shopping. Word quickly reached all of the cops on duty that night, and they'd walk in, find something—or five things—that they liked, and then walk out. I checked the shit in as fast as I could, but there was no way to get ahead of them. Much of the merchandise never even made it inside, because cops were taking it right from the wagon. There were several fur coats that never got inventoried, and large stacks of pawn tickets simply disappeared. Those cops then went to the pawnshops—in uniform—and claimed everything as stolen merchandise. Yeah, *they* stole it. I inventoried hundreds of items, while scores of others disappeared.

I was just a rookie. *Is this how it is?* I was boggled. My partner was there with me, and—thank God—his hands remained clean.

"Leave it alone, Joe. Nothing you can do about it." He shook his head in disgust.

So there it was: *Leave it alone.* We were supposed to be the good guys, and now I was supposed to leave it alone. As a rookie cop, this substantial bust was going to make a name for me, but the desk sergeant told me to go home. "Good job, Joe. We'll finish this up." I learned later that the thieves had been released, and that my inventory had been discarded. Every bit of the stolen goods was gone.

The thing is, I don't think those guys believed they were corrupt. This precinct was Harlem—one of the roughest in the city. But that was no excuse. It amazed me that so many corrupt cops actually thought they were the good guys. I think they had convinced themselves that they were just catching a break: *I'm finally getting something out of this job.* Like they deserved it. Not too long in the future, Frank Serpico would come along and do what I wish I'd had the balls to do. But the corruption he would one day expose would make the crap I witnessed look like a trip to the candy store.

It probably was not a great idea to go down into the subway in Harlem all alone after midnight, even—maybe especially—for a cop, but I didn't want to be around any more blue uniforms after I'd checked out that night. I sat at the front of an otherwise empty car, except for one guy at the back. He looked like a punk, but I ignored him. Instead, I languished through an internal self-lecture that was based on my past beliefs, and that guided my future behavior.

I will not do it. On that train, I made a vow to myself that I would never do anything to bring shame to my family. I would never do anything that would get my name in the paper. I didn't want to be *that* cop, and I would not let these guys drag me down. I was not so stupid that I couldn't understand the progression. One bad cop makes it okay for the next to go bad. *Take it. It's no big deal.* Then, once a guy takes something for the first time, the second and third times become easier, until he's the guy saying *It's no big deal.* By this time, I'd already taken the five bucks. Slumped in the hard subway seat, I wished there was a way for me to undo the past. But I could only look forward and say, *I'm not that cop.* I managed to stay true to my word and to myself. In future years, Serpico's testimony and the ensuing Knapp Commission investigation would land a lot of cops' names in the newspaper. I was glad mine would not be there.

When I got home that night, I checked on my sleeping family. Number five, Joseph Jr., lay in his crib kicking and tossing his arms, but he seemed happy. Our bed was still made. I picked him up and carried him while I made my rounds. I didn't want to go to bed, but knew I would have to eventually. I had to go pick up a van the next day that I was buying. I needed it, because a friend of a friend had hooked me up with some work delivering Avon products. Plus, the family was now too big to take the train every time we went someplace. As long as I worked the 4:00 pm-to-midnight, or the midnight shift—12:00 am-8:00 am—I could spend my days doing deliveries. That extra money paid for the Ford Econoline, and left a bit more for family needs.

Joseph held my nose as I walked down the hall and glanced in at the others. *Out.* From my father's room came the sound of snoring. He'd had a stroke before my mother passed away, and was paralyzed on his left side. The arm, which hung in a sling, and the leg, which was reinforced by a brace, were now cooked noodles. He had six other adult children, and he ended up with the one who had run away from home in order to get away from him. Payback, I guess. The others each had their own excuses for not taking him in, so he'd landed with me. I'd never blamed my siblings for not stepping up, but I was also not happy about being *given* the short straw. But he was my father, so what was I supposed to do? The kids seemed to like him, and he them. Robert would come home from kindergarten and show his grandfather the gold star his teacher had placed on a picture he'd drawn or colored, and the old man would give him a big smile and a nickel. That's the same old man who'd kicked the crap out of me at that age. But with only one good leg, I guessed he wouldn't be kicking anybody any more.

"Hey, Robert, be a good boy, and go get me a pack of *Pell Mells*."

Dad gave the boy some change and Robert ran down to the corner for the Pall Malls and then ran back home to deliver the cigarettes and to collect his next nickel. At least Robert was happy. The others collected their share of nickels, too. My father received a pittance from Social Security each month. I'm still waiting for my first nickel.

I found Barbara curled up with a book in the living/dining room at the back of the apartment. I gave her a kiss, she took the baby, and I sat down next to her.

"How was work?"

She cooed and kissed Joseph.

"Good."

I didn't tell her about my experience that night. I had never mentioned the five dollars I'd received from Johnny or the desk sergeant who had robbed the electronics store. She didn't need to know that I only arrested the bad guys who did not wear badges. But she knew it had not been a good day.

"Why don't you get some sleep?"

"Yeah."

I got up and gave her and the baby a kiss goodnight. "I love you."

"I love you, too."

The walk back to the front of the apartment was grim as anticipation of nightmares filled my head. *I don't need this shit.* In the bedroom, I slid the holster from my belt and opened the dresser drawer to deposit it. There followed a moment's hesitation in which I pulled gun from holster, placed it to my head, and heard its dreadful call. *Pop.* I blinked the thought away, pushed the still-holstered weapon to the back of the drawer, and then got ready for whatever would come once I shut my eyes.

CHAPTER 21

Emergency Service

DEATH IS HARDEST FOR THOSE who do not suffer it.

I had learned this at the feet of my dead friends in Korea. I'd lived it kneeling beside my mother's coffin in Brooklyn. And I felt it in Barbara's embrace when her father had passed away. It may very well be the cornerstone of my existence until the day *I* suffer death and leave the hardship of survival to others.

I have also learned that death is particularly hard for those who have delivered it.

In 1962, Tactical Patrol Force was bussed up to Bedford Stuyvesant in north, central Brooklyn. A classic New York City, shit-versus-fan scenario played out and the precinct called for reinforcements. The local crazies protested and rioted over some nonsense or the other, and Vietnam wasn't yet a twinkle in the city's already bruised eyes. Bed Stuy was about as bad as it got in a city that was going straight to Hell. Officers from all over Brooklyn— Tactical Patrol Force, Precincts, and Emergency Service—attempted to control a crowd that had become more unruly and dangerous by the minute. A thunderous, reverberating boom startled both sides of the madness. Then another. Somebody was tossing heavy steel barrels from the roof of a building down at the police. *I'm gonna kill this SOB.*

I got to the roof just as he muscled another sixty-pound bomb to the edge. My gun was drawn, and I took aim.

"Stop, you son of a bitch, or I'll shoot you."

He lifted the barrel and cocked his arms for the toss. I had a clear shot for what would be a clean kill, legally speaking, yet I raised the gun and fired above his head. He propelled the barrel over the ledge, then ran and jumped to the next roof, free to threaten more blue lives on another day.

As I'd raised the gun and the assailant had fallen below its aim, a moment of Irish-crystal clarity descended upon me. Only my vision—so many years before—of a future together with Barbara came close in its crispness.

The instant I'd altered my aim, I knew I would never kill or shoot another human being again—even animals like that one on the roof. I could not do it anymore. Korea was so long ago, but I'd left behind more dead bodies in that country with my name on them than anyone had even bothered to count. Dozens, scores, maybe hundreds a day, for days at a time, during months of battles, fell to the mighty cannon at our hands. Pull the cord—*Got 'em.* Two degrees this way—*Target hit.* Three degrees that way—*Good show.* Adrenaline and fear make a dandy cloak for the horror of taking lives in astonishing numbers—complete exhaustion allows you to sleep even when your humanity tries to deny you righteous slumber. But, soon enough, the day arrives when you must account to yourself.

It hadn't at all been as personal as I had once thought it was when they'd been shooting at me. Now, I understood that *Kill or be killed* works both ways. The North Koreans—even the crazy Chinese hordes—had merely wanted to survive. They didn't want to be there any more than I or Parrish or De Stefano. I remembered that, more often than not, Red prisoners had been *happy* to be captured. Why not? We no longer tried to kill them. Perhaps they'd been just as relieved not to have to kill, as well. All I know is that there is a cord that begins at my soul and ends in hills, valleys, and rivers all over Korea. Its tug is tangible. I am forever attached to other souls with no names—or faces—of men I've laid to rest, and I do not want any more attachments. I'll die first.

Wally never seemed to have this problem. 1 Truck was in Bedford Stuyvesant that day, as well, and Wally stood at the back of his truck with a Thompson submachine gun in order to protect all of the heavy armament within, when some of the rioters approached, and made their intentions clear.

"We're taking the truck, pig."

Cigar in mouth, Wally held up his gun.

"You just come and get it then."

I told you, when Wally laid down the dare, people understood his intentions. Wally's the guy who invented *Make my day.*

"You'll pay for this truck with your lives," he said.

A four-year old could read the truth in the wide eyes below his arched brow. The rioters backed down and were lucky for it. There was not a chance in a Clint Eastwood movie that Wally would have let those people take his truck. He would have killed them first, and finished his cigar second.

Just because I'd resolved to never again shoot anyone, didn't mean I couldn't talk a good game. On another night, I was in Bedford Stuyvesant on foot patrol with a partner, and he made an open-bottle collar. The rule was, you got your ass off the street as soon as possible after you made an arrest, so he did. But I stayed behind, which I shouldn't have. A short time later, I rounded a corner and witnessed a stabbing. *Jesus Christmas.* The guy ran into an alley and I followed. It turned out that the alley was a dead end. No problem. When I caught up to him, I realized that his weapon was only a screwdriver, while—of course—I had a gun, and all I had to do was show it to him. I cuffed him up and walked him toward the street. The Puerto Ricans outside the alley yelled to him in Spanish, and he yelled back to them. Despite my inadequate language skills, I knew what was happening, and understood that my life was in danger.

"Hablo Ingles?" I said.

He shook his head. *"No. No hablo Ingles."*

"Well, you hablo this, asshole." I stuck my gun in his spine. "You tell your friends that I'm coming out with you. One of 'em so much as touches me, you are the first to die. Then I'm taking whoever else I can with the last five bullets. Tell 'em. So I can understand."

His English came out remarkably fast, and everyone moved away from the alley. When we got out to the street, I stopped the first car to approach and opened the back door.

"I need you to take me to the police station."

The woman in the passenger seat said, "We're not taking you anywhere."

I needed to get away from there before the locals changed their minds. I knew that they would not think twice about killing a cop, and I also knew that I would not actually use the gun.

"Then I'm going to place you both under arrest, and *I* will drive your car to the station."

The nice couple drove my prisoner and me to the station post haste. With heartfelt sincerity, I thanked them for their trouble.

Of course, my refusal to use my gun had put more than my own life at risk. Just like a Marine on the battlefield must be able to count on his brothers, a cop on the street has to know that his partner has got his back. I confess that there had been times when the cops around me were in danger due to my reluctance. My fellow officers and I had once found ourselves in a barricade situation in which a gunman had holed up in a building. Each cop was sent to a specific location with instructions to shoot if the gunman showed himself. With my secret knowledge that I would not shoot this man—even though I knew that I or another cop could lose his life—I got in position and held my gun ready for show. In an inadequate response to a dangerous situation, I merely prayed that he would not show his face anywhere in my watch area. To everyone's relief—none more than mine—the gunman eventually surrendered.

New York City had a lot of pain-in-the-ass areas where people always wanted to start something. One night, I walked a neighborhood street and people yelled at me from their stoops and windows. More and more people joined the fun and, soon enough, they got in my face. I called in a 1013 (officer needs assistance) and several squad cars showed up. One car drove down the street, and the officer within repeated an announcement through the bullhorn:

"When I get to the end of the street and turn around, anyone still on the street will be arrested."

People disappeared, because they saw *TPF* on the car. Those three letters painted on the hood, the trunk, and both sides meant they absolutely would go to jail. People knew TPF, and they understood that all bullshit stopped with us. Desk sergeants hated us because we brought in offenses that their cops were told to ignore. We didn't give a crap, because we were told not to give a crap. In TPF, there were very few craps given. We'd drag them in by their toes, and have those desk sergeants figure out the charges.

It happened that way once on Carroll Street in Brooklyn—78th Precinct—in the neighborhood where I'd grown up. An Irish/Italian wedding (I could have told them that was a bad idea!) broke up, and everyone was on the street. The Italians gave the Irish shit, and the Irish gave their offensive shit right back. Most of the shit, of course, was in the form of a fist. I was with the bride (The Italian half of the blessed union) and she started to give *me* a hard time.

"You keep it up, lady, and I'm placing you under arrest."

Next thing I knew, the partygoers were like the UN, and they were all united against me. An uninvolved citizen called in a 1013 on my behalf, while I batted away Paddys, Ronans, and Callahans, as well as Alfredos, Carmines, and Giovannis with my nightstick until the squad cars showed up en mas. *If I've got to swing the stick at you, you're going to jail.* But we placed the big mouths under arrest, as well, and put them in cars. The desk sergeant sorted out the mess back at the station.

The opportunity to help people in need was what I'd always envisioned. Walking a beat in crappy neighborhoods, constant harassment, people who'd gleefully kill you for the fun of it, and cops who were petty criminals in their own right, had never been part of the bargain. I wanted out of TPF, so I visited Chief Klotsbach at 1 Truck of the Emergency Service Squad for the second time. The first time had been when Wally had talked to the chief on my behalf while I'd still been in the academy.

He'd told Wally, "When your brother comes on, have him see me."

So, I'd gone down there right out of the academy.

"Get a little time in on the job, will ya kid. Wear the uniform for two years and see what it's like. Then come talk to me again."

Two years later, in 1963, I was back. The only thing I'd needed then was to get out of TPF, and that wouldn't be a problem, because TPF officers who'd done their time could get just about any assignment they'd wanted within the department. After a February meeting with Klotsbach, I'd been transferred to ESS in March. Of course, my hope had been for an assignment to 1 Truck in lower Manhattan with Wally. I didn't need my older brother looking out for me anymore, but, as far as I was concerned, there'd been no better cop on the force with whom to work. I knew what he was like, and I was proud of him. Only the previous year, Wally had been awarded the Catherine O'Dwyer Medal for Lifesaving, one of the highest honors the city bestowed upon a police officer.

The only thing worse than a jumper is a pissed-off jumper. Wally's jumper had been on the ledge of the seventh floor of the once-grand Hotel St. George on Clark Street up in Brooklyn Heights, just south of the Brooklyn Bridge. The guy had been bound and determined to empty the contents of his room onto the sidewalk below before he made a splash himself. He was crazed. Wally's team ascended to the roof above, prepared a rappelling line, and then Wally propelled himself away from the ledge. Before the jumper knew what happened, Wally had landed on him and shoved his shaking body through the window and into the arms of police officers who had rushed the room on cue.

The only thing that would have made me prouder, would be working at this man's side on 1 Truck. Klotsbach put me on 8 Truck in Brooklyn. *I'll take it.*

I didn't know the first thing about Emergency Services, but they'd trained me for a full day, so I was ready. Back then, Emergency Service Squad was the equivalent of being an Emergency Medical Technician (EMT) or a paramedic. Today, my grandsons, Joseph, Jonathan, and Dustin are all either EMTs or Paramedics. Those kids are doctors compared to what the department had taught me. We'd been dispatched to car wrecks, fires, heart attacks, suicide attempts, and a host of situations where people were either injured or in peril. When not on an emergency call, we were expected to conduct ourselves as any other cop in the city would. Emergency calls were *our* job, even if precinct cops had arrived first. Other jobs that we responded to were often turned over to the precincts. Of course, traffic violations—which I did my best to avoid—were handled as you'd expect.

My pet peeve on the job was vehicles parked on a hydrant—I didn't care that parking sucks in Brooklyn. There'd been a pizza place in the 90th Precinct where, every day, the owner had his truck on the hydrant that was in front of his place. I finally wrote him a summons. Next day, the truck was there again, so I wrote him up a second time. This went on for a week. Every day, he got a summons. Eventually, an ESS lieutenant called me into his office.

He said, "I understand you're getting a little crazy with summonses for this pizza parlor."

"Yes, I am. He keeps his truck on the hydrant."

"Don't you think you should let up on the guy?"

"No, I don't."

"Well maybe you should," he said.

I knew what was going on. The precinct got free pizzas from this place in return for the parking spot in front of the hydrant. I didn't care. I'd seen plenty of this shit before. When I'd been in TPF, I had a desk sergeant ask me to go pick up a couple loaves of bread at a bakery around the corner. When I asked for the money, he told me that I didn't need money at this place.

"Pick up your own bread then. I don't want any part of it."

In the case of the pizza place in the 90th, I asked the lieutenant, "Are you telling me to stop writing this guy?"

He said to me, "Oh, no, no, no. I'm not saying that."

He hadn't quite winked, but he didn't have to.

"Okay. Fine then."

I continued to write up the truck, and I got another call. This time his order was, "Stop writing the pizza guy."

"Fine."

I stopped writing summonses all together. I got called on that later, because we were supposed to write at least one a day, to show that we were out there. "Everybody or nobody" had been my response to the inquisition.

When I told one of my partners what was going on, he said, "I got this, Joe."

He started writing up the pizza truck, and Pizza Man found a new place to park.

Look, a free lunch is a free lunch, and I've understood that since my cheese-sandwich days in grade school. If a deli owner didn't charge me for a sandwich, I was grateful. I figured he wanted to show his appreciation for the police. There could, however, never be any expectations in return for that free sandwich. And I never asked to get something for nothing. Believe me, there wasn't a cop in the city who had a problem with a free lunch. But most would not accept anything if something was expected in return. Most of us had no expectation whatsoever of a gratis meal. And most would not even go back to the same place the next day if the owner gave them a sandwich on the house. We weren't supposed to ever accept anything—I understood that.

Here's the way it usually went: I'd order my eggs, or pastrami, or pizza, and when I was finished eating, I'd hand over a bill large enough to cover the meal. The waitress or owner would make the change at the register, I'd fish out the appropriate tip, stuff the rest in my pocket, and say, "Thank you." Later, I might buy a coffee someplace and discover that the restaurant had either made the correct change, or had merely converted my large bill to smaller ones and some coins. Neither of those outcomes bothered me, and I appreciated the latter. I wouldn't go back the next day or even the next week, because I didn't want the owner to feel I expected more. I didn't take advantage. Some guys, however, would eat at the same counter day after day, and not leave so much as a tip. Now, if the deli owner had parked his truck on the hydrant after giving me a free sandwich, I'd probably go talk to him about moving it, and explain that I'd have to write him up if he didn't. We all decide where to draw our own lines, I guess.

Years later, I'd get that hydrant itch one last time. It had hit me hard and fast. My partner and I cruised Crossbay Boulevard, and I spotted a Cadillac at the hydrant in front of a fancy restaurant. This hadn't been brilliant police work on my part. The car in question—white convertible, with a stripe of blue stars down each side—had begged to be noticed.

"You gotta be kiddin'!"

I swung the squad car around and pulled up behind it. *Jackpot.* The license plate read *Elvis 1*. My partner and I looked at each other in disbelief. Then we laughed.

"I'm writing him."

"No way, Joe."

"Are you kidding me? Yes, I am."

"You haven't written a summons in years. You gonna start here?"

"It's Elvis! I gotta do this."

"I'm telling ya, Joe, Ann'll never speak to you again."

Shit. Ricky Mamone was my favorite partner in Emergency, and his wife, Ann, was a doll. I couldn't believe he'd tossed Ann in my face so quickly.

"How 'bout we just go in and bust his chops?"

"No. Leave it alone. You can't go in a fancy place like this and harass a celebrity."

So, I let Ricky talk me out of it, but I should have written the summons. Why should Elvis have gotten a pass on the hydrant just because he was famous? Of course, his fame was the whole reason I wanted to do it. Today, it would be much more fun to say, "I wrote Elvis Presley a summons" than "I could have written Elvis Presley a summons." I should've written him up. If only that were my greatest regret.

The Emergency Service Squad was good for me, and I started to like being a cop. My hope to help people had finally come to fruition. Another cop might find releasing a young boy's penis from the grip of his zipper beneath him, but the relief that kid felt made me feel good about myself. And the appreciation of the boy's parents, who took our names and badge numbers and sent a nice letter to our command, made me feel much better about the people of the city. Where I'd once been disrespected and taunted merely for the badge I'd worn, I now received appreciation, respect and, at times, praise. Oh, there'd still been plenty of the former, but the latter got me through. Johnny Amandine had taken his TPF ticket-to-anywhere and moved to narcotics—he'd wanted to be a detective. We'd had divergent goals for our time on the force, and that was okay. I'd no desire to spend my days dealing with the city's underbelly, and he'd no wish to rescue kids who were in too much of a hurry to safely pull up their zippers. That's life.

In January of 1964, I moved my family to Long Island. I'd bought my first house. Barbara's stepfather had passed away in December, and Maisie lent us her $1,500.00 death settlement for a down payment on a $14,000.00 house. So, we loaded up the van, and we—me, Barbara, my father, Barbara's mother, six kids, and another in what had become a busy oven—moved to Lindenhurst on the south shore. Of the five bedrooms in our new house, we had two to spare for what would soon be seven kids. It was the greatest. I felt like I was going to The Hamptons after my shift each day.

But there was an issue with one of my children at home. One of the boys had what I'd figured—or hoped—to be a medical problem that neither my ESS skills nor my temper could deal with. Robert was almost seven years old and Barbara still needed to wash his sheets three or four times a week. Angrily insisting that he get his ass out of bed when he needed to piss had no effect. We finally took him to the doctor.

A thorough examination ended with these words from the doctor: "This is not a medical problem. I recommend that he see a psychiatrist."

I'd never been a big believer in psychiatry—not for sane people anyway—but, despite my best efforts to convince the doctor that my son was not crazy, he'd been persistent. I hadn't a clue what else to do, so I took the proffered paper with the name and phone number, and made the appointment. Disbelief, shock, anger, and shame combined to boil my skin and melt my heart at the psychiatrist's words.

"Your son thinks you don't love him."

This was stereotypical, horse shit psychobabble, the likes of which could only be uttered in a sappy movie. But there they were: *He thinks you don't love him.*

"Of course I love him. I love all my children."

"I'm sure you do, Mr. Lynch. The problem is, *he* is not sure."

Even as I felt stunned and confused, the answer swirled around me and squeezed the life from me: *I've become my father.* I could have curled up and died at the very thought. When I'd been my son's age, I'd been convinced that my father did not love me or even care about me, and he'd never taken the time to do anything about that belief. Not once in my life had I heard my father say, "I love you." Never. The man was living with me and my family in our humble at best (but grand to us) home—I bathed the man, for Christ's sake—and he'd yet to show even an inkling of gratitude.

I tell them, don't I?

I resolved to correct the problem. Barbara, Robert, and I piled into our Econoline—a cargo van that I'd spent some extra money on in order to add windows down the sides and to purchase a couple of bench seats that I could bolt to the floor in the back in order to turn it into the family car. We set out on the thirteen-mile drive home from the city-paid doctor. Even at the age of six, kids know how to tell you what you want to hear.

"You know I love you, right?"

"Yes."

"Because I do."

"Yes."

On that day, I made a pledge that my children would never doubt my love for them.

A kiss and off to bed. "I love you."

A kiss to greet them at the door. "I love you."

A reminder during the Jackie Gleason show. "I love you."

A spanking for a bad deed. "I love you."

Spotted playing basketball with friends. "I love you." Usually followed by a red face, laughs from buddies, and an "I love you, too, Dad," because each of them knew I'd expected to hear it back.

I'm confidant that each of my children—despite a disciplined upbringing during which exemplary behavior, honesty, and respect had been nonnegotiably enforced with a firm hand—would testify to the love that they have felt from me throughout their lives. The love they continue to show me, Barbara, and each other to this very day is further testament to the cycle that had finally been broken at their generation through a visit to that psychiatrist, and the ensuing soul-searching on my part. There is no greater legacy than that. Each time I see my adult children offer a kiss and say, "I love you" to their brothers and sisters makes me happier than a Korean pig in shit.

After the visit to the psychiatrist, my boy swallowed a little red-coated pill of nothing more than sugar each night, convinced it would prevent him from wetting his bed. The problem quickly disappeared.

CHAPTER 22

Bridge To Humanity

IT WAS A MISERABLE, RAINY day. The Belt and Southern State Parkways formed a thirty-mile rush-hour parking lot. What should have been a forty-minute drive took close to two hours after an 8 a.m. to 4 p.m. shift. I pulled in the driveway at about 6:15—dinnertime. I grabbed my holstered gun and the brown paper bag that contained my uniform off the seat next to me. Barbara was long familiar with the meaning of the bag: the uniform went from bag to washer without her ever touching or looking at it. The day had turned to shit long before my arduous drive home.

With my coat held over my head, I rushed into the house through the side kitchen door, right from the driveway, and stomped rainwater from my shoes. My father was sitting at the table. I'd hoped he would be in his bedroom at the back of the house. No luck.

"Hi."

My tone was not cheerful, but he didn't expect it to be.

He snuffed a cigarette in his silver Knights Of Columbus ashtray—the Knights' diamond-shaped logo stood from the center of the shallow tray on the bottom diamond point and had slots at each of three remaining points in which lit cigarettes could be rested. A blue swirl of smoke drifted toward the open window next to him. There must have been a dozen cigarettes in the tray.

"When are we eating?" he asked.

There was no sign of supper on the stove, in the oven, or on the counter. Lightening flashed outside and provided momentary brightness to an otherwise gloomy day.

"Is that rain coming in the house?" I asked.

He looked through the window—wind and rain beat at the Dogwood on the front lawn—then picked up a cigarette pack from the table and shook it. Nothing came out. He yelled into the living room as if I wasn't standing there.

"Helen."

He always called Ellen "Helen."

"Get me a pack of cigarettes."

I wanted to smack him.

"Her name is *Ellen*."

I'd told him that hundreds of times. I'm sure he did it just to piss me off. Ellen stopped correcting him years ago.

He picked up the filthy ashtray, and dumped it into the paper bag he kept on the floor next to him for his garbage and the tissues with phlegm he coughed up from dawn to dusk. Eleven-year old Ellen ran into his bedroom and got a pack of Pall Malls from the carton on his dresser.

"Here you go, Papa," she said with a smile.

Her sweetness was returned with indifference.

"Thank you, Ellen," I said. "I love you."

Ellen turned toward the living room, and the prick who fathered me slid his cane between her feet. She stumbled toward the doorway.

"I love you, too, Daddy."

When she'd settled back in front of the television with the others, I addressed the old man. "I ever see you do that again, I'm gonna break that cane across your back."

He knew I was full of shit, even though we both knew that I thought I meant it. He nestled the new cigarette pack between his slung arm and his torso and made quick work of peeling it open with his right hand. Then he tapped a cigarette partway out on the edge of the table, pulled it the rest of the way between his lips, flipped the Ronson lighter with his thumb, and lit it up. There was never more than a minute or two between his cigarettes—four packs a day. With no corner grocery store on 11th Street, we now bought them for him by the carton. Almost ten bucks a pop. Saved him a lot of nickels, though. He didn't acknowledge my anger.

"Shut that window," I said.

In the living room, the kids and a couple of their friends, along with piles of folded laundry, covered every inch of furniture and a good part of the floor.

"Have you all done your homework?" I asked.

"Yes, Dad," was the reply from most.

Robert jumped from the middle of the sofa and ran upstairs without a word. His friend from across the street, Johnny Dalton, looked at me from the far end of the sofa.

"You eating with us?"

"No, Mr. Lynch." He jumped from the couch. "I gotta go home for supper."

I asked Ellen, "Where's your mother?"

"Downstairs."

The basement was where Barbara did the laundry and where we kept the bulk of our non-perishable food. Otherwise, it was a big open space that—at times—the kids played in. Through the living room and into the back hall, I made a quick stop to the right in my bedroom and tucked my gun under a folded blanket on the top shelf of the closet. Back in the hall, I passed the open entrance to the living room and pulled the basement door just beyond and on the left. Barbara sat on the bottom steps. She didn't turn, although she had to have heard the door open. This could have only meant one of very few things. I leaned my head to the right and looked through the kitchen. The most likely reason took a long drag from his Pall Mall, and our eyes met. He turned and looked out the still-open window. *Son of a bitch.*

"Shut that goddamned window," I said, and this time he complied.

At the bottom of the stairs Barbara wiped tears from her cheeks.

"What did he do this time?"

"Same stuff. Nothing is ever good enough."

The *same stuff* usually meant he'd bitched about his food, complained about the kids—whom he saw as servants now, rather than cute grandchildren—barked orders, or told Barbara that she didn't do things right.

"I'm sorry."

"It's okay."

"No, it's not. He's an ungrateful bastard. I'd like to break his neck."

"He's your father."

"Yeah."

It was the same thing I'd repeatedly told myself: *Honor thy father. I'd like to honor him with a gravestone.* But it wasn't true. I'd never wished death upon him. As much as I did not love him, I don't think I ever hated him. I hated having him in my home, though. And I despised the way he treated my wife or called my daughter *Helen* or accused the kids of stealing his money or hacked up phlegm all day or looked out that freaking window.

After I gave Barbara a hug, she looked at the bag by my feet. She wiped away another tear. I wasn't sure whether it was left over from the anguish caused by my father, or if it was a new one sparked by the day she then understood I'd had.

The bag represented a body in Brooklyn. This one had been in a tub filled with water and blood. All we'd had to do was get the body—a big one—in a bag, but it had been soaking in the tub for days, and every part we'd pulled at with our gloved hands fell off. The tub wouldn't drain. So we tipped the tub on it's side, and water, blood, and body splashed to the floor. We pushed the parts of somebody's loved one into the bag. A person who'd had more mundane life experiences than I would certainly suffer horrible nightmares after such an awful scene. At least I didn't have to worry about that.

Barbara picked up the paper bag. "I'll get this in the wash."

"Thank you. I love you. I'll go get some Chinese."

Chinese food had been a seldom-seen indulgence in the house, but we had an army to feed.

That night, dogs chased me and the other man who, when I'm awake, I almost felt like I knew. After all, I'd been seeing him four or five times a week in my dreams.

I don't spend much time examining the creatures, but they are of the junkyard variety—large, unkempt, and vicious. As in the other *chase* dreams, I know that capture means death. The snarling and growling grow closer and inform me that this death will be particularly grue-some. I fall and watch the boots of the other man put distance be-tween us. Then the dogs lunge. I flail, kick, scream, and scratch.

Then I awoke.

Barbara stood at the bedroom door with a book in her hand and concern in her eyes. I just stared into space. *I don't know how much longer I can take this shit.* After I convinced her to go back in the living room, I sat at the edge of the bed and studied the closet door. Soft shadows, formed by the combination of trees in the backyard and lights on the elementary school beyond, swayed on the surface. I thought about the man in the tub—a suicide. From the bed, my mind found the gun under the blanket in the closet.

In The City That Never Sleeps, real-life nightmare scenarios play out with alarm-ing frequency. Early Friday evening, August 5, 1966, Joe Thomann and I patrolled the Williamsburg neighborhood of Brooklyn, and we received a call alerting us to a jumper on the Williamsburg Bridge. A man was atop the north tower on the Brooklyn side of the bridge. We responded, and arrived on the scene first. After we blocked traffic, we devised a plan that required Thomann to walk up the sus-pension cable with a harness, while I ascended the stairs within the tower. In the interest of full disclosure, I admit that the cable was never a real option for me, be-cause the thought scared the crap out of me, so Thomann surrendered the stairs.

The first level within the tower was a fifteen-foot, vertical, rail ladder with an enormous girder to scale at the top. Then came the stairs. The unusually low-for-August temperature—low 70s—was a Godsend as I bound the stairs. Nonetheless, sweat soaked my uniform as I emerged at the top of the tower almost 200 feet above the roadway. There was no time for sightseeing, yet I was aware—in an out-of-body sort of way—of the commanding view of Brooklyn, Manhattan, the East River, as well as the entire universe beyond. My eyes closed momentarily in reflex so I could regroup. My breath came heavy. The sun—and fear—heated my face. I opened my eyes with my head down and first saw my feet, and then the roof surface of the tower. On either side of me, I found the substantial cable saddle housings that stood over 6 feet tall, and I followed the outer cable with my eyes.

Joe Thomann was less than a quarter of the way up. He stepped purposefully up the 18.5-inch diameter suspension cable, with his harness attached to each of the two waist-high safety cables on either side of him. At about every 15 feet, a vertical rod attached the safety cables to the suspension cable below them. This meant that every time he reached the rods, he had to unclip each of his harness lines and reattach them on the far side of the rods. It was going to take him forever to reach me. It'd been a necessary evil, though, because this escape route needed to be blocked from the jumper. If he got out on the cable, the outcome would be disastrous. Below, new arrivals on the scene prepared to cover the remaining cables.

On top of the tower, there was only me, the saddle housings, and the view—no sign of the jumper. I eased to the river side of the tower—looking north—and peered over the edge. The East River lapped 500 feet below. An electrical pulse surged through my body and terminated at every nerve ending within. With no structures around to provide reference, it may as well have been 5,000 feet. And considering that it was about 450 more feet than certain death required, the exact height didn't matter much. As my friend, Reflex, pulled me back, I caught a glimpse of blue denim and sneakers below me. My jumper had lowered himself to a ledge about six feet beneath my perch. He lay on his stomach with his legs dangling over the edge of darkness.

I felt he wouldn't jump. I figured that I might have to talk him in—convince him that he didn't want to do it—but if he were going to do it, he would not have gotten himself into such an awkward position. When jumpers jump, they jump. They don't hang around and think about it. Once they do that, they often change their minds. It's all too scary once they've had the opportunity to ponder the next move. Because the level I stood on was a perfectly good diving platform, I felt sure he'd gotten down there merely to hide from me. I considered my next move. One thing was certain: I wasn't about to drop to that ledge with him—we'd both need rescuing, and it'd be pretty easy for both of us to make an unintended plunge. I needed to get him up to me without either one of us doing something stupid.

"What's your name?" I asked.

He looked up at me but didn't respond. Black kid—maybe nineteen—dressed in dungarees, white undershirt, and well-worn black Converse sneakers. He looked scared shitless. I could relate.

"Why are you doing this?"

Nothing.

"Talk to me." My tone was gentle. "Why are you doing this?"

"My girl broke up with me."

Jesus Christmas. The kid's heart was broken, and I didn't have a clue what the hell I was doing. I sat on the edge with my feet dangling above him. He shifted and told me to stay away. My opinion about him not jumping was changing.

"You think you're gonna hurt her by doing this? You're just gonna hurt yourself."

"It already hurts."

"I know it hurts." I didn't know. Barbara was my first real girlfriend, because I'd been so damned shy with the girls. I couldn't even imagine the hurt I'd have felt if she had left me. But I could imagine jumping off this bridge even less. A bullet to the head was the only form of suicide I could envision. *Pop.* Done. At any rate, if there were any good reasons to take your own life, a broken heart wasn't one of them. I believe there's plenty of love to go around for everyone.

"What's your name, son?"

"Eric."

"That's a good name. I want to show you something, Eric."

I lifted my ass and fished my wallet from my back pocket. From it I plucked a recent photo of the family. I'd had a professional photographer—a friend of a friend—come to the house, and he'd taken the photo right in the living room with all of us on the sofa. Eight kids now: Matthew, Ellen, Robert, Marianne, Joseph, Kathleen, Schanna, and Christopher.

"I want to help you, Eric. But I want you to look at this photo first." I reached down as far as I could with the photo. "That's my kids. If something goes wrong, they don't have a father anymore."

He looked at the photo as best he could. I was sure he got the idea.

"Imagine the hurt they are going to feel."

There were tears in his eyes. I held the photo a little longer.

"You got family, Eric? Mom, dad?"

"Yeah." Eric looked down at the water.

"Imagine their hurt."

He looked at the water again.

"I want to die."

"No you don't. You want the pain to stop."

The tears streamed down his face.

"I want to help you. Will you let me help you, Eric?"

He nodded. I put the photo away and as I got on my stomach, I glanced down the suspension cable. Joe Thomann had stopped maybe a third of the way up. There'd been nothing he could do. I extended my left hand to Eric and he grasped it. This was the most terrifying moment to me. Other than my own weight, I had no purchase. Today, a cop would not be allowed to go up there without backup, much less in the absence of a harness. If my partner had been with me, he'd at least be able to grab hold of me. Instead he watched the climax of the show from his spot above the roadway and hoped for a happy ending.

Eric grasped my hand, and I gave him a tug. He pulled back, and my body shifted toward the edge, so I used the only tool I could think of—threat. I pulled my gun and pointed it at him.

"If you pull me, I'm gonna shoot you, Eric. I'm not going over. Understand?"

He nodded.

"Okay. Just slide your legs up onto the ledge. I got you." When his legs were up, I said, "Now, get to your knees."

With Eric on his knees, I stood up and holstered the gun. I knew he wouldn't pull me. Maybe I'd overreacted a little. Then I helped him up to my level, and he dropped to his knees and sobbed. I stroked his head with a gentle hand. "It's okay, son."

I then helped him to the doorway that led to the stairs. On the suspension cable, Thomann almost ran the fifteen-foot sections between the vertical rods on his way back down. *Crazy son of a bitch.* Eric and I stepped through the door into what seemed like another universal dimension. An ominous and frightful world had been left behind, and the steel door behind us kept it at bay. All that was left was 200 feet of staircase and ladder. On the way up, I hadn't noticed the breeze whistling through the open grid work of steel girders that evoked the Eiffel Tower in Paris. I unbuttoned my uniform shirt, and the air cooled the sweat on my body. Eric felt weak, which made me concerned about the descent. The clang of rushed footsteps on rusted stairs below brought relief. Phil Reeves was the first guy to reach us. Bill Riley was right behind him.

"Jesus Christ, Joe." Phil's stern, bug-eyes startled me. He held out a harness belt. "You got a death wish?"

I did not. The idea of dying had certainly crossed my mind in the past, perhaps more often than is healthy. I'd even wondered at times if I'd be able to do it myself. *Pop.* Maybe I'd actually thought I *should*—end the nightmares, the fears, the anger, the shame, the confusion. Done. But I did not *wish* to be dead. I didn't wish to forfeit the life that God had given me—the life He'd intended me to cherish. I wished to be free—rid of shackles and weights of uncertainty and doubt. I wished to be safe—purged of torment and assaults from my own mind. I wished to be in control—able to keep rage and depression at distance. I wished to be normal.

I took the belt without comment and wrapped it around me.

Bill secured a belt around Eric's waist. "You okay, kid?"

Eric nodded. It would be the closest he'd come to speaking the entire way down. I wondered what was going through his mind as three cops crowded around him and held, tugged, and cradled him every inch of the descent. Maybe he thought about his girlfriend and the pain she'd caused him. Or that he should have made the leap as soon as he'd gotten to the top. Perhaps he felt shame and embarrassment at having not done so. He looked defeated. A quarter of the way down, Joe Thomann reached us. Up the cable, down the cable, up the tower—a real stud that guy. He smiled, and gave me a light slap on the cheek.

"You fucking moron."

I sensed the humor in his tone, but my own smile felt phony.

When stairs turned to ladder near the bottom, the going got tricky and the harnesses that connected Eric to my waist were a blessing. The last thing anyone wanted was for this kid to suffer a broken leg or worse. Riley held a firm grip on my harness belt, while I planted my feet atop the massive girder and kept the lifeline between Eric and me secure and taut. Reeves guided Eric's every move as he helped him over the girder and down the ladder. Camera flashes filled shadows inside the dark base of the tower for milliseconds at a time as film captured physical events while emotional reality slipped through its one-dimensional grasp. Below me, no fewer than six cops helped Eric and each other to secure footing at road level.

Eric was brought to an ambulance, and I became lost in a sea of familiar faces, flashing emergency lights, cheers, and the car horns of impatient commuters who just wanted to get home to their now-cold suppers.

I watched the activity around me through someone else's eyes. The body I now occupied buzzed like an electrical breaker whose circuit had been stuck in a half-open position. The ESS truck provided support when I could no longer convince muscles to do the work themselves. Ears heard words, but mind failed comprehension. Somebody guided me to sit in the truck and we sped through city streets that seemed familiar, although I could not place them. At the station, I lay in a bunk and saw views of the city from above the East River. The tower below my feet soared ever higher, and the river grew distant below me, until I tumbled down, down, down into a deep sleep.

When a cop finishes a job, it's done. A life saved doesn't change that. I didn't check up on Eric later. We didn't exchange phone calls or meet each other's families. He didn't keep me informed on the progress of his life or send pictures of his children in later years. There'd been no almost-jumped reunions on anniversaries of that day. It was done. But just like the connections to lost souls in Korea that I have carried throughout my life, I am eternally tethered to the boy in the blue dungarees and black Converse sneakers, with the once-broken heart. People told me then that I was a hero, but when I think back on that day, heroics is not what I recall. What I remember is a young man's pain. It is the opportunity to help a person in need that I cherish.

At home that night, I held my wife and children close. I told each that I love them. I cried.

CHAPTER 23

Minefield

NOBODY CHASES ME THIS TIME. The unknown man is not with me. I do not fear for my life. My life *is* in grave danger, though, and I believe I will die. The gun is pressed against my temple, the hammer is cocked, and I wonder if I will feel the bullet when it crashes through my skull. *Will I hear it?* I hear my breath, a sharp hiss with each inhale, controlled and elongated exhales. The gun slides against my skin ever so slightly, and my eyes close. *Nothing.* When they open again, the world rushes by me in darkness.

I think about Barbara. How I sometimes hold her close in front of the kids. I kiss her and tell her she's beautiful. "I love you," I say. I kiss her some more, and laugh with the children at her embarrassment. She and my eight children are everything to me. The children know I love them, but they may not realize how important they are to me. I don't have a lot of time to do things with them. Two jobs, three jobs—whatever it takes to put food on the table. But I'd do anything for them that falls within my tiny sphere of influence. If this bullet was meant for any of them, I'd step in front of it without hesitation. I'd give my life for each and every one of them.

But would I preserve it?

Tears soak my eyes, and sweat rolls into the creases of my brow. What will they do without me? How will they face life with this knowledge? A bump—*Thump, thump*—and I am jarred in the front seat of the 1967 Ford Fairlane station wagon. I'd bought the car a year ago, because I wanted to have a real car for my family. Now, Barbara doesn't feel like we're going out to fix someone's furnace every time we climb in the van to shop for groceries. My head bounces with the bump, and the gun slams my head. My eyes instinctively shut. *Nothing.* When they open this time, I take the gun away from my head, release the hammer, and drop it on the seat next to me. Heat fills my face; shame smothers my heart.

It was the worst kind of nightmare, because I was awake. It felt surreal, but I can assure you it was acutely real. The 1:00 am traffic on the Belt Parkway was light. I stayed at exactly fifty-five MPH, and the few other cars on the highway passed me as though I was doing thirty. Earlier, I'd sat at the side of the highway—pulled into the grass of the shoulder near Plumb Beach on the south side of Brooklyn, and then I'd shut off the lights. Sporadic traffic zipped by to my left—*thump, thump* as the cars in the right lane cruised over an offensive pothole. To my right spread the vast darkness of the Rockaway Inlet. Lights from working-class beach bungalows twinkled in the distance and offered up their restful serenity. I chose to embrace the darkness. *Thump, thump.*

I'd picked up and unholstered my gun. It's weight felt powerful, and the oily smell was soothing. The comfortable relationship I'd always experienced with weapons, however, had—over time—morphed into dysfunction. This very sidearm had taunted and teased whenever I'd tried to ignore it. The farther I'd pushed it away—the deeper I'd buried it—the louder its call had become.

Just see the center of the darkness, relax, and this relationship is done. With only the inlet as witness, I'd brought the gun to my head, and focused on the vast nothingness before me. *Thump, thump.*

A flood of thoughts—God, family, friends—had filled my head and confused me. In the end, I didn't want my family to know that their father and husband had committed suicide. Visions of Barbara facing neighbors were too much. Those people already looked down on me because I was a cop and because I had so many children. *I know they do.* Barbara's friend—her name was Barbara, as well—who lived across the street from us, was the one neighbor I trusted to treat her well. Otherwise, the rest would talk. There was just too much shame there. So, I'd dropped my service revolver on the seat and pulled back onto the Parkway. The potholes and dips in the asphalt that normally pissed me off beyond measure had gone all but unnoticed until I hit one particularly offensive pit in the center lane that grabbed the front right tire and did it's best to drag the car to the next lane. I'd felt the impact in my spine. It only took a couple more miles before the gun had found its way back into my hand. I'd lifted it back to my head, pulled the hammer back with my thumb, and held a firm finger to the trigger. It had occurred to me that if I hit a pothole—*Thump, thump*—and the impact caused my finger to compress the trigger, then maybe it was meant to be. It's hard to believe that people can feed themselves that kind of crap and actually believe it. Many of our beliefs are, after all, merely a product of convenience. *Thump, thump.*

Of course, I'd again found all the reasons not to do it—this time—and the gun had sat beside me on the bench seat until I'd pulled into the driveway at home. Perhaps the rule for shooting oneself in the head mirrors that of jumping off a bridge: when shooters shoot, they shoot.

That had been the first time I'd taken specific steps to end my life. Suicidal thoughts had filled my head for some time, though. In those days, I spent a lot of time alone—in the car, lying awake in bed, and at various extra jobs. At one of those jobs, I'd washed windows at nice homes in Nassau County for a buck a window. My reflection would look back at me from plate glass, and mock me: *This is what you do, big shot?* I didn't have a problem with doing the windows people couldn't be bothered with. Food, clothes, school supplies, birthday gifts were all more important than pride. And, frankly, I'd never been ashamed of hard work. It would have been nice to do my menial tasks without my mirror image, though. *Every time I turn around, there I am.* Alone with my thoughts and a squeegee, I was often visited by the unknown man. He was a great runner, but not much use to me otherwise. Firing squads would materialize and take aim. I'd flinch as their rifles exploded. And vicious, snarling dogs snapped at my feet from below the ladder. It was never good enough that they all dominated my sleep hours, now they followed me to work. Conscious and subconscious blended—sleep and awake had difficulty distinguishing themselves.

My squeegee glided across a window. Displaced soapy water, which ran down to the sill, revealed my transparent glass image that blended with the sheer white curtains behind it, creating a shrouded effect. The ghostly figure stared me down in a feelingless taunt. *Korea* it whispered. Yeah, I think about Korea from time to time, too, while I toil. More often than not, it is The Chosin Reservoir and The Missing Days.

I remember that we had been making our way through Nightmare Alley (an aptly-named coincidence) where the snow and ice covered mountain soared to the left of the narrow road. Deep ravines dropped to our right, and skeletal treetops poked from monstrous snowdrifts. *Nowhere to run to; nowhere to hide.* But we were still alive, and we continued to move. The Howitzer was still with us, and we rotated rides on the back of the prime mover. My feet screamed with pain, and I was not sure whether they were cold or hot—frozen or on fire—even while the deuce-and-a-half carried me along at a walking pace. I wanted to climb down and walk—*Maybe getting the blood flowing will warm me*—but when it was my turn to dismount, the agony proved unbearable. I walked anyway. The wind whipped through the mountain pass and warmth found a distant place to hide. I remembered that we had lost the gun sometime after that, but the details were sketchy. Patrick Parrish was gone. *Oh, God. Not Patrick.*

The Howitzer and prime mover were destroyed and lay at the bottom of a deep ravine with all of my earthly possessions and Bryan's three hundred bucks. What few photos I'd taken since we had arrived in Korea would be preserved on undeveloped film wrapped around the spindle within my camera, which was tucked away in my pack where even the North Koreans would never be able to get to it—memories gone the way of The Missing Days that followed shortly thereafter. Then, all I had in my memory banks were Item Company, the patrol, and the ambush. Something happened during The Missing Days, even if it had been innocuous—my bet is that it was not. The flipped pages that were the archives of my experiences always revealed the same clean, untouched leafs. *Or have they been erased?* Either way, there was nothing there.

My reflection sneered at me. *You know how to end this,* it said. And I thought about the way. *Pop.*

Like many people, however, I did some of my best thinking in the car—especially at night when the traffic wouldn't distract me. White lines formed a string of dashes that appeared in the pool of headlight illumination and created a Morse Code message that rivaled the garbage flashed at us by the LST in Wonsan Harbor years before. *Dash. Dash. Dash. Dash. Dash.* Like my life, it meant nothing. I'd floated into another minefield and, this time, there was no rescue party. I visualized the mines that I had never seen that night in Korea and imagined poking one. *POP.* I wished my life had ended then. Of course, it had been death by explosion that I would have chosen over the drowning. It's hard to imagine a worse way to die then by drowning. I should know—it was what I was doing now. I had pulled myself up for air so many times and could no longer reach the surface. I was tired. I longed for a deep breath of cleansing air—just one breath—but the will to fight for it was lost. Fear filled lungs that longed for peace and, as I sank below for the last time, I searched for the mine that would end the agony.

I continued to go through the motions, though, and life moved on. There were moments of good that bolstered me for short periods at a time. In 1967, I received the Catherine O'Dwyer Medal For Life Saving for my efforts on the Williamsburg Bridge the prior year. I called my brother, Wally, with the news. Only five years before, Wally had received that same award from the city. We were now the only brothers in department history to have both been honored thusly, and I couldn't wait to tell him. To me, the medal represented the qualities that made a cop good. I relished the idea that our names could now be spoken in the same breath, more for our shared accomplishment than for having a mutual sperm donor. When he'd joined me for the award ceremony at City Hall on June 28th—and then again on August 9th for the recorded television celebration—I could not have been more proud. I'd never had to worry about having Wally's approval before that day, but now I also had the sanction of the best cop in the city. It meant everything to me as a police officer.

Barbara and my eight children had also been in attendance on the first day at City Hall, which made the day perfect. Nothing could have been better than to share that moment with my family. For the three oldest kids, the highlight had been visiting WNEW TV Studio Five a couple months later where all of the awards were presented a second time—for the cameras—during a banquet dinner. Nine-year-old Robert had been enthralled with the TV cameras, and would eventually operate similar cameras for a living (I'm not certain there is a connection). On our way out of the building, Joe Thomann ducked into Sonny Fox's Wonderama studio, and returned with a handful of TV funny-money for the children.

"Here you go, kid."

His mild lapse in police etiquette had been well appreciated. At home that evening, Robert found his grandmother, Maisie, and told her that the Mayor of New York had shook his hand. By her reaction—a crushing bear hug and near tears—you'd think the kid had met Jesus himself. John Lindsey was no Jesus.

I didn't need to do a thing in order to bring joy to my family on those days—just put them in the car and let them tag along. They'd had a new experience and seen their father under a softer light. For that brief period in time, I was genuinely happy.

But the city had done it's best to sap the joy from that day. When first notified that I'd be awarded the medal—the city's Medal of Honor—I also learned that Joe Thomann would be awarded an Excellent Police Work ribbon. That son of a bitch went up that suspension cable, and was offered a pat on the back by the department and the city. We'd taken the call, arrived on the scene together, formulated and executed a plan, and saved a young man's life—period. He'd deserved whatever I got. It just pissed me off that the department would treat him so poorly. I went to the award commission and let them know.

"What else could you possibly want?"

"I don't want anything for myself. I want you to show my partner the respect he deserves."

After reevaluating, they'd upped his award to a commendation, which—in NYPD terms—is a pretty high honor. He should have gotten the medal, though. Joe, being of good fiber, never held it against me, but I—on the other hand—continued to see him relinquishing the stairs to me. I put the two-ounce, fourteen-karat-gold medal from Tiffany and Company in the drawer alongside the old Bronze Star.

The 60s, which were a pretty shitty time to be a cop in New York City, limped toward a close. In 1968, the department transferred me to ESS 9 Truck in Queens. Same job, different assholes. There had certainly been many opportunities to do good, and I cherished them. But race riots and Vietnam War protests set the entire city on edge. Hate for cops rose to an all-time high. The peace, love, and Molotov-cocktail crowd—with their long hair and clown outfits—really confused me. How could one speak through violence in the name of peace? Those draft dodgers held up two fingers to signify peace, even as they berated the young boys who came home with bullet wounds and missing limbs after they'd fought for that peace. *It's all about the love, man.* And then they'd spit on the vets. They were a new breed of asshole that repulsed me.

We'd dispatched to Queens College in the Kew Gardens Hills neighborhood of Flushing on the occasion of one of those protests. Every available unit from the precinct, TPF, and ESS had been on hand. The students had not been rioting, but the protest was getting loud and unruly, so we'd been assigned to keep it under control. There'd been the typical line of containment, to which I'd been assigned. A young lady—I'm being generous—walked up to me and spat in my face (her way of saying, *Peace*, I guess). *Bitch.* I flexed my hand around my club and brought it down on her head. Okay, that had only been a fleeting thought. I'd actually remained lucid enough to understand that she'd been trying to provoke me into doing something stupid—perhaps violent. Maybe she'd wanted us to arrest her for the sake of the TV cameras. Three or four big, bad cops carrying off a nineteen-year-old girl by her arms and legs would have made great television. Instead, I hacked up my best glob and spit it back in her face. Her stunned silence had been worth whatever repercussions I'd suffer. Fortunately, there'd been none. She mustered up her best indignation, and ran off screaming.

"He spit in my face. Did you see that? He spit in my face."

Nobody cared. Although George Vega, one of my partners, nearly spit up his last meal.

I called after her, "Come back, and I'll do it again."

This was the kind of crap that I brought home with me. While my response to her had been greatly satisfying, she—and so many others like her—would never know what she'd done to me. *Pig!* We were there for *them*, and they called us pigs. We carried their children out of burning houses, provided first-aid to their mothers at the scene of a car accident, arrested the people who snatched their sister's purse, and they called us pigs—they spat on us. Every bit of crap, every indignity, was tucked away in my heart where nobody could see it. It undermined my soul like termites to a house. The outside looked fine, but the structure was weak. Eventually, the house has to come down, and that is what I took home.

I don't remember what it was. Some asshole—maybe a sergeant partnered me wrong, a citizen didn't like his hydrant summons, or some jackass called me pig—got to me. It wasn't hard to do. And I brought it home. It'd been after a day shift, and I got in about 5:30 pm to find a house full of kids, windbreakers and sweaters hung from the banister at the bottom of the staircase, hats and toys and who-knows-what strewn around the living room, and remnants of afternoon snacks on the kitchen table. A *Get Smart* rerun blared from the television.

"Why is this place always such a goddamned mess?"

I threw the coats on the floor. The children did what they always did—stared in stunned silence for fear of being the one to be singled out.

"Pick those up and put them where they belong!"

No one moved. It was the scene from *It's A Wonderful Life* in which George Bailey yells at his kids and rants about all the things that are wrong in his little world—a scene that was repeated often in our home.

"Joe." Barbara stood at the back-hall entrance to the living room. "That isn't—"

"Don't tell me what is and isn't. What the hell do you do around here all day?"

I knew exactly what she did around there all day. She took care of nine kids now. The place was like Camp Pendleton with one person in charge of the mess hall, laundry, kitchen, and cleaning. She broke up fights, convened court, and sent offenders to the brig. She put up with my father's crap when he played the role of sour commandant, and she treated his ungrateful ass like he was her blood.

"This place is a goddamned pigsty," I yelled at Barbara. "And they call *me* a pig."

I knew immediately that there'd be no taking it back. Shame gripped me, and it grew more thick with every breath. The tears welled and streamed down my beautiful wife's face. When she cried, it made me more angry—the only coping skill I understood. She turned and slipped into our bedroom. The kids remained frozen. The look in each set of eyes spelled fear but—to me—it only looked like hate.

"Shut that TV off, and put this shit away."

They scrambled. I wanted them out of my sight, and I knew they'd stay upstairs until called down for supper. The truth is, I wanted *me* out of *their* sight. I hated to see those young eyes boring in on me—some pooled with tears—when I was like this. They'd witnessed my anger plenty of times before, but they'd never heard me utter such hurtful words to their mother. Such words had never crossed my lips.

In the kitchen, the old man stayed silent. He knew damned well not to speak to me when I was like this. He didn't have to. His eyes said it all: *What a fucking asshole.* They almost seemed to laugh. This from—of all people—*my* father. He turned and looked out the window at whatever the hell it was that he found so interesting out there.

Good. The eyes made my skin itch—all of them. I could feel them crawling on me at times like this. *Everybody just keep your eyes off me.*

The worst three days of my life followed, during which only need-to-know words had been spoken in short monotones. Barbara stayed out of my sight whenever possible, and—other than the youngest who didn't understand—even the kids spoke only in measured necessity. I was unsure of my own state. Anger? Depression? Guilt? Grief? Self-loathing? Who knows—maybe all. I'd have bet dollars to donuts, however, that it had just looked like anger to everyone else.

I wished she'd just divorce me, and I feared that she would. I never wanted to lose Barbara, but I felt it would be for the best—for her, for me, and for the kids. *Just kick me out and be done with it.* It was pure selfishness on my part. I could work my three jobs every week, support my estranged family, go home to some crappy apartment, and then live my misery beyond the knowing eyes of the people I loved the most. It is said that they are the ones you hurt, and it's true. But, through no fault of their own, having them around hurt *me*. Without them, there would be no shame or guilt to suffer every time I lost my temper over some stupid little thing, or administered an unwarranted face slap or other punishment. As witnesses, they made me feel worse about myself than any self-hatred I could have mustered on my own.

How the hell was I supposed to feel when I called the person who loves me the most a pig? I hated myself more than I'd ever managed to hate anything. I'd never even been able to hate my father, for Christ's sake.

After three days, I mustered the humility to apologize.

"I don't remember what you did to piss me off so bad," I said. "But I forgive you."

That's the way I'd always apologize to Barbara, and she always understood. It was too difficult for me to express the shame over what I'd said, so I made a joke and all was forgiven. As was always the case, we both laughed, kissed, and held each other close.

"I love you," I whispered in her ear.

I didn't know how I'd become that person. I understood the externals—the things I couldn't control: nightmares, finances, and the garbage I dealt with in the city. Nine kids (we'd stopped with Mark) the old man, car troubles.

Police work, extra jobs, little sleep. Something had to give somewhere, and I could excuse myself an occasional implosion. When I'd been young, everything had rolled off my back—even my father's firm hand. Sewer-to-sewer ball or a game of wadded-paper football was all it had taken. Junior Sheehan and I would have a good laugh at the old man's expense, and everything would be right. I'd been a happy kid, and—besides my mother and Barbara—the Marine Corps had been the best thing that ever happened to me. It had been what I'd needed in my life—or so I'd thought.

I remembered my mother's words to me when she'd learned that I was at Parris Island: *You've made your bed. Now, you can sleep in it.* Was this my bed? Could she really have been so prophetic? I had thought that I'd proved her wrong so long ago. Aside from a broken nose, I'd excelled at Parris Island. No prouder Marine—a sixteen-year-old kid—had ever taken to the parade field on graduation day. I thrived on the discipline and training at Camp Pendleton and—at the very least—had carried myself well in a gruesome war far from home. Then I'd returned and shaped new Marines back at Parris Island, where I had read that heart-crushing letter from Ma nearly four years prior. *You've made your bed...*

After the Marine Corps, everything had started to change. Like sunburn, I hadn't felt it happening at first. By the time I realized that my skin was heating up, it was too late. The heat would build even as I got home from the beach, and by morning the blisters would have formed. I guess I'd started to feel the emotional heat in Germany about the time I'd yelled at Barbara about the cigarettes. If anybody had ever told me that one day I'd talk to a woman—*any* woman—like that, I'd have laughed at the lug. Women were to be respected at all times. But there I'd done it. And it wouldn't be the last time. Over time, the burn curve became more dramatic until the sun had scorched me beyond repair. By the end of the 1960s, my skin had peeled and deep layers of scar tissue had been exposed.

I hated what I had become, but I had no idea how to get out of that bed. When I was happy, I was the happiest guy on the planet, and—thank God—I still had those days. You never met a sillier guy or heard a louder laugh. I always loved to laugh, and everyone loved to hear it. Just when they'd let their guard down, though, watch out. My blisters would reveal themselves at a moment's notice. I've never cried over spilled milk, but my kids sure have. I'd wished that I knew how it had happened. How I'd allowed myself to become so angry. How depression had gripped such a happy person. How self-love had morphed into self-loathing.

CHAPTER 24

And I Wait

WHERE'S MY BULLET?

In 1971, cops were dropping all over the city. By the end of that year, fifteen New York City police officers had lost their lives in the line of duty. *What—I'm not good enough?* I'd played Pothole Roulette in the car several times. Off duty, I'd become obsessed with the weapon, and found myself handling it often. In order to protect my family, I'd decided that I couldn't be trusted with my own gun. I didn't want them to live with that stigma. Additionally, if I killed myself, they'd get no pension. I needed to die in the line of duty. Now, if I was killed in the line of duty, my children's father would have died a hero, and the family's financial needs would be met—Barbara would receive a lifetime pension. So, I began to leave my service revolver in my locker at work whenever I checked out after my shift—it never came home with me anymore. On the job, it was empty. I had ammunition on my belt, but unless I was at the firing range, no bullet ever saw the inside of the chamber.

And I waited.

I knew that the day would come when it'd be necessary for me to pull my sidearm in order to protect myself. When that happened, I'd be defenseless, and I would be shot. *Hero Cop Killed in the Line of Duty—Family Gets Full Pension.* Suicide by Cop, wherein someone with a death wish points a gun at a police officer and is subsequently shot and killed, has always been a common phenomenon. Mine was the same idea turned around—*Suicide by Perp.* It was perfect, really. Someone who didn't wear the blues may have thought it was a faulty plan, because my gun would be found empty—*Cop Commits Suicide by*

Perp. Not so. I had no doubt that the brothers would take care of me as well as—and more to the point—my family. When the gun was discovered to be empty, it would then be loaded. That may or may not happen today, but back in 1971 New York City, it was a given. If it could be helped, no cop in the city would have allowed another cop to be tagged with suicide on the job. No police officer would have stood by as another's family lived with that shame. No Brother in Blue would have seen that family left without security for their future. We took care of our own.

Somewhere in the city—several years before—there had been a cop who'd shrugged into the uniform one morning, slipped into the passenger seat of his partner's car, drank the coffee his wife had sent him off with, sneered at rush-hour traffic, laughed at raunchy jokes, and died of a heart attack before ever reaching the station house. His partner continued the drive to work. Upon arrival, the partner alerted other officers and, together, they moved the warm body into a squad car, and then went inside to check in the dead police officer for an abbreviated day at work. A cup of coffee all around, and then a couple of guys went out to *discover* that one of their brothers had died on the job—better benefits for the grieving family. We take care of our own.

In another case that came closer to home, a young officer stopped his car someplace in New York City, took out his service revolver, and put a bullet in his own head. *Pop.* A sea of police officers responded. When the detectives arrived, one of them removed the gun from the dead officer's car and tossed it in the trunk of his own car. Without a weapon, suicide is impossible. *Good Cop Shot In The Line Of Duty—Family Receives Pension*

The *murdered* cop was given a hero's send off. Thousands of cops from New York City, and the surrounding counties came to the funeral in order to honor his sacrifice and grieve their loss. Where the family of a suicide victim would have been left to mourn on their own, millions of people in the Greater New York City area shared this family's load. That alone is worth something.

I'm not saying it's right in either case. I'm just saying I know what happens. These two good men had good families, and the loving hand of the uniformed brothers had provided for them. So I waited for my moment. I hadn't been looking to be a hero. I just wanted to be dead and for my family to be taken care of—financially and emotionally. *And when some son of a bitch shoots me, I hope he goes away for life. He'll deserve it. I may have provided the opportunity, but he'd still need to be the kind of shit head who would point a gun at a cop and pull the trigger. At least his bullet will find a willing target.*

So, I'd go out on the job with an empty gun, and I'd wait. An added benefit to an empty gun was that if I—in a moment of weakness—decided to turn it on myself, I'd have the extra step of loading it, which would give me pause for thought. The problem was, my plan—well conceived as it might have been—put other cop's lives at risk. The way I saw it, I wasn't gonna use it anyway—empty or full, but at least with a loaded gun, I could have changed my mind in order to save a fellow cop's life. It was unlikely that I'd be afforded the luxury of time to load, if I found myself in such a situation.

One time, Bill Riley and I patrolled Queens in a squad car and a woman ran up and stopped us. Someone had just assaulted her, and stolen her purse. The suspect had a gun. I didn't think, *Here's my chance.* That wasn't the way it worked. Like Riley, I wanted this guy. He'd gone into a narrow alley that cut through a block and linked the streets at either end. Riley went around one end, and I took the other. When I made it into the alley, my partner was already there. He stood, gun drawn, with stiff arms extended at a group of bushes that were up against an apartment building.

"Drop that gun, and get the hell out of there."

My sidearm was comfortably tucked away in its holster. I'd reached for it as I ran into the alley and thought, *What the hell is the point?* A handgun skittered across the pitted concrete from the base of the bushes, and the criminal came out.

"Down, down, down," Riley yelled. The guy got on his knees, and Riley shoved him so that his face met the damp concrete. Only then did Riley relax a bit. We searched the assailant, and discovered that the son of a bitch had a second gun. I retrieved the weapon and Riley cuffed the bad guy. Twice, his eyes locked on my holstered gun. He remained silent, but when he looked at me, I flushed. We both knew what this meant: I'd screwed up. Maybe this clown could have gotten to his second gun and fired a lucky shot—probably not. Still, there *had been* a second gun in the mix, and a second cop who had not covered his partner's back. It was stupid, and I felt ashamed. But I continued to carry an unloaded weapon.

Weapon at my side or not—loaded or unloaded—my radar was always up. As a teen, I'd been fully *unaware* of my surroundings. Like the time when Junior and I had hitched a free ride on the back of a Trolley right in front of Red The Cop. That's what all the kids in the neighborhood called him: *Red The Cop*. Adults just called him *Red*. He was a great guy, but he didn't take any crap from "the hooligans," as he liked to refer to the young troublemakers on his beat. The guys I'd palled around with didn't really fall into that category, but boredom sometimes leads to indiscretion. Jumping the trolley for a block or two didn't meet the hooligan standard as far as we'd been concerned, but Red hadn't been fond of the habit—I'm sure for safety reasons as much as for economic ones. When our feet landed on the back platform, a shrill whistle filled the air.

Junior spotted him.

"Shit! Red The Cop."

He pointed over my shoulder, leapt to the street, and disappeared through traffic. I spun around. Red The Cop was already off the sidewalk, and running across the street toward me. I panicked. I jumped, and my feet planted together on the street in preparation for a quick getaway. I wasn't so much afraid of Red The Cop as I was of Red The Cop telling my father. I spun away from him and sprinted straight into the path of one of the new Streamline trolleys that came from the opposite direction of the car I'd been on. The impact threw me about seven feet and—luckily—the trolley stopped before it ran over me. I jumped up and ran all the way home in total ignorance of Red The Cop on my tail the entire way. When I reached the front stoop, I sat my ass down to catch my breath, and Red The Cop stomped to a stop right in front of me. *Jesus Christmas, where'd he come from?*

"Jaysus, Mary, and Joseph, sonny."

He spoke in a thick Irish brogue through huffs of breath. Sweat trickled from his orange hair over his pink forehead. I waited for him to bop me with his stick.

"Are ya alright, bye?"

"I'm fine."

"Ya coulda got yaself killed."

He took me by the collar to report to my father, who turned out not to be home. Red The Cop told the story to my brother, John, and explained that he'd run the six blocks just to be sure I hadn't been hurt. John gave me the bop on the head I'd thought I'd get from Red The Cop, and the entire affair was officially put to rest.

At some point over the years since that ill-conceived trolley ride, I had become hyper sensitive to my surroundings. Situational awareness had been part of the training at Parris Island and even at the police academy. If you were not aware when at war, you were dead. But what I now experienced was some kind of suped-up version of the military-learned skill. Nothing happened that I was not aware of. The way people breathed, smelled, or sucked their teeth was noted. Every person who entered an establishment was catalogued. I noticed what they looked at and how long they looked at it. I registered whom they spoke with and I sensed their moods. I made a mental checklist of clothing and distinguishing marks or traits. When I spoke to someone, I noted their hands, their eyes, their sweat. I noticed who just walked out of the grocery store across the street while I conversed with a friend on the sidewalk. This sensitivity to my surroundings amounted to more than just good police training, although it helped on and off the job. Mostly, though, it kept me on edge and could trigger any of a number of reactions in me. Sometimes the reactions were favorable.

I had my son Christopher in the station wagon with me over in Amityville a few miles from home. I drove south on Broadway toward the downtown area. Up ahead, a police car had been stopped on the northbound side of the road. The officer was up the curb talking to someone. Christopher talked about school, but my attention was firmly affixed to the situation up ahead.

Uhuh. Uhuh. As we approached from the opposite side of the median, I ze-roed in on the guy the cop spoke to. Dungarees, old white sneakers, military jacket—probably from a surplus store, because I could tell this guy had not served. He was agitated. Christopher said something that sounded like a distant radio emanating an indistinguishable drone. "Wait a minute," I said. He stopped talking. My left foot hovered over the brake pedal (a driving skill I'd learned on the police force). And there it was. The punk in the military jacket hauled off on the young police officer, and the cop dropped to the ground. My left foot slammed the brake pedal. The assailant flashed toward the median up ahead, and my right foot pushed the accelerator. The piece of shit ran into the road ahead of me, and my left foot went back to work on the brakes. My right hand turned the wheel to the right; my left hand extended from the driver's-side window and grabbed the guy by his coat. Then my right foot accelerated the station wagon up the curb, my left foot slammed the brakes, and shithead bounced off the left fender and face-planted into the sidewalk. My fourth son thought his father was Batman. Every step had been a reaction tipped off by a vigilance that I didn't understand. In this case, it had been for the good. But at other times, I was the crazy guy who snapped at a rolled eye or a breath of exasperation that nobody else even noticed. I was the guy who always expected something to happen and was eternally prepared for it to do so. What might merely startle others, would trigger a de-fensive display of terror, anger, and flying fists. Be assured, when I snapped, it was rarely for the good.

Despite my insane fear of dogs, a few have made their way into our home over the years—for the kids. The first one—I don't even remember his name—was a mean son of a bitch that even the children had grown leery of. I called the dogcatcher and had him taken away. I kept my distance while the catcher snared him and guided his snarling, growling ass to the truck. That dog was definitely the stuff of nightmares, and I was glad to see him go. Our second, Pepper, was a mostly harmless Black Lab mix who the kids got along with well. From my bedroom window at the back of the house, I saw that a friend of one of my younger children had decided it'd be fun to tease the dog and toss some rocks at him. Pepper had finally had enough and lunged atop the child. I dove, hands first, followed by head through the window that was ten feet above the concrete-paver patio, rolled, and landed on the dog before I even realized what I'd done. I dragged Pepper off the stupid kid who was unharmed other than the piss in his pants. The poor dog had merely protected himself and managed to refrain from actually biting, but he was done. The dogcatcher took him away later that day.

Then came the puppy with the broken tail. I'd sworn there'd never be another dog, but there he was. Tiny—he couldn't have been more than six or seven weeks old—shaking, and with a broken, bloody, raw tail that bent at a ninety degree angle. There'd been an explosion at an apartment building above an Off Track Betting office in Queens. The entire building had been destroyed and there'd been no survivors—other than the puppy with the broken tail. There didn't seem to be an evil bone in his body, so I brought him home.

I climbed out of my 1971 Volkswagen bus and zipped my heavy coat. Some of the children were on the front stoop so, with hands in my coat pocket, I went to that door.

"Hey, I got something for you guys."

The puppy—a Fox Terrier—with the now-bandaged, broken tail (which would forever remain bent at a ninety degree angle) emerged from my right pocket cradled in my hand. *Instant hero.* The poor thing was scared shitless, but quickly warmed up to the children. One of the older ones—apparently foreshadowing his own future drinking issues—named him Budweiser on the spot. The name stuck and, before long, I couldn't imagine calling him anything else. Like the liquor that—through people close to me—had infected my life, Budweiser became a big pain in my ass. But I loved that dog like no other before him.

For the seventeen years that he scurried around my feet, shit and pissed on the floor, and begged for food at the kitchen table, our relationship was one of respect, love, and frustration. To this day, I believe that Budweiser lived his life with the events of that horrific day at the OTB office just under the surface. No one had ever met such a nervous dog. Just call his name and he'd piss at your feet. Any loud sound would send him scurrying under furniture with a trail of piss behind him—sometimes crap. The Fourth of July and every thunderstorm was torment to him and, in turn, me. I don't know how I'd afforded all those paper towels. Any other dog would have been gone after a month, but there'd been an understanding between Budweiser and me that transcended the occasional bare foot in fresh crap. I'd yell at him and he'd high—ninety degree—tail it under the table, and squirt his liquid fear all over the floor.

I guess the dog had PTSD—I don't know. PTSD hadn't been the *in thing* yet with the guys coming back from Vietnam. But it wasn't too far off. They'd get that diagnosis in 1980. I wasn't interested either way. Not only did we have the hippies and the draft dodgers, we now had to suffer the whining from these guys coming back home to cry for everyone to see. *I seen some things, man.*

No shit you saw some things. It's a goddamned war, asshole. You think we didn't see some things, man? Maybe if you get off the drugs you can handle it like a man. It made me sick.

That's the way it was. The Greatest Generation had given way to the Crybaby Generation. I wasn't offering anybody any tissues. I had my own shit to deal with. They wanted to know why there'd been no "Welcome home." Where the hell was ours? Crush the enemy with humiliating defeat, and you get your "Welcome home," I guess. That didn't happen in Korea and it certainly didn't happen in Vietnam. The American people didn't even notice us come home. *Korea Armistice Signed; Hostilities Cease Today.* On July 27, 1953, similar headlines announced the good news across the country. The typical reaction was, *'Bout time. What's for supper?*

Nobody gave a crap, and they still don't. Most people could tell you about Pearl Harbor, Iwo Jima, Normandy, and any of a number of other famous battles that occurred during World War Two. They'll talk to you all day about Vietnam. But whatever happened to Osan, Inchon, Seoul, The Chosin Reservoir, Old Baldy? Forgotten—like they never happened. Unless people watched the eleven seasons of M*A*S*H, they probably never heard of the

Korean War. Shit; that show hadn't even really been about Korea. They just used that setting to make a statement about Vietnam, which had still been in full bloodbath when the series began. The protests and media frenzy generated by the war in Vietnam had shoved any lingering memories of Korea aside. Ours became the *Forgotten War,* and those of us who fought it had been forgotten with it.

The day would come when I'd understand our Vietnam War vets better. I'd learn that they were not much different than I. In the early 70's, however, that day was a long way off.

My oldest son, Matthew, was close to finishing high school and nearing draft age. That concerned me, of course, but I was prepared for the worst. His hair was getting long, and phrases like *Far out, man,* and *I can dig it, man,* and *Go with the flow, man,* spilled from his mouth. Everything every kid said in those days ended with, *man.* He tormented me about getting bell bottoms. In his bedroom, love beads hung from the shelf over his desk. If I ever caught him wearing those damned beads, I'd ring his neck with them. I was in that room one day discussing an impropriety on his part, which means he was getting some hell for some stupid thing he'd done. On the desk lay a new necktie I hadn't seen before—or bought. It was an expensive adornment that neither of us could afford.

"Where'd you get this?"

"A&S."

"When?"

He looked at the tie. "Yesterday."

"How much was it? Look at me."

"I don't remember."

"Where's the receipt?"

"I don't have it."

"Did you steal this?" It'd been written all over his face.

Nothing.

The boy had gotten his share of clobberings from me and, looking back, I don't blame him for not wanting to answer.

"DID YOU STEAL THIS?"

Matthew hesitated. "Yes."

My fist balled up and sailed directly at his face. I could see his cheekbone collapse before I made contact and managed to divert before tragedy struck. Instead, my fist crashed through the plaster wall and broke the doorframe beside his face. The heat of my rage matched the fear in his face as I pulled my hand from the wall. White dust specked my knuckles, which had already started to ache.

"You're going to pay to have that fixed."

"Yes, sir."

"Who was with you?"

"I—"

"Who was with you?" I seethed.

"Bob."

It didn't surprise me to learn that Bob Gentry had been involved. He was quite charming when he'd needed to be, but I could tell he was a little shit—a regular Eddie Haskell whom I did not care for.

"Take that tie and get in the car. If you get arrested, you can stay in jail."

I took him to Abraham and Strauss where he returned the tie and offered his apology. I had no doubt to its sincerity. Luckily for him, they did not press charges. What kid shoplifts neckties, for Christ's sake? He went to a Catholic high school where ties were worn. If he'd needed a new one, I would have bought it for him—granted, not as nice as the one he'd five-finger picked for himself. But my boy had been a bit of a ladies man. I don't know where he got that from—certainly not me. I'd had to talk to him on occasion about the proper way to treat a girl—always with respect—because he made me a little nervous. "Always treat young ladies with respect." Which, in addition to speaking to them properly, never laying an angry hand on them, and being kind in every respect, meant absolutely, positively, and unequivocally, no sex.

"Keep your pants zipped and your hands to yourself."

So with regard to the necktie, my guess was he'd needed to dress to impress. *Fine. Just stay dressed, and come to me if you need the money.* Not that I would have bought him a necktie that cost more than all the clothes on my body combined. A few weeks later, during a private conversation at the kitchen table, Matthew confessed to me that he'd stolen the tie to gift me for Father's Day. That Father's Day had since passed. Instead of the tie, Matthew had given me a nice card in which he'd written, "I love you"—the best gift a father could receive from his boy.

Matthew was not drafted after high school, and did both himself and me proud when he chose to enter The Citadel. I figured that, in about four years time, my boy would be an officer in the United States Marine Corps. But a school athletics injury that had left a piece of surgically-implanted stainless steel in his shoulder disqualified him from entry to Officers Candidate School at Quantico, Virginia after graduation from the military college. So Matthew did the next best thing and became a cop in his new home of Charleston County, South Carolina.

While Matthew had been away at college, I'd gone back to school in order to better my chances at success. By this time, the sergeant's exam had befuddled me three times. With so many jobs to work, I'd never taken the time to study for it. In addition to washing windows and the previous job delivering Avon products, I'd done everything imaginable to earn cash. Polish and refinish floors, deliver Ford Ramblers from the rail yard in New Jersey to the dealerships in New York, return lost luggage from the airlines at Kennedy Airport to pissed off people on the Island who never tipped, hang out (it hadn't been the official job title, but that's what it amounted to) at a recreation center in a shitty part of Islip—I didn't care, as long I was getting paid. Even cleaning up after baseball fans had left Shea Stadium looking like the Fresh Kills Landfill over on Staten Island, was among other low-pay, low-reward, menial jobs that I'd been happy to do. Everyone knows somebody who knows a guy who has a line on a job, and that network ran deep on the NYPD. I took good advantage of it. Whenever the sergeant's exam had been offered, however, I'd show up tired and wait for luck to intervene. Or maybe I'd hoped the scoring curve would one day adjust just enough for a couple of stupid guys to squeeze through. By this time, however, the curve had moved away from my limited knowledge, and kept me farther out of the promotion loop. So, I cut back from the second and third job routine long enough to enter college and finally make something of myself. And I did well—at creating more stress.

But I'd also found out just how stupid I wasn't. It's nice to see an A on a report card, but seeing the abbreviation for the Automobile Association of America made me ecstatic. It got to the point where a B killed me. Never in my lifetime experience would I have believed that I was capable of such a thing. When I'd been in the Army, my high score on the G.E.D. had given me a temporary lift in scholastic self-esteem that, over time, had drifted away, like a balloon over treetops. Now, report card after report card from the New York Institute of Technology offered manifest proof that I was a smart, forty-something college student who could accomplish anything through hard work.

"Shut that TV off and go outside." I would yell from the kitchen, where my books and paperwork covered the table. "I'm trying to study."

"Stop running around like goddamned circus animals up there." My voice carried up the basement stairs and through the closed door. "I'm trying to do homework, for Christ's sake."

"Knock it off out here." I'd appear from my bedroom at the living room entrance, and the bickering would stop. "I've got a test tomorrow."

A scan of the room revealed nothing but stunned faces—all but one.

"And wipe that shit-eating grin off your face, Quinn."

John Quinn always flashed that nervous grin when I'd yell. I wanted to wipe it off his face for him. He busted up laughing at the phrase *shit-eating grin*—and ran out the front door with his hand over his face.

I looked at Robert. "Why do you hang around with that idiot?"

Now, everyone laughed. I may have cracked a smile myself as I slammed the bedroom door. *Jesus Christmas.* Quinn was a good kid.

For the first time in my life, I'd thrown my heart into education. And the heart rebelled. At the age of forty-five, two years after I'd entered college, it lashed out and attacked me. Once I'd replaced the second and third job with school, money got tight. I'd been squeezing pennies that had already been squeezed. It was like olive oil: extra virgin, virgin, kind-of virgin. My pennies had been through the press so many times that they looked like the girls in Times Square—nothing virginal about them. In addition to the money mess, there was homework, studies, tests, job, traffic, nightmares, kids, and aging parents—something had to give.

The woman had been pinned under a train on the El. She was dead. With only enough room for one person to get under the train to retrieve the body, I found myself in the precarious position of navigating open beams below me, and struggling to free the folded body of the deceased woman. It was strenuous work. I finally pulled the body out and stood it up against the platform where other officers pulled it up. Then they helped me up.

"You okay, Joe?"

I didn't even know who asked. I leaned against the train car for support—I had no strength—and looked down at my uniform. It was evident that I'd be brown-bagging it. A couple of guys put the woman's remains in a body bag.

"I think I need to go to the hospital."

When I got to the emergency room, I was told that the emergency doctor was asleep. "Do you really think you need to see him?"

I happened to feel a bit better, so I left and returned to quarters. I went out sick right there at headquarters and lay down, because I was *not* better. The shift ended at four that afternoon, but I stayed there that night and went home in the morning. I stopped at the police surgeon's office in Massapequa, Long Island on the way and he checked me out.

"You need to get to your family doctor right away." Nothing about my heart. Just, "Go see your doctor right away."

I went home and lay in bed for two days—fully clothed. I couldn't move. I was an Emergency Services cop and I didn't recognize a heart attack when I was having one. The elephant crushing my chest, however, finally wrapped his trunk around my neck and whispered in my ear, "Go to the doctor." And the doctor told me, "Call your wife and get her over here."

The EKG told the story. "You see this? You see this? You should be dead. You could've died."

So, here was the funny thing—if you have the right sense of humor: I'd waited and waited for my bullet, held the gun to my head so many times, and wished for a time machine to transport me back to Korea where I could have stood in Patrick Parrish's boots at the right moment. I had planned ways to meet death for a decade. Now I had a beautiful opportunity—a heart attack—how simple. No suicide for the brothers to cover up. I could get off the table in the examination room, jog out to the car, and be dead before the third step. The Grim Reaper held before me his beautiful gift on a black platter, and I wanted to beat it off with an ugly stick. *Oh, God, I don't want to die.* I have no explanation for me.

Three weeks in the hospital were followed by three years of expecting to die at any moment. I was scared shitless every single day. The department moved me to light duty on my way out the door. My last day on the job was December 31st of that year—1976. I began terminal leave on January 1st, and received full pay through March 27, 1977—my official retirement day. A sergeant and I went out on the same day for the same reason. He'd made it five more days. Dead. I knew that time was short. Three years later, I found myself still alive, and I finally convinced myself to get a grip. *Stop worrying about it.* I retired at forty-six and I'm eighty-six today. I've nearly bankrupted the city's pension plan with that lousy $1,600.00 per month they gave me. Ha!

CHAPTER 25

California Dreaming

Since my early teens and the train rides into the mountains to a world of wonder that seemed like heaven, it had always been my intention to one day live in glorious Pennsylvania. I'd treasured the summers during which I'd transformed into another person (someone without a care for Brooklyn or the man who came home drunk and beat me with his belt) and nights enveloped in a comforter of stars that spread across the still sky—a sight otherwise unimaginable to a city boy.

In the early days, I'd envisioned a simple white house on Main Street, with a small porch out front, from which I'd wave to neighbors as they passed on the sidewalk. Or maybe I'd have a porch-to-porch chat with the folks next door. I'd listen to the radio in the living room—with not a bed in sight—and sip a cream soda or two. There would be a tidy and inviting outhouse of my own out back. Tin lunch pail in hand, I'd make the short walk across Mill Street Bridge and clock in at the Standard Steel Mill only five minutes after leaving the house in the morning. Maybe I'd enjoy a cup of coffee with the boys—surely I'd like that stuff by the time I reached adulthood—before I'd set off to make railroad wheels or, better yet, tank parts for some future war our nation might be lucky enough to march off to. Of course, I'd find a special lady to share it all with and—like my grandparents—we'd live a simple and magnificent life.

In later years, my dream had continued. Much of it remained the same, although the outhouse had become a bathroom—maybe two, when I considered all the children I'd have. And as I'd made my way through the ranks in the Army, the steel mill no longer enticed me, either. With time, I harbored the idea of a fashionable home just a few blocks off the town square in Lewiston, where the Embassy Theater and an ice-cream cone are only a leisurely walk away. It'd be nice to put some distance between me and the gritty-collared Main Street in Yeagertown. By the time I'd settled into the blue uniform of the NYPD, that dream would have to wait until I'd retired. The dream, however, had solidified into a plan. It would take me forty or more years from those early days in order to make it a reality, but I knew the day would come.

Although my retirement had arrived almost six years sooner than expected, the plan had already been squashed beneath my aching, tingling feet. Over the years, the effects of the frostbite I'd acquired in Korea had become troublesome. The ache in my feet had become a pain in my ass—particularly during winters. Other than the two stints at Parris Island and my time at Camp Pendleton, I'd always lived in cold climates. But that situation had to change, so Barbara and I made plans to move to San Diego. I'd remembered the pleasant summer breezes off the cold Pacific Ocean, and the cool, but never unpleasant winters—the perfect climate. Barbara's sister, Bea, had long ago established a home there, so it was an agreeable choice to both of us.

As we formulated the plan for our move, and soon after my heart attack, we lost Barbara's mother. My heart ached all over again. Maisie loved me, and I her. Outside of Barbara, she had always been my biggest supporter. If my wife and I had a disagreement—*if I yelled at her*—Maisie would tell Barbara, "You be nice to him; he's a good man." Yeah, she'd stick up for *me*. "He works hard for this family. He loves you so much. Go apologize." In her eyes, I could do no wrong. A decades-long habit of smoking Kools had ended her life with lung cancer. She'd help around the house all day, and then take her breaks with a cigarette and a glass of Ballantine, while she stood at the end of the kitchen counter by the wall phone. I never saw the woman sit down. She'd even take her meals at that same spot—never at the table with the rest of us—and when she was in her bedroom upstairs, she'd smoke at the open window and watch the kids play basketball in the street. I cried as if I'd lost my own mother all over again.

They say that lost love is a terrible thing, so I'd been fortunate not to lose any more with the passing of my father the following year. I'd never once wished for his death, but when the time came, I was glad. It was not a spiteful glee; rather it'd been a welcome relief. What seemed like a never-ending chapter had finally closed. I'd been lost in a story that had repeated itself over and over. Sadly, the plot never advanced. The main character had continued to bitch, moan, and cause stress throughout the family. He'd put a strain on my relationship with my siblings, who refused to help with him. Eileen had a room that she saved for Bobby's occasional visits from his home in Bermuda where he worked for NASA. The rest of the year, that room remained empty. Jimmy couldn't help himself, much less the old man. With alcohol, he'd destroyed his own life, his family, and any hope for a stable existence. John, Wally, and Raymond just flat out refused. For his entire life, the old man held power over his children through the tension he wrought.

Back in the early 1970s, Wally's eldest son, Billy, got married in Ohio. He'd worked for Greyhound at the time, and got a great deal on a bus charter so that the entire family could cruise to Ohio together in comfort. On the way home, Jimmy sat across the aisle from me at the center of the bus. He'd made good use of the open bar and gotten sloppy drunk—his favorite form of inebriation. Our father sat quietly at the front of the bus smoking his Pall Malls.

"Look at him. He oughta just die," Jimmy said.

The conversation had turned ugly over the previous few miles. I leaned in close to my brother.

"Why don't you just shut your mouth now," I said. It wasn't a question.

"Fuck that son of a bitch." A cloud of cigarette smoke lingered about his face, and the fog of alcohol permeated his head. "He ain't never done a goddamned thing for us."

"What the hell have you ever done for him?" My voice rose with Jimmy's belligerence. The cockles of those around us followed suit.

"All that fuck ever knew was his belt and his boot."

"He's still your father." The words seethed through my teeth. I emphasized each with a tap to the side of his head from the back of my hand. "Show a little respect."

Five rows back, Bobby moved from his window seat to the aisle. Too late.

"And the old lady never did a thing to—"

The back of my fist cracked his face, and blood appeared below his nose. Bobby barreled in between us, and Wally lunged from behind over two seats—and whomever sat in them—and landed on Jimmy.

"You son of a bitch. I'll fucking kill you," Wally growled.

A small army pulled, tugged, and muscled us all apart, even as my fists swung wildly catching pieces of Jimmy's face. I was no longer that fifteen-year-old kid in my mother's kitchen. My older brother wouldn't have a prayer against me now. And Jimmy didn't know when to tell the alcohol to shut up.

"Oh, the big shot cops are gonna beat up on their little brother."

Bobby shoved him to his seat. Jimmy looked around him to the old man.

"Fuck that cocksucker."

Bobby, who was one of the gentlest and most reasonable men I'd ever known, grabbed Jimmy by the shirt.

"Another word and I'll take your teeth out."

Bobby's threat stunned Jimmy into silence. The old man pushed himself from his seat and waved his cane from the front of the bus.

"You want me? Come and get it, you asshole."

"Fuck you, prick."

"Shut the hell up, Dad." The reprimand had come in chorus from Bobby, Wally, and me.

Within spitting distance of Yeagertown, Pennsylvania, everyone finally settled in for the silent four-plus hours ride that remained. The beauty of our surroundings had been lost on me as Barbara took my hand. In hers, I felt the moisture of her recently wiped tears. Jimmy had been relegated to the back of the bus near the now-closed bar. Bobby and my nephew, Tommy, kept an eye on him until they'd all fallen asleep.

Each of my brothers, my sister, and I had known that Jimmy's words—spoken more harshly than necessary—held a great deal of truth. None of us loved our father, and his death would be a blessing. This was not, however, a sentiment that needed to be verbalized on a bus that was crowded with family—or even to each other in private. It might sound like a wish.

Shortly after that trip to Ohio, I'd elected Wally to take over. I'd had it with my father, so I put him in the car, drove him to the big house on Avenue N in Brooklyn, and deposited him along with a carton and a half of Pall Malls in the dark living room. Later that day, Wally called me.

"What's Dad doing at my house?"

"I don't want him anymore."

"I don't want him, either."

"Tough shit." In the short pause that followed, I could hear Wally blow out his cigar smoke.

"I'm bringing him back."

"Take him to one of the others."

"They don't want him."

"I've done my time. Figure it out."

When I returned from work the next day, my father was at his usual spot at the kitchen table. The Knights of Columbus ashtray overflowed with a day's worth of cigarette butts. Wally and I didn't speak to each other for five years.

Those five years had ended with a simple question from one of the guys at work.

"Hey, Joe, your brother doing any better?"

"Whadda ya mean?"

He looked at me like I was crazy.

"He's in the hospital."

Tomato-red cheeks betrayed my embarrassment. My brother and hero—the two of us had been famous within the ranks of the Emergency Service Squad as the only set of brothers on the force to share in the honor of the Catherine O'Dwyer Medal For Life Saving—had (unbeknownst to me) been in the hospital for two weeks. Not only had his family not called to tell me, but there had not even been any notice from any of my other siblings. The men on my truck had known about it while I'd languished in the dark. So I gathered up all the fence-mending tools in my paltry arsenal—shame, humility, love, and tears—and went to see my brother.

Soon after Wally got home, he volunteered to take in the old man, and our father lived with him for what became the final year of his life. The end had come as a relief to everyone.

Eight months later, in July of 1978, our whittled down family climbed into my newly-acquired 1976 Ford Esquire station wagon, and set out for California. I'd bought the two-year-old car—the finest I'd ever owned—from my youngest brother, Ray. Matthew and Robert lived in South Carolina, and Marianne stayed behind in Lindenhurst for school. Ellen came with us to reunite with her husband, who had gone ahead of us to start work. Joseph, Kathleen, Schanna, Christopher, and Mark would find a new home with Barbara and me in Poway, California, a suburb of San Diego.

It had broken my heart to leave my siblings behind. That last drive west on the Belt Parkway rolled by in a wide-awake dream of childhood games and beatings, family joy and grief, work pride and heartache. I resisted the urge to look left at Plumb Beach—maybe I'd been afraid that I'd give myself away—but I thought about my secret stop there years before. Family good-byes already behind me, the Ford Esquire glided onto the Verrazano Narrows Bridge without the tempting—and, perhaps, stalling—side trip to Park Slope or the Gowanus Canal neighborhood of my childhood.

Brooklyn—the home I loved—shrunk in the rearview mirror. New York City had been my life, yet a part of me yearned to be rid of it. It didn't seem fair, but years on the department had soured me to the city that would forever be a part of me. The reality of my self-imposed exile filled me on the west side of the Goethals Bridge and the southbound lanes of the New Jersey Turnpike. Any remnants of New York City had disappeared from the mirror, and only second thoughts and apprehension spread before me on the vast highway that carried hundreds of cars making speedy work of putting New York in their past.

Poway is a short drive north of the city of San Diego—cowboy country. In 1978, many stores still offered hitching posts out front for their customer's horses. It was the perfect place to listen to my Country and Western records. During my Army years, I'd developed a love for Hank Williams, Merle Haggard, and Conway Twitty.

I'd found Poway to be quiet, peaceful, charming, *and hot*. The cool Pacific breezes I'd remembered at Pendleton were not up to the thirty-mile trek inland from the ocean. This often left Poway about ten degrees warmer than the coastal cities. And when the Santa Ana winds blew in from the eastern deserts, all bets were off. *But it's a dry heat*. Don't let anybody fool you—it's a goddamned convection oven. My skin flaked, and my nose bled. My sinuses were more clear than they'd ever been before, which allowed hot air to pass through like an oil-fired furnace. *Shit*. It didn't take too long to adjust, though, and the first winter had sealed the deal for me. Today, I could not imagine a better climate. But, with much time on my hands in retirement, the climate had also been ripe for depression, anger, and self-doubt, the likes of which any Country and Western artist would be envious come song-writing time.

Somehow, unseen by my family, the nightmares had managed to stow away in the station wagon, and make the cross-country trip with me. The laid-back Southern California chewing-tobacco country lifestyle had offered no relief. By the time I'd made the move west, the nightmares had already occupied my sleep for twenty-six years. That's twenty-six years, times five nights a week. I can do the math, but don't see the point. The geographical change had been no match for a tortured mind that always knew where to find me. Reading, watching TV, washing dishes, and doing laundry had been keep-busy work meant to hold my subconscious at bay. It didn't work. If I hadn't given my service revolver away, I would have put a bullet in my head while watching yet another rerun of *I Dream of Jeannie*—I'm sure that someone, regardless of his situation, must have done that at some time or other. It was obvious to me that I needed to get off my ass and do something.

But "off my ass," meant on my feet. Over time, I'd made friends with the owner of the convenience store around the corner, and he'd offered me part-time work. It got me out of the house for up to twenty hours a week, offered some welcome socialization, and put much-needed household money in my pocket. It hadn't been much, but every little bit helped. We'd worked out a system in which he paid me under the table so that my Social Security benefits would not be affected. It wouldn't make sense to earn eighty bucks a week, and then lose my disability in a system that punishes people for helping themselves. The job, however, hadn't lasted long. Twenty hours of pay meant twenty hours of standing on my feet while I rang up Coors Light, Slim Jims, Marlboros, and Skoal. I'd spend half my pay on Susie Q's and coffee, which served to make the load on my feet even more arduous. As much as I'd enjoyed the job, I just couldn't manage it physically. I went home and caught back up with Major Nelson and Jeannie.

In 1980, the Vietnam boys finally got their wish. It hadn't been good enough that they'd moaned and complained to no end about how bad they'd had it. Now they needed a diagnosis for their complaints: Post Traumatic Stress Disorder (PTSD). I don't know if that made them happy or not, but they got it. The diagnosis eventually cleared the way for VA-sponsored health care— more drugs, I guess—and disability benefits. Can you imagine? *Monthly checks because war sucks.* I'd seen it all now. I was well into the years in which I'd held great disrespect for two groups of people: the guys who took college and teacher deferments in order to avoid the war, and the boys who bravely served but then came home to bitch about it. They all disgusted me.

I drove up to Laguna Hills, California, just over an hour north of Poway, and thought about my own war—the one in Korea, not my mind. The sound of distant mortars in Pusan filled the car. In 1950, the fight had been miles away, but we'd heard our destiny as we made our way into the harbor on my nineteenth birthday. It was there, on the welcome mat of war, that I'd met Father

Otto Eugene Sporrer, the man whose steady faith would comfort me before I'd prepared my first round for the cannon. After five days of relentless battle, I'd met him again for mass in the clearing on the hill in Sachon.

"I didn't know it would be this hard, Father."

"Remember that God is with you every step of the way, Joe."

"I know he is. But so many guys have died already."

"They sit with God now."

It wasn't exactly what I'd wanted to hear at the time, but I'd understood that he was in no position to make promises about life and death.

"Keep a clear heart, Joe, and know that God resides in it. He will be with you through the worst. Remember: Every moment, every thought is a prayer, and God is listening. Stand tall and fight for right. The outcome is in your hands through God."

I'd attended mass that day and a couple more times in the Pusan Perimeter, then again near Seoul after the landing at Inchon. I rarely saw the Padre at the Chosin. Although he'd been assigned to the 11th Marines, he'd spent much more time with the 5th Marines, who'd needed his strength, courage, and conviction of faith even more. My last encounter with the Catholic priest had been at Masan near The Bean Patch after the Chosin Reservoir campaign. As an officer, Father Sporrer had been housed in an elementary school with the other officers. The Navy chaplain, however, was a Marine through and through and, as such, spent a great deal of time mingling with the enlisted men. On Christmas Eve, he'd heard my confession for the last time. Later that evening, Marines piled into the school's auditorium dressed in parkas for a midnight mass. A single stove made poor work of heating the large space. A few overhead bulbs and candles on the altar provided dim light. Even though the stove caught fire halfway through the service, the celebration proved to be as close to perfect as Christmas away from home could be.

As we'd mounted up to move to Pohang, Father Sporrer had been shipped out for Japan and then back home. Although I'd seen him on only few occasions up to this time, his departure came as worrisome news. After all, he was my connection to God in that place.

In the back of a replacement deuce-and-a-half for the trek to Pohang, his words had come back to me.

"Every moment, every thought, is a prayer, and God is listening. Stand tall and fight for right. The outcome is in your hands through God."

I worked hard to keep those words within easy reach from that point on.

On this clear winter day in 1984, I'd found St. Nicholas Catholic Church in Laguna Hills. As a boy from Brooklyn, my idea of a church had always included large-stone walls, soaring steeples, and dark, contemplative interiors. After six years in Southern California, however, the modern mission style that distinguished St. Nicholas from my childhood churches had grown on me. Otto Sporrer had built his church from the ground up and opened its doors in 1967, right about the time that the Lagunas and surrounding areas had given up their open spaces in favor of the dream lifestyle. It was a beautiful church in a growing, desirable community.

In the rectory suites, the retired Navy chaplain emerged from his office.

"Heard somebody's looking for me."

Over thirty years had passed since that Christmas Eve mass adjacent to The Bean Patch. The receding hairline had marched to the crown of his head, where it met the remaining thin, gray, strands. Although his slender frame and face had filled, and large, thick, wire-framed glasses covered everything from brow to mid cheek, his sturdy countenance—even at seventy-two years of age—was unmistakably that of a Marine. The eyes—filled with wisdom and compassion—had not changed.

I extended my hand. "Joe Lynch, Father."

"Call me Otto." He looked me over and nodded. "Do I know you, Joe?"

"Yes, Father."

"Korea?"

My eyes widened. "You remember me?"

His laugh was sudden and cheerful. "No. No. I'm afraid not. But you look the right age. And you are certainly a Marine."

"So are you, Father."

"Humph. Thank you. That means a lot to a Navy guy." He turned and motioned with a hand. "C'mon. Let's chat. And we're not in the military any longer. Call me Otto."

"Okay, Otto. Thank you."

The office, although comfortable and nicely appointed, was nothing fancy. We sat in wooden armchairs in front of the desk. He smiled at me.

"Cannon Cocker?"

I nodded.

"God, I loved the 11th. First in?"

I nodded again. "Went over on the Henrico."

"Oh boy. *Un*-Happy Hank. I didn't think you boys would make it in that bucket. They'd lifted me over to Pickaway before you diverted to Oakland."

"I remember."

"The 5th Marines fought hard in The Perimeter, but they couldn't have done it without the artillery. You guys were something else."

"Thank you, sir. Otto."

He nodded and tightened his grip on the arms of his chair. Then he pushed himself to his feet.

"Let's take a walk."

We entered the church from alongside the altar, and then walked down the center aisle.

"I retired from the Navy in '65. When I came in search of a parish, Cardinal McIntyre handed me seven acres of dirt and told me to build a church."

"You did a good job."

"The job I did can't be seen in these walls, Joe. You've got to look at the congregation, and the other lives we've touched."

His eyes scanned from left (pews, windows, high ceiling) to right (altar and crucifix).

"It is a nice church, though, isn't it?"

Then he affixed a square gaze upon me.

"So, to what do I owe the pleasure?"

"I just wanted to thank you, Father. I think about you often. You got me through that war."

"You and God got you through."

"Your presence was my assurance that God was with us."

I looked at the cross that hung from his neck.

"Every moment, every thought, is a prayer, and God is listening. Stand tall and fight for right. The outcome is in your hands through God."

"Sounds like something I would have said."

"You said it, Father. And I took those words to heart."

"Did you attend my masses?"

"Every one I could. And confessions. You heard my confession right after we'd arrived."

"Pusan?"

"Yes, sir."

"Little clearing by the train platform?"

I went chill. "Yeah. That was it."

He looked over the pews. The closed-door confessionals enjoyed some time off at the moment.

"I remember a young corporal. He seemed a bit anxious that we didn't have any of those around after I'd agreed to hear his confession."

My eyes felt wet when he'd turned back to me.

"But he got right down on his knees, and said his peace while all his buddies watched. Humph. Didn't have much to confess as I remember." He placed a hand on my shoulder. "Nice to see you again, Joe."

"Nice to see you, too, Father."

"Glad you made it. All your parts in place?"

I flexed my fingers beside my legs. Neither of us looked at my hands.

"Thankfully."

"How has it been since?"

I felt as though he knew my story.

"Okay, I guess."

"Just okay? God wants us to be more than just okay, Joe. Remember those words you spoke a little while ago: Every moment, every thought, is a prayer, and God is listening. Stand tall and fight for right. The outcome is in your hands through God."

"I try. I fight every day."

"We saw a lot of bad things over there. I do my best not to think about it."

"Me, too."

"The boys had a tough time in Vietnam, too."

"So I hear." My unsympathetic tone had not been intentional.

"You don't like that, do you?"

"We all saw it, Father. We were told to deal with it. That's what I do."

"Times change. People change. They're calling it PTSD now."

"They can keep it."

"You know, I felt the same way when they came back. 'Sissies.' That's what I thought. But maybe there's something to it."

We walked back toward the door.

"Start with forgiveness, Joe. Forgive the new breed. And forgive anyone else you need to. And don't forget yourself. Forgive yourself, Joe. All healing starts there—with forgiveness."

Father Sporrer reached for the doorknob.

"Father?"

"Yes, Joe?"

"Would you hear my confession?"

He dropped his hand from the knob.

"I'd be delighted. Come on. I've got a nice confessional I think you'll like."

Forgiveness had been on my mind, if not my plate, for several years. I confessed to Father Sporrer that I had never forgiven my father. My relationship with the Navy chaplain had then come full circle—confession to confession—and at this, our final meeting, I made a vow to God, through the priest, that I would learn how to forgive.

In the car on my way home, I thought about the old man. *I forgive you. You son of a bitch.* Well, Father Sporrer had not said it would be easy. The biggest obstacle to forgiveness had been my father's belligerence toward my wife. The process took years, but forgiveness is best served slow-cooked. The effort expended—deep thought, ongoing prayer, and continued use of the words *I forgive you*—made it more palatable. Today, I can look in the mirror and know that my father's misdeeds shaped the man I have become. I no longer have the need to say, *I forgive you,* for it is complete. I can now think of my father and say, *I love you.* There is no regret for not having said those things while he was alive, because I believe he knows.

While I worked on forgiveness, months turned to years. School kids turned to adults, children brought grandchildren, marriages came and went, and lives trickled away. My brother John—the oldest—left us in 1989. Devastated is the only way to describe my feelings. I crumbled. He'd gone into the hospital, and was dead before I could even get on an airplane. At his funeral, his wife, Mary, told me about his Purple Heart, which he'd been awarded during World War Two. He'd been a truck driver in the Army Air Corps, and German bombers had attacked his convoy in Belgium. The truck in front of his took a direct hit. Shrapnel from the exploding vehicle erupted through his windshield and embedded itself in his head. And there, much of it had stayed, even as his body lay in the casket. I was crushed that he had never told me, but I understood—after all, there are many things my brothers do not know about me. I wondered about Wally. *And Jimmy. What scars does Jimmy medicate with all the liquor?* I didn't ask.

September of 2000 saw my youngest sibling's death. At sixty-one, Raymond's heart had stopped beating while he slept. The day before, his doctor had given him a clean bill of health so, that night, he'd gone to bed enveloped in a healthy aura, but he never woke up. Previously, Ray had been on the heart-transplant list with congestive heart failure. But over time, he'd shown progressive recovery and been removed from the list. A miracle. And then my baby brother was gone. The phone rang and the world spun in the wrong direction. Natural order said "Oldest first," but then the youngest was flung away. I received the call early in the morning, right after what I believed was my worst nightmare ever, only to learn that life could beat anything my subconscious could dream up.

At the funeral home in Queens, a man named Alex introduced himself to me. His clothes were filthy and his skin was not far behind. We shook hands, and I made a mental note to wash up at the first available opportunity. Alex was a homeless veteran.

"We all came," he said.

I looked around the room. Homeless people—men and women—gathered in groups and sat alone. A few family members spoke to a couple of them. Ray had moved to Queens after his divorce and, since his retirement from the Brooklyn Union Gas Company, he'd volunteered with the homeless at his church's shelter. It was another surprising revelation I'd learned about a sibling only after his death. Ray had fed them, clothed them, slept with them, hugged them, and kissed them. He'd told them jokes and that he loved them. They'd been his friends. I felt dirty—not because of the handshake, but because of my internal reaction to it. They'd come to say goodbye to the man who had treated them like people rather than like homeless nobodies. They'd come to see my baby brother off. The pride I'd felt fed the sadness.

It had been a bad time—*the worst time*—to lose my brother. Only four months earlier, the entire family had been crushed by the death of my grandson. The pain caused by the loss of seventeen-year-old Jonathan—Matthew's first son—was still raw. How could God, the universe, the roll of the dice, do this to us? I'd arrived in Charleston for Jonathan's funeral only to find Matthew in the hospital. His heart was about to explode, and I was afraid I'd lose him, as well. My eldest boy had been inconsolable and I was at a loss to help him. When Ray had arrived from New York, his perfect blend of calm assurance, heartfelt compassion, and loud humor made way for moments of peace and joy. Matthew was released from the hospital the following day, and we—with no less than one thousand other people from Jonathan's school and community—said our goodbyes. Much of the standing-room-only crowd listened to the service from outside the church.

Having spent many years away from the church himself, Raymond had found his way back. During communion, he would always say, "I love you, Lord Jesus," when he received the host. And to this day—in memory of Raymond—I say, "I love you, Lord Jesus," when I receive communion. I couldn't stop saying it now if I tried. I think of my departed baby brother every time the body of Christ descends upon my tongue.

CHAPTER 26

Reunion

FOUR WALLS: BEDROOM, OFFICE, LIVING room, kitchen—it's all the same. Whatever the room, there are four walls that hold me in. I limp and shuffle from one room to the next, but nothing changes. In the office, I turn on the computer—I never would have guessed I'd have one of those—and play solitaire. It keeps my mind off my mind, as well as off the walls. I've even learned to make spreadsheets on the computer. I love spreadsheets. I love the order. I love the discipline that it takes to keep them current. Where does my money go? It's in a spreadsheet. What loans am I paying off and how much interest have I paid so far? It's in a spreadsheet. Who owes *me* money, and what payments have *they* made? It's in *several* spreadsheets. I review my spreadsheets every day to make sure they are current. I love it when I get a check from one of the kids. It goes right on the spreadsheet. Then I write a check to my bank so I can keep my house, and I enter that in another spreadsheet. When they visit, I congratulate them on their prompt payments, and I show them the spreadsheet. They are so very impressed. It's all so neat. Thank God for spreadsheets. Sometimes I miss doing them by hand, though. I used to write each number in it's own little box with care. Always in ink. Never a mistake. Very satisfying. But now the computer even tallies up everything for me as I make entries. Totals at the bottom of the page show principal paid, interest paid, total paid as well as principal remaining. Enter a number, and everything changes. No more calculator to run my tabs. I love it. And I love solitaire.

I wish I were dead.

Ten minutes to Wapner—or whomever is presiding over *The People's Court* these days. Spreadsheets and solitaire and death will just have to wait. I leave the computer, and limp to the four walls in the living room. A framed photo of Jonathan rests on a shelf above the television. In it, he stands by a fireplace that is decorated for Christmas. His easy pose—hands in pockets of comfortable chinos—and handsome smile beneath a Nike baseball cap, belie the internal torture that ended his life shortly after this photo of him was taken. The medical examiner ruled his death an intentional overdose. *Intentional overdose.* I know what that gentle turn of phrase means. The Nike Swoosh seems to hold a hidden meaning, and it breaks my heart.

It's December now, and my own home is decorated for the greatest holiday of all. But the excitement, fun, and joy of Christmas will be shadowed by the deaths of Jonathan and Raymond earlier in the year.

The next day I staged a breakout. I left the house of four walls, and drove down to the city. It was December 8, 2000—the fiftieth anniversary of the Chosin Reservoir Campaign, and for me specifically, the anniversary of the ambush. A reunion of the Chosin Few—the name given to those who survived the distant yet always-present battle—would commemorate the occasion. Men flew into San Diego from across the country, booked expensive hotel rooms, and paid the price of admission for meals, guest speakers, field trips, and brotherhood. With no money to spare for such an extravagance, I drove a half hour and acted as though I belonged. No one questioned me.

Aged Marines and soldiers—who no longer concerned themselves with pumped chests or sucked guts—milled about and got reacquainted with old chums, and made new friends. I waded through the smiling faces and searched for any I recognized or, perhaps, a familiar name slapped on a chest with sticky paper. I didn't have a nametag, because I hadn't paid for one.

Then a hand found my shoulder, and a voice said, "Joe."

I turned and—even after fifty years—recognized Stanley Zabodyn, who stood a half head over me.

"Stanley." Tears jerked their way to the corners of my eyes.

He pulled me in for a hug. I was so comforted by his embrace that one of those tears slipped through my closed eye, and ran halfway down my nose. I felt as if I'd already come home.

"Do something with that," he said, when he pulled away and saw the tear. "I got some people for you to see."

Stanley took me to a table, and my heart was instantly filled. Harold *Digger* O'Dell jumped from his seat, limped a single step on legs of different lengths, and crushed me in his arms. I felt as if he'd just pulled me in from the edge of a cliff.

Another guy leaned back in his chair and watched us. He sported a shit-eating grin. When he finally got my attention, he slyly pressed the pads of his thumb and forefinger together and brought them to his lips. I already knew. Then he inhaled deeply.

I pointed at him. "Kreiger."

"Got a rosebush full of diamonds,"

Stanley, Digger, and I joined in.

"Got six Cadillacs."

"Don't bother opening the door, man,"

"I'll just float through the keyhole."

We all laughed, and men at nearby tables applauded. They had no idea what we were going on about. They just saw some old guys replay good times. And Paul Kreiger was, of course, the funniest guy at the fiftieth reunion.

"Hey. Anybody got a Tootsie Roll?" The question boomed from an approaching newcomer.

Kreiger scooped a handful of the chocolate treats from a bowl at the center of the table, and tossed them at John Gruber. John stuffed the one he caught in his chops like an unlit cigar. There was a bowl of the dense, chocolate candies on every table—a reminder of the welcome treat for hungry Marines in the Chosin. They had either been placed there out of reverence or as a bad joke. The Tootsie Rolls had held such an important role in the Chosin—and any remembrance thereof— that a representative of the candy company had also attended the reunion.

I gave John a hug. "You look great, pal."

I don't know that I would have characterized John Gruber as a friend all those years ago. At Pendleton, he'd been an acquaintance. In Korea—as he'd wired our communications between the Howitzers, fire control, and the forward observers—we'd crossed paths often but spent little time together. And, of course, we'd both attended the occasional mass. But, fifty years later, if you ran into a guy you served with in war, he was your friend. We were each so glad that the other had survived.

I sat him down beside me, opened an envelope I'd been clinging to, and spread a newspaper article between us on the table.

"Holy Jesus, Joe. Where did you get this?"

"It was in the New York newspaper the next day. My mom saved it."

John lifted the paper and studied the photo. His eyes glassed over as he scanned the solemn faces of what we would now call kids at Father Sporrer's field mass in Sachon.

"I didn't even know anyone took a picture."

"Me neither," I said. "I found out when I got home and my mom showed me."

"God, we look like babies. Well, except Buckles. Look at the size of that goon."

We had a fond laugh laced with memories of the sergeant everyone respected and loved, as well as the circumstances that had surrounded our first mass in Korea.

He ran a finger over the image of Sporrer. "I wonder if he's still around."

I shook my head. "Died in '93."

John looked up from the photo. "Kept in touch?"

"Yeah. No. I went to see him once at his church not too far from here. A fine man. Sorry he's gone. That's the second time he's left us."

John went back to the newspaper clipping. "What's with the circle? You wanna make sure you don't forget which one you are?"

"Ha! Ma circled me before she'd even cut it from the paper. Wanted to make sure all her friends knew which one I was when she showed it around."

"Mom's are like that." He studied the photo a last time and allowed his finger to find his own image, just behind mine. There knelt a young John Gruber with short, mussed hair, and dressed down to his Marine Corps issued t-shirt.

"I usually clean up for church," he said. His smile spoke nostalgia.

"I think God understood."

"You think—" He looked at me and then back at the paper. "You think I can borrow this?"

My mouth said, "Yeah," as my mind wondered about the possibility that I'd never see it again. "Of course you can."

"I'll guard this with my life, Joe. Soon as I make some copies, I'll send it back to you."

With complete confidence that John *would* protect it with his life, I wrote my address on the envelope and relinquished temporary custody of the clipping over to him. As fate would have it, the life with which John Gruber assuredly guarded the newsprint-bound memory ended soon after that reunion, and I never saw the clipping again. Given the choice, I'd have John back.

At the Chosin Reservoir, the Deuce-and-a-Halves carried mostly men who could no longer carry themselves, with the rest rotating in short shifts through the sparsely remaining spots. Stanley Zabodyn, his legs black with frostbite from below the knees down to his feet, sat in the back of Patrick Parrish's big truck. The pain in his legs, as well as the torment caused by Korean Back, made the journey unbearable for him. On the road, ice crunched below boots that, in turn, were filled with more ice. Frostbite wretched every man to varied degrees. Wind beat down the mountain and blistered the convoy. Loosely-formed tornadoes of white, powdery snow crystals scooped up by the wind swirled in the air and stung whatever exposed skin they could find. Time slipped and bent around the fighting withdrawal from the reservoir and encapsulated the Marines in a never-ending journey of increasingly questionable consequence. And then, in a moment, all time had ceased for Patrick Parrish and many others in the snail-paced convoy.

Machine-gun fire from the high ground had spit up chunks of ice, dinged vehicles and shattered windshields. Patrick's prime mover lurched to a stop. Bullets sprayed through the windshield and penetrated the corporal's chest. He managed to push the door open and stumble to the road. In the back of the truck, Stanley took two bullets. He rolled out of the bed and down to the road. Staff Sergeant McAbee ran from the Prime Mover that was next in line, and threw himself on the exposed Patrick in order to protect him from further injury. Stanley struggled to the side of the road and down a shallow embankment. Every able-bodied man took up hasty position and returned fire on multiple enemy positions. Like a crab carrying a rock below its belly, McAbee shuffled Patrick closer to the truck—Patrick was of no help. From his position of minimal cover, Stanley heard my distant voice call to him through the deafening racket, and with the little strength he could muster, cried out.

"I'm hit, Joe. Oh God, I'm hit."

"Hold it." Everyone at the table in San Diego turned from Stanley's recount of the harrowing attack on the convoy at the Chosin to me. "I wasn't even there, Stan," I said.

"Of course you were there. I can't even tell you what it meant to hear your voice. You were looking out for me."

"Stan, I wasn't there. I was in infantry by then. I'm sorry, but that was someone else calling to you."

Digger's, John's, and Paul's gazes ping ponged between us.

"When were you in that ambush?"

I didn't have to think about it long. " Fifty years ago today. December 8."

"Patrick Parrish died on December 4th, two days after Simmons. I was wounded on December 4th. That's four days, Joe."

"I'm telling you, I was in the infantry when Patrick died." Thoughts of The Missing Days skittered across the back of my head, and left hairs on end where they had trod. "I wasn't there."

"Joe, it was a goddamned mess, but I know what I know." Stanley looked to Paul Kreiger for backup.

Paul held up his hands. "Don't look at me. I'd already been evacked with a bullet of my own."

"I was a bit ahead of you guys in the convoy," John said, "I learned about Patrick after the shooting stopped."

"McAbee was distraught." Digger deftly maneuvered the conversation. "He gets Parrish under cover of the truck and realizes the kid isn't gonna make it."

"Was Joe there?" Stanley asked.

"I was driving the mover behind Patrick. Couldn't say for sure, though. I would think maybe."

"You would think maybe?" Stanley rolled his eyes. "That's specific."

"I was with the infantry by then," I insisted.

"I know Joe volunteered sometime around then—before we got back to Funchilin Pass. Koto, maybe. I don't know."

"This was before Koto-ri," Stanley said.

"Okay. Maybe before. I don't know. Mighta been after I lost *my* truck. It'd been hit hard and died a quick death. Warmed my hands in the steam coming off the engine. But it had the Howitzer coupled to it, so both had to go. McAbee dropped a thermite grenade down the muzzle of the gun to seal the firing block to the frame, and we pushed truck and gun together down the ravine. I know you were there for that, Joe."

"Oh yeah," I said. "First, we tried shooting the gas tank to blow it up. Ha! Remember that?"

Digger laughed the laugh of sad nostalgia. "All of us shooting at the tank waiting for that thing to blow. Nothing. That's when McAbee says it's got to go over. Damn thing must've gone hundreds of feet. Spectacular and sad to watch all at the same time. All our stuff—packs, sleeping bags, everything—was in that goddamned truck. Your gear was in the truck, Joe."

"Yeah. Lost my camera and Bryan's three hundred dollars. But that camera had some photos I wished I hadn't even taken. Atrocities. I'm glad it's gone. Probably still there—untouched. We just had our minds on getting the hell out of there, and everything went over. I hate that place. What I would have given for one of Paul's keyholes then."

"McAbee called in a strike on the truck to make sure nobody'd get it," Digger said. "Corsair comes screaming down the mountain above us, and passes so close I coulda reached out and touched it. Unbelievable. Then it continues down the valley and drops a bomb on the truck. Bryan's three hundred bucks is in pennies now. And you got no worries about those photos ever showing up."

Everybody laughed, and then Digger continued.

"So, a few days later, Stanley and Patrick got hit. McAbee was in the truck with me and we watched Stan roll off the road and Patrick drop to the ground. Patrick wasn't moving, and McAbee ran right to him—shots firing all around him. It was total chaos. The snow was falling from the sky, but we kept getting hit with wisps of snow shot *up* by all the bullets. Strangest thing to see—snow coming at us from top and bottom. Anyway, after the shooting finally stopped, I made my way over to McAbee. He'd rolled Patrick onto his back, and I asked if he was gonna make it. McAbee didn't say a word—just shook his head. I looked at Patrick, and other than his eyes rolling in his head, he wasn't moving. Couple minutes later, he's gone. McAbee took it hard. He shoulda got a medal."

"They don't give medals for saving dead guys," Stanley said. It was a solemn thought expressed aloud.

"Don't matter. He threw himself on Patrick," Digger rebuffed. "Rounds pinging all around him. He exposed himself to protect the kid."

"McAbee's a fucking hero," Paul offered.

Digger nodded. "He should've gotten a Silver Star. Anyway, McAbee said he was fine after it was over. You could see it in his eyes, though. Took it hard."

"I loved Patrick," I said.

Stanley took a sip of coffee. "Yeah. We all did, Joe. Good, good kid."

Silent reflection followed until Stanley spoke up again.

"The whole convoy was backed up by Koto, because the bridge had been blown at Funchilin Pass. Nowhere to go."

"Here, we think we're done," John said, "And the Air Force drops these humongous bridge sections from them cargo planes."

"Flying Boxcars," I said.

"What a sight that was." John shook his head. "Two giant parachutes on each one. Engineers build a new bridge and we're off. Unbelievable."

"You guys were off. They evacuated me from Koto-ri," Stanley said. "I don't know what I was more scared of, losing my legs or taking off on that frozen airfield. Them pilots were good."

"How's the legs?" I asked.

"Still get me around." He slapped both legs. "Ha! I can do that, because I barely feel a thing. Gotta place 'em with purpose when I walk, though, so I don't go ass over canteen. Better than a wheelchair, though. How bad you get it?"

"Not bad. Just the feet. How'd you know I got frostbite?"

"You were at the Chosin. Shit, Joe. You forget that, too?"

The others laughed.

"Right," I said. "Sometimes they tingle, sometimes they hurt, sometimes there's no feeling. Like I've just got dead weights down there."

"VA taking care of ya?" Stanley asked.

"Oh, Hell no. I take care of myself."

Stanley surveyed the other guys.

Paul took the cue. "You should go see them, Joe. Get your money."

"What money?"

"Disability."

"They don't owe me anything. I'm not disabled. I've just got shitty feet. Ha ha!"

"Shitty feet are a disability, Joe," Stanley said.

"Let them use that money for the people who need it."

"You need it. They print enough for everyone."

Digger asked, "When's the last time you worked?"

"Oh, I don't know. Fifteen, twenty years?"

"Why so long?"

"The heart attack and my feet."

"Your feet?" Paul asked.

Stanley held out both hands to me in case-closed fashion.

I waved him off. "I don't want anything from them."

If you are not a combat veteran, I don't think I can make you understand what that reunion meant to me and, I'm sure, the other guys. Hell, even a veteran of our modern wars may not fully grasp it. The Chosin Reservoir Campaign and withdrawal is in a class of its own. Based on the relative number of enemy forces and the conditions—both weather and terrain—it may well have been the single most desperate situation the US Marines have ever found themselves in. It is the singular event that defines the life of every man who was unfortunate enough to be there. Maybe a reunion of Titanic survivors could parallel the feelings—or first responders to the World Trade Center.

They say that as you are about to die, your entire life flashes before your eyes. In the embraces of these men at the end of the night, images of the Korean War mimicked the pre-death slide show I will one day see. We were not the first men to share an experience that others couldn't hope to understand, and we wouldn't be the last. But as we hugged, a reunion of souls took place. Fifty years earlier, we'd been chosen to fight as one, we'd been chosen to survive, and on that day in San Diego, we had been chosen to reunite. We *were then*, and *are now*, The Chosin Few.

I walked Stanley to the elevator on my way to the parking lot.

"Promise me you'll get over to the VA, Joe."

"We'll see."

"We'll see nothing. Just go."

He pushed the elevator button, and I gave him a last hug.

"I'll catch up with you tomorrow," I said.

"I love you, Joe. Means the world to see you."

"I love you, Stan."

I left him waiting for the elevator and made my way to the exit.

"Hey, Joe," he called.

I turned back. "Yeah."

"You were there."

Jesus Christmas. I waved a dismissive hand and continued to the exit.

"No. I wasn't."

From behind me, the distinctive ding of the elevator followed me to the doors, as did Stanley Zabodyn's equally crisp laugh.

At the time of the fiftieth reunion, Stanley and I had been sixty-nine years old, and after all those years, I could forgive him for mixed up memories. Like I told him, he'd probably heard someone else. In the car on my way home, it also occurred to me that a delirious man might have heard a nonexistent voice at his darkest moment. The guy had been severely frostbitten, his dull fatigue was transformed to heightened anxiety during the attack, and two fresh, hot rounds had seared his body. I'd imagine all that could have conceivably caused the man to hallucinate. He'd heard the voice he wanted most to hear—that of his absent best friend. The thought chilled me. And then there were The Missing Days. Did Patrick Parrish's death fall within The Missing Days? Did Stanley Zabodyn's near death? Were those events enough to cause my mind to erase nearly a week of memories? Or did something more terrible happen back there? Perhaps—and more likely—it had just been my own fatigue. I wanted to know.

Hilly, snowy, icy terrain spreads in all directions but I pay it little attention. I run as fast as I can on the rough, frozen road. I am aware of the crunching sound my boots make on the churned-up ice. I slip but adjust my balance and manage to stay up. It's brutally cold yet I sweat beneath my heavy parka. Another fella—a Marine—runs a few yards ahead of me. I have no idea who he is, but I know he's a Marine because the yellow leggings are a dead giveaway. He glances over his shoulder and I know he can see the fear in my face. I am terrified because he is putting space between us, and our two pursuers are closing the space behind me. I have no doubt that if they catch me they will kill me. I look back over my shoulder. The determined look on their Chinese faces sends a shutter through my core. *Chinese.* I will myself to run faster but am unsure it has any real effect. The deep breaths I steal freeze my lungs. My ankles roll with the frozen rocks beneath my feet and with the uneven ground. My boots continue to find purchase even as they slide on a treacherous decline. Another look back at my Chinese pursuers, and right foot collides with left calf—*Don't fall.* The road rushes up at me, and I extend my hands in order to break the fall. *Stay up.* Deep, rough, frozen tracks on the road, from a tank that has recently crumbled the ice, scrape and sting the skin of my left cheek—*Gonna need to clean that out*—as I slide like a backpack tossed from a speeding Jeep. Ice crystals fill my nostrils and lungs—*dust pneumonia.* The two men are on me before I can finish the thought. I flail and kick and punch and scream.

I bolted upright in my bed at 3:30 am, the morning after I'd left Stanley waiting for the elevator. The blankets were nowhere to be seen, and Barbara stood beside the bed in her nightgown. The sheet beneath me was soaked with sweat and smelled like disease. My heart pounded, my breath came in gasps, and my mouth was dry—almost dusty tasting. The nightmare was identical to one I have had a hundred—a thousand?—times before, yet it was so different. The other man with me, although he offers me no assistance and appears to be okay with leaving me behind, is clearly a Marine. I am a Marine. Most troubling of all, was the look on the faces of the two men who chased us. Actually, it was that they had faces at all—never in the past have they had faces—and those faces were clearly Chinese. I did not allow myself to consider the location. The nightmares have tortured, tormented, terrorized, and terrified me for fifty years. Never before have I been so rattled.

Only three weeks had passed since the reunion before Paul Kreiger phoned me.

"I'm telling you, buddy, anyone who was there and shows signs of frost-bite, is eligible for disability. I get 40%. Stan gets more, but his legs were pretty fucked up."

It took another week for Stanley to call.

"Paul says you haven't gone to the VA. You need to go down there, Joe."

"I'm not going down there. I'm fine."

I wasn't fine. My feet hurt and my life had been turned upside down. Since the reunion, the nightmares had come rapid-fire and had intensified in severity. There was no hint of a blank or even nondescript face in any dream. My pursuers were always Chinese now. Firing squads were now manned by a row of Chinamen who grinned behind Sten Machine Carbines that fired deadly 9mm rounds. Gone, too, were the standard junkyard dogs of mundane nightmares. In their place appeared snarling, salivating, long-toothed, Chinese-faced junkyard dogs that would surely rip a Marine to shreds. White hospitals and office buildings and hotels had given way to snow-covered valleys, gorges, hills, and mountains.

I now know that the dreams are about Korea. There is no ambiguity about this. Somehow, the happy—and at times somber—reunion has revealed this to me. I am uncertain that knowing is good. But none of this was what Stanley called to talk about, so I kept it to myself.

"I'm fine, Stanley."

"You don't have a pot to piss in, Joe. Go get what they owe you."

"They don't owe me nothing. I volunteered to do a job, and that's what I did—my job. People got hurt. It's expected. Jesus, I've got sore feet, Stan. Digger's got one leg shorter than the other—after he spent a year in the hospital. You were shot. Twice. And me? I got sore feet."

I didn't add that I'd also gotten fifty years of awful dreams—awful. Dreams that had never revealed their motivation. Dreams that had tormented me. Dreams that had taken my sanity. Dreams that had led to anger, confusion, fear, self-loathing, and suicidal thoughts and tendencies. I had never believed my life could get worse until I'd learned that the war had done this to me—that I was weak enough for the war to do this to me. Five decades. Five goddamned decades of just wanting to end the misery. Five freaking decades of pushing through instead of living. And when I learn the reason for the dreams, instead of revealing a path toward relief, the nightmares become more terrifying and more frequent. No, I didn't add this for Stan's benefit.

Stanley stayed quiet. I could almost hear the rusty wheels turning.

"You know what cops do when they retire, Joe?"

Here we go. I ran my free hand through my hair. "What do cops do, Stan?"

"They start a second career. The first pension is nice, but it ain't enough for a guy who retires after twenty to make a life all the way through old age. You only got 75%, for Christ's sake. And you been living off that shit for twenty some-odd years, because you couldn't start a second career. Yes. They do owe you."

"You rehearse that with Paul first?"

He chuckled. "Yeah. Not bad, though, huh?"

"It was pretty good."

"And you know I'm right."

"I'll go down there when I can."

"Yeah. Fit it into your busy schedule."

The phone calls from Stanley, Paul, and occasionally Digger, went on that way for the better part of two years, until Stanley talked me into busting open the piggy bank in order to fly to Houston for the next biennial Chosin Few reunion. Since Stanley lived in Houston, I stayed at his home. The trip would not have happened otherwise. It was at this reunion that an intervention of sorts took place. This intervention had nothing to do with alcohol, drugs, food, sex, or spreadsheets. In fact, it had nothing whatsoever to do with addiction. Only feet.

"Jesus Christmas. Lighten up. I'll go. I promise."

"So help me," Stanley said, "If you don't go, I will fly out to San Diego, and I will drag your ass down to the VA myself. We are not going to talk about this again."

CHAPTER 27

Disillusion

I TOOK MYSELF BACK FIFTY-THREE years to Korea, and remembered things I'd rather not. Nothing remarkable stood out that might explain the nightmares. The ambush, in which so many others had been killed and injured, was the stuff any self-respecting nightmare wishes it could conjure, but there had been no chase on that long-ago night. There was always a chase in my dreams—or at least the assumption of chase.

I'm with another Marine—haven't the slightest clue who he is. A soldier is there, too, and he could be George Burns for all I know him. His wrists are bound behind his back with barbed wire, blood trickles into his palms, and he flexes his fingers, presumably to mitigate the pain. The only other person present is a Chinese guy—a soldier—and he has the only gun. He holds it to the face of the American soldier. "Why are you doing this?" I ask. "Shut up," he says. I believe he is going to do it—put a bullet in the kid's face. I act quickly. I lunge at him and get him to the ground. A fierce struggle ensues and I do my best to get the gun from him. This is the point when the other Marine should get into the fight. *Anytime now.* Nothing. He stands there as I tire and the Chinese soldier gets the best of me. His gun is pressed into my neck and he pants with anger. When he stands me up, the other Marine avoids eye contact with me. I say nothing. Any chance for escape has passed. Any anger at the Marine is pointless. *Why didn't you help? You're a fucking Marine!* The Chinaman shoves me back in place and presses the gun harder at my neck. I close my eyes. When he releases his grip on the front of my parka, I open my eyes to see him take a step back. Then he levels the gun to my face. *Here it comes. Through the keyhole. At least I'll be out of this place. The Marines will find our frozen bodies and get us home. No man left behind.*

The Chinaman draws his face into a grotesque smile. The thought of being killed by this man with the crooked, brown teeth sickens me. Then, in one fluid motion, he turns his gun to the American soldier and pulls the trigger. One bullet to the center of the face. I gasp for air at the sound of the shot. The Chinese soldier laughs. My throat burns with bile. The body of the American soldier drops to the ground.

After the dream, I could not go back to sleep. This, without doubt, is the most disturbing nightmare I've ever had. Thoughts tickled my consciousness and I did my damnedest to push them away. But my mind seems to have a mind of its own. Finally, it blurted to me, *The Missing Days.* Since the reunion, I had struggled through this so often. It just seemed so obvious: the Chosin Reservoir and The Missing Days. I knew that if I could only remember, I could lay the unknown Marine and the new soldier to rest, as well as banish the Chinamen and Chinadogs for good. *Wish in one hand, and shit in the other...*

I never knew when the depression would hit. The truth is, I'd lived in a near-constant state of depression and it had become my normal, so I usually didn't recognize it any more. It was no way to live, but the proper way was so distant, I had no frame of reference to provide even a glimmer of hope that I might one day attain it again. When I had reason to smile or laugh, the edge was smooth. The luster was dull. Even my anger had lost its dynamic highs. It seemed to retain the same old effects on those around me as they'd cringe and avoid or acquiesce, so I guess the outward manifestation remained the same. But an internal cloak surrounded it now, and tempered the rage. There was no satisfaction. The cloak held the chemical reaction to the anger back, and my heart didn't race as fervently or as long. The cloak would contract, and I'd fall back into indifference. Sometimes, however, the depression was overwhelming—for others.

The day had been like any other. 6:00 am coffee washed down a handful of pills that regulated my heart, blood pressure, and perhaps as a side-effect, my general state of being. My internal clock had made sure that I got to those pills at the anointed time. I'd flipped the blanket off my legs and torso— they never cover my feet because even the weight of a sheet is too painful for them—picked up the remote, and shut off the TV (the television masked the Howitzer-induced tinnitus so that I could sleep). As I swallowed each pill, I made entries into my last-remaining, hand-written spreadsheet that showed each pill and time taken so that there would be no confusion. I padded to the front door and realized that this had been a nightmare-less night. *Humph.* My version of a weekend. I retrieved the newspaper from the driveway, and then sat in the living room to read about how much the world sucked.

While Barbara slept in (she still stayed up until three in the morning), I washed my breakfast dishes and threw in a couple loads of laundry. I always did laundry with the same care with which I updated my spreadsheets. Whites, lights, darks. Bleach, no bleach. Gentle, heavy duty. Cold, warm, blister-inducing. Whatever didn't go in the dryer was hung from a bar in the garage. Hangers or folded, though, it was all accomplished with precision. If something needed to be ironed— well, that required somebody else's expertise. Later in the day, Barbara prepared a simple lunch of leftover chicken and peas from the night before. The food was good but inconsequential. It was merely meant to keep me alive long enough to clean the dishes and take my afternoon nap. After a rousing round of computer solitaire, I turned on the television in the bedroom, shut the door, and climbed into bed for my two-hour nap. Everything went according to my rigorous schedule.

The event that followed made up for the lack of a nightmare the night before, and brought my *weekend* to a devastating end. Refreshed from a restful sleep, I took on the arduous task of reading Tom Clancy's *Without Remorse*. The 768 pages would keep me busy for a week—maybe more. Dullness permeated me and the words merely floated through my consciousness without meaning. Just as Mr. Clark was about to pull the trigger on another drug kingpin, I set the book aside and retreated to my office and the solitaire. Solitaire doesn't care. It pays no attention. Happy, sad, or angry, it remains indifferent. It is patient. Play slow, or play fast, it waits in silence for the next move. Expert decisions, or bonehead mistakes, it does not judge. It just doesn't care. Solitaire had become my best friend.

"I can't do this anymore."

I turned in my seat. Barbara stood at the door holding herself. Her eyes were red. I merely blinked.

"You have to see someone. The doctor. A psychiatrist. Someone."

She'd been on me for weeks—or was it months?—to go to the doctor for my depression. I had no desire to do any such thing. I had no desire. For years, I'd lived in a "maintenance" level of depression. It rarely changed. But since the first reunion and the realities it revealed, the intensity had increased in perfect parallel to the intensity of the nightmares.

For five decades, Barbara had seen me at my best and at my worst. But she had never seen this, and she was scared. The Thousand Mile Stare had become my only expression. There was no happy, sad, or angry. There was nothing left on the inside for me to show on the outside, and she was scared. She was the only person on the planet who knew my history, and she believed that this might be the end for me. We didn't talk. She prepared meals and I washed the dishes. I sat at the computer and stared at digital cards on the monitor but didn't move them. I wondered if they were my countdown deck. Finally, Barbara gave me the ultimatum.

"You have to go, Joe. I can't take this."

I looked at the cards.

"Bea says I can stay with her."

So, there it was. Over fifty years of my shit, and she'd had it.

"Ellen's home. We're going shopping."

The air rushed out of the house with them as they left, and I couldn't breathe. What the Korean War—with all the guns, and mortars, and bayonets, and grenades—had not been able to do, mere words had accomplished with a single shot. The wound had been fatal. *Let's make it official.*

Thump, thump. Pop.

The Great California Earthquake, which the world had forever predicted, had finally arrived. And the epicenter had erupted beneath my home. The fissure proved deeper and wider than any that had ever preceded it, and the world changed. Without balance, I searched for something to hold on to, but my hands grasped at non-existent purchase. My legs turned to noodles and support eluded me. I stumbled down into a depression that even I could recognize. First, I struggled to gain control and pull myself free. Then I didn't care. I languished and sunk deeper with no desire to pull myself out. *What's the point?*

This life—the life I often hated, the life that brought me occasional great joy, the life that, like my father, kicked me when I was down, the life that, unlike my father, lifted me back up and brushed me off, and the life that had brought me a family I could always count on to be at my side—was over. The body had to merely accept its fate and lie down. So, I would help it along.

I walked into the bedroom. Shadows of the tree out back swayed on the closet door—an effect of the spotlights from the elementary school on the other side of the creek. In the closet, I lifted the folded blanket on the top shelf. *Where is it?* Of course it wasn't there. That was on Long Island. When Barbara's cousin, Brian, had joined the New York City Police Department, I'd gifted my service revolver to him. It had never even made the trip to California with me. I hadn't needed it—didn't want it. *I want it now.* Brian had requested my badge number from the city, but they had already reissued it by the time he got on the force. That hadn't mattered. The gesture alone had made me so proud. And he was destined to be a great cop no matter what number was on his shield. The son of Barbara's Uncle Tom—whom I cherished for his humility and integrity—Brian came from the finest stock. *But, I want my gun back.*

I relished the remembered weight—*I miss that*—it's elegance and power. I closed my eyes and inhaled its oily aroma. *With one hand, I release the cylinder. The bullets slide in with precision ease. No play—just right. With the slightest flick of the wrist, I snap the cylinder back into place. For old time's sake, I spin the cylinder with my left hand. It moves freely and smoothly. Just like new. "Thanks for taking such good care of this, Brian." "No problem, Uncle Joe."*

Brian always called me "Uncle Joe," because of our age difference. I liked that. It made me feel like we were blood family. That boy loved his Uncle Joe.

CHAPTER 28

The Beginning

EVERY ENDING USHERS IN A new beginning. It cannot, nor should it, be avoided. Your car takes a crap, and you either get a new one or you start riding a bicycle. Break up with your best girl, and you might find another best girl, or you might become a priest. Retire early from the police department, and you could start a new career, or you could choose to become the greatest solitaire player in the world with a flair for spreadsheets. Yin and yang. Martin and Lewis. Endings and beginnings.

For a week, I waited to wake up. *This can't be real.* I thought my mind had conjured a new line of torture for me. In lucid moments, all I thought about was how to get a gun. None of my children in Poway owned a gun. That would have been convenient. *I'm just gonna borrow this, Joseph. You'll have it back in a second. No. Put those away. I just need one. Thanks. Pop.*

They'd come to my funeral and see me in the coffin. *A fresh hole in my temple. Blood trickles down the side of my head, and soaks the white satin casket liner. They say "Goodbye," as if I'm boarding a bus for Los Angeles. A tear forms in the corner of my eye, but my pain means nothing.*

For the next week, Barbara cried a lot.

I didn't know how to end my life, but I knew that I couldn't live without her. So, I decided to appease her.

On the way to the doctor's office, the guy in front of me slowed down as soon as the light ahead turned yellow. Then he stopped and waited for it to turn red. I sat behind him for forty-five seconds and thought about a gun. A week ago, I'd have wanted it so I could shoot this asshole for making me sit at a light. On that day, I didn't even notice that he was an asshole. I didn't notice the wasted time at the light that would have, on any other day, infuriated me. I just thought about the gun and potholes and lost opportunities. *Thump, thump. Pop.* I thought about Plumb Beach and the twinkling lights of Rockaway across the vast, dark bay. I felt the breeze cool my sweat atop the Williamsburg Bridge, and I visualized 500 feet of thin air between the East River and me. *So many opportunities—so little courage.* So many years had gone by during which Barbara could have moved on. A horn blew from behind, and I realized that the car in front of me was already gone. I pulled away from the light, and it didn't even occur to me to scold the clown behind me. *Get off my ass, shithead.* I didn't notice that he gave me the finger as he sped around me—Barbara kept it to herself until later.

Barbara told Dr. Heller everything—my entire life story in a minute flat. I liked him, and I did my best to be responsive to his questions. I put up with his pokes and penlights and tongue depressors and thermometers and blood-pressure cuffs and even the cold stethoscope.

"I want you to see a psychiatrist, Joe."

I knew how this would end: the psychiatrist would tell me that I don't think my father loved me. *Thanks for the news flash.*

"I don't need to see a psychiatrist. I know what's wrong with me."

"What's wrong with you, Joe?"

"I don't think my father loved me."

He looked at Barbara and then at me. "You making a joke?"

I nodded.

"Because you don't look like you're making a joke. I think you should go see her."

"There's nothing wrong with me. It doesn't matter."

"I'm sure there is nothing wrong with you, too, Joe." He tapped the keyboard on his computer. "But it does matter, and it won't hurt to see her."

He jotted down the information from the monitor.

"She's at Scripps. Go over there now. I'm going to call ahead for you."

"I'll make an appointment."

"Sounds like another joke. She'll make time for you now."

We found Dr. Fredrickson at the Scripps Clinic and, as promised, she made time for me.

"So, what's going on, Joe?"

"My feet hurt."

"Why?"

"Frostbite."

"Unusual for San Diego."

I saw that she already knew exactly what I was talking about. Scripps is minutes away from the VA hospital in the third largest veteran-populated county in the country. I knew I wasn't the first old soldier to sit on her couch. Her quip nudged a half-hearted smile from me. Pretty girl—maybe forty—cracks a joke, and it's the right thing to do.

"Korea, right?"

"Yeah."

"Chosin?" The Chosin Reservoir wasn't the only place guys got frostbite, but it was a safe bet.

"Yeah."

"Marines?"

"Yeah."

"Tell me about it."

I gave her the watered-down version, which included Chinese hordes, shitty weather, rough terrain, and a long, miserable walk. Missing were any details about dead Marines, frozen bodies, grueling battles, and the ambush. She was easy to talk to, seemed interested in whatever I had to say, and my words flowed in a fifty-cent history lesson that I'm sure she already knew. Then she wound up.

"Dr. Heller says you're depressed. What's that about?"

The throw from left field hit me directly in the throat. The muscles there thickened and my voice shut down.

"One thing that you will learn, Joe, is that you can say anything here."

"Why can't my wife be here with us?"

"How long have you been married?"

"Fifty years."

"Wow. Congratulations. That alone is quite an accomplishment. I'm sure she is very supportive."

I looked down and nodded. "Yes, she is. I don't know why she's so supportive."

"Why do you say that?"

"She puts up with a lot of crap. She should've left me a long time ago."

"She must love you very much."

"She must."

"I'm going to guess that you share a lot with Barbara."

"Everything."

"Good. The reason I asked her to wait outside is that, even though you freely share with her, there may be times when you hold back some details or feelings. Maybe to protect her. Maybe to protect yourself. I want to have this time with you to feel things out. You need to feel free to say whatever is on your mind. There is no judgment here."

Solitaire. "Okay."

"We may invite her in at another time. Can you tell me what brought on this depression?"

"Nothing brought it on." She didn't respond. "Everything. Maybe I'm just getting old."

"Ever had issues with depression before this?"

I'd thought I'd been there to talk about what was going on in my life at that time, so her question startled me, and I could feel the four walls of her office close in on me.

"I ask you that, Joe, because I just want to see if we can identify any patterns. Occasional depression is common. We all have external influences that bring us down from time to time. The death of a loved one is a great example. We allow ourselves to feel the pain—to grieve—and then we move on. But some people are unable to function this way. For them—"

"On and off," I said.

"Excuse me? On and off?"

"You asked if I've had issues with depression. On and off."

"How much on?" she asked.

"Most of the time. Then I snap out of it for a while."

"How long is a while? Weeks? Months?"

"Days. Hours."

"Do outside influences help with that?"

"Family. Church. Sometimes I just wake up feeling good. Like if I haven't had a nightmare the night before."

"Do you have them often?" she asked.

"Most nights."

"What is 'most nights?'"

"Four, five, six times a week."

"How long has this been going on?"

"Fifty years."

Her eyes remained locked on me. Then she looked down at her lap and pursed her lips ever so slightly. It was the closest thing to emotion I'd detected in her. I felt ashamed.

"I'm sorry," I said.

"What are you sorry about?"

"I don't know."

"I'd like you to tell me about your nightmares."

She listened as I described my faceless pursuers, the brown-toothed Chinaman who shoots the soldier, Chinese-faced junkyard dogs, chases across dirt and rock covered terrain and through a white hospital. I recounted the night fights in which Barbara had been the victim of my attempted self-preservation.

"Who else have you told about these nightmares?"

"Barbara. And now you."

"Are you familiar with PTSD?"

My heart jumped. I shook my head and then stopped.

"It's a Vietnam thing."

"You don't think it affects men from the Korean War?"

"I don't know."

"Joe, how often do you think about suicide?"

I don't think about suicide. Why would you— "Constantly," I told her.

"When was the last time?"

"On my way to the doctor this morning. Maybe in your waiting room." I rubbed my palms on my slacks. "A couple of times right here."

She looked at my hands. "Have you ever acted on it?"

"A couple times. Obviously, I didn't do it."

"Is a couple two?"

"Maybe six. Maybe more."

"Would you like to tell me about it?" she asked.

I thought about that. "Barbara doesn't know."

"Just between you and me."

"It was in New York."

I shared the details of the pothole game that I'd invented.

"I finally stopped carrying my gun home."

"That was a good choice. But what about at work? You had to carry your gun."

"I kept it unloaded."

"A cop in New York City carries an unloaded gun on the job? Another suicide attempt?"

She missed nothing.

"My family would've been taken care of if I got killed on the job."

She nodded. "I get it. So, really, you attempted suicide every day you worked. Your *maybe* is now hundreds of times."

"I guess so."

I wiped my palms again—by now my slacks had wet spots above the knees—and then I balled my hands alongside my legs. She studied my discount-store sneakers.

"Have you seen the VA about your feet?"

I pictured Stanley leading me by the ear into the VA.

"I was gonna make an appointment."

"Okay. Good. I work at the VA one day each week."

"What a coincidence."

"Dr. Heller knows that. I'd like you to meet me there this Thursday. We'll get you started with a claim for your feet. Get you some proper shoes."

"Okay." Proper shoes sounded nice.

"And there are some people I'd like you to meet."

"What people?" I asked.

"The VA has a PTSD clinic."

My face flushed, and I fought to hold back the tears.

"I'll show you around. What you do is up to you. In the meantime, we'll make an appointment for you to come back here, if that's okay."

At least she wasn't brushing me off. I was glad, because I liked her.

"Yeah. If you think so."

Thursday morning found me filled with apprehension. There'd been no nightmare the night before, because there'd been no sleep. I paced from room to room in search of something to do, but not even spreadsheets could keep my mind focused for more than a few minutes. I looked forward to the possibility of new—and, I hoped, free—shoes, but not to the likelihood of hospital nonsense. The opportunity to see Dr. Fredrickson again was good with me, while meeting others was less so. If I had to admit that I was crazy, I'd much prefer to limit that admission to the kind doctor at Scripps. I wanted to involve fewer rather than more people. Crazy is a private thing. If at all possible, I'd even opt to keep that news away from myself.

We met at 10:00 am sharp. Dr. Fredrickson walked me to a reception area, where she got me signed in. We then took a seat to wait.

"You are going to have your feet examined first."

"Then my head?"

"Ha." She smiled in deference to my great sense of humor. "Well, I guess eventually. Look, Joe. It's obvious that your issues are service related. Barbara's ultimatum has merely exacerbated your feelings. But it got you here, so that's a good thing. A doctor will look at your feet. Another will talk to you about the dreams, depression, and suicidal thoughts. Together, we'll come up with a treatment plan that the VA will pay for. Eventually, they will determine your disability rating based on your feet *and your head*. You'll be compensated for that."

"They're going to give me money because I have nightmares?" The thought had seemed ludicrous.

"You haven't worked since you were forty-five, Joe. Let's examine the reasons."

"I had a heart attack."

"What caused it?"

"Stress. The job—lots of jobs—the city, the nightmares, the depression, thinking about killing myself, nine kids, money, my father. Shit—excuse me—I'm sure there's more."

"A lot of those are directly related to the nightmares. And here's the thing: heart attack or not, you should have been removed from that job anyway."

"Why?"

"Because of the suicidal thoughts. You carried a gun. You were a danger to yourself, as well as others."

"I could have driven a bus," I told her.

"Straight off a cliff?"

"We don't have those in New York."

She gave me a pat on the knee and stood up. "Somebody will escort you to your next appointment when you are finished here. I'll catch up before the meeting."

"What meeting?"

"I don't want to ruin the surprise."

"I think you'll like this group, Joe."

Dr. Fredrickson and I stood in a hallway just off the waiting room. Men of varied ages passed us and entered a room to my left. Inside, others had already gathered with coffee and friends. Dr. Fredrickson introduced me to Jeremy, the therapist who facilitated the group meeting of combat veterans with PTSD. Despite my discomfort, I was already on board. Nothing I had ever done before this point in my life had changed anything for the better. I felt defeated, and I wanted someone to take care of me. I wanted someone to make me better. Dr. Fredrickson seemed willing to be that person, so I chose to follow wherever she led.

The old familiars of Jeremy's group checked out the new guy when I walked in with him. Most of the guys looked Vietnam era to me, and some of them took the guesswork out with hats that signified so. These were no kids anymore. *Where did all that time go?* Several younger men there had been from more modern wars—I guessed the first Gulf War. And then I spotted the unexpected. A gentleman about my age turned from a discussion he was having and watched me. He wore a Korean War Veteran hat. My surprise must have shown. He excused himself from his conversation, and approached with an extended hand.

"Pete. How are you?" he said.

"Joe. Nervous." I looked at his hat again.

"Take it you didn't expect to see any contemporaries, Joe."

"No."

"Ha. When I first came in, I figured it'd be a bunch of Nam guys and me—the one Korean War guy with a loose screw."

"Yeah." My eyes scanned the room.

"C'mon. You'll like this."

Pete escorted me to where two other men sat on the far side of the room.

"Frank and Willie, meet Joe." Pete rocked a thumb back toward me. "Joe thought he'd be the old guy in the room. Joe, meet Frank and Willie."

Frank and Willie both pushed themselves from their seats. Frank's hat gave him away: WWII, Navy.

"USS Baltimore," he said with a point to his cover.

"Squirrelly," Willie said in reference to the Baltimore's nickname. "Frank was with the first shore patrol at Hiroshima after we dropped Little Boy."

"Willie here's a soldier," Frank said. "Normandy."

I shook their hands, and held them a bit longer than I probably should have. "You men are my heroes. I'm a Marine."

"Chosin?" Frank asked.

"Yes, sir."

"Well, you're one of mine, kid."

That was the last mention of battle-specific service throughout the entire one-hour meeting. I'd expected plenty of talk about gruesome firefights and bloody battles, but nobody mentioned war. Each man talked about his prior week and how his life was going. Something had sparked Hank's (a Vietnam vet) anger during that week. He talked about why that anger had emerged in such a caustic way, and how he'd then dealt with it. I got the impression that Hank had been around this group for a while, and had learned how to successfully get his anger under control—this week's event had been an unusual one for him. Vincent (another Nam vet) had been around a while, as well. He talked about a recent nightmare in which he'd been chased in the jungle.

"When I fell in the dream, I woke up."

Jeremy asked, "How'd you feel?"

"Fine. I rolled over, put my arm around Steph, and went back to sleep."

"How long had it been since the last time you had that dream?"

He shrugged. "Couple'a weeks."

"How was Stephanie?"

"She didn't even wake up. Couple years ago she mighta gotten a black eye or a fat lip."

I was stunned. I caught Jeremy with his eyes on me.

"What do you think about that, Joe?"

I'd wondered if he'd steered the previous conversation for my benefit. Evidently, Dr. Fredrickson had briefed him on my situation.

"I'd like to go two weeks without a nightmare." I hated the sheepish demeanor I was sure I'd projected.

Jeremy turned back to Vincent. "How often did you have the dreams when you first came here?"

"'Bout every night. Some nights, more than once."

"How often now?"

"Once in a while. Doesn't matter much, though. They really don't bother me anymore." He shrugged. "Just a dream. Roll over and go back to sleep."

The thought choked me. *I want that.*

"What's that, Joe?"

I looked up from the floor in front of my eighteen-dollar sneakers. "Oh." I shook my head. "Nothing."

In the course of an hour, almost every negative aspect of my life had been discussed, without so much as a peep from me: anger, self-hate, self-doubt, guilt, shame, suicidal thoughts and attempts, and nightmares, which someone referred to as night terrors. There'd been tears and laughter, tough questions and easy support, but most important, there'd been acceptance without judgment. In later weeks, I'd realize that this first meeting had not been a "put on" for my benefit. There'd been no rehearsed scripts from which everyone received some negative aspect of the new guy's life to talk about. Instead, each meeting went pretty much the same. Guys shared successes and setbacks, as well as their hopes and fears. The difficulties in their lives were astonishingly similar to those in mine, and at times, I'd actually shuttered. But I felt like an earthquake victim who'd been trapped in the rubble of a building for a week. The giant collapsed concrete slab that had smothered me for so long was slowly lifted from above me, and I caught my first glimpse of light. It was—of course—much too soon to know if I would survive, but the first sensations of what I'd later realize was hope seemed to caress my skin as the rescuers from our group gathered around and gently pulled me from my prison.

That first meeting ended with a group prayer:

God, grant me the serenity to accept the things I cannot change,
The courage to change the things I can,
And the wisdom to know the difference.
Keep coming back. It works if you work it.

Then I approached Vincent. "Joe Lynch," I said.

"Vincent DeMarco, Joe. Welcome."

"I'm chased in my dreams, too."

"Not surprised. It's a popular theme. We gonna see you next week?"

I looked around the room. Hand shakes and hugs and slaps on the shoulders brought the gathering to a slow end.

"Yeah, I'll be back." I turned back to Vincent. "I want what you got."

"What's that?"

"Sleep."

Over time, *Vincent* became *Vincenzo* and then *Vinnie the Guinea—ha ha!* In other words, Vincent became my friend. A handshake became a hug, and then turned into a kiss on the cheek. "See ya next week" became "I love you." And it hadn't stopped with Vincent. We didn't buy beers and hang out at the beach together, but the guys in that group all became my friends—a family of sorts. Without hesitation, shame, or fear of judgment, I could—and did—tell them anything I cared to. There were no secrets, because I figured if I was going to do it, I was going to do it all the way.

By the time I'd attended my third meeting, the others in the group had learned about my father, could describe each nightmare I'd had, and understood the intricate rules of Pothole Roulette. Not a single man thought the last was an odd device for suicide—some called it "Creative." I could tell which of those men were most likely to succeed and which would probably struggle. It was all about the attitude. The guys who simply came to be "cured," or didn't take the advice seriously, were destined for failure. But the men who said, "Show me the way," and then followed, were the men to watch. If a fella said, "Tell me what to do," and then did it, he was destined to excel. I became one of those men. I soaked up everything anyone had to say, and then I fit their ideas, advice, and experience to my circumstance. I attended meetings after group counseling after private sessions. Anger management, yoga, medication, meditation—anything I was advised to try, I tried.

The day I'd walked into the VA, my life had been over, so there'd been nothing left to lose. I'd been informed from the start that there'd be no magic wand waved over my head—anything I wanted, I'd have to go get. Well, I wanted it all. I wanted to stop the nightmares. I wanted to stop the anger. I wanted to believe in myself. I wanted the emotional numbness to go away and be replaced by feeling. I wanted to like me. In that diverse group of men, I'd discovered the possibility that I one day would.

Now, make no mistake about it, meditation was as foreign to me as the Korean Peninsular had been fifty-two years earlier. A week before I'd gone to the VA, I'd have thought you were swimming in a bowl of Fruit Loops if you'd suggested meditation to me.

"Show me how," I asked, and I was shown.

My mantra was simple and to the point: "God help me." I was willing to do the work, and just as willing to ask for human and Divine help. "God help me." And God did help me. I learned the fundamentals of meditation in a group setting, and then I brought my practice home. I'd sit in a bedroom that had long ago been abandoned by one of my children, and clear my head of all thought. "God help me. God help me." I'd concentrate on my breath, as well as the words. If anything that I did not need floated into my consciousness, I would acknowledge it, thank it for stopping by, and then send it off with a soft pat on the ass. That had been the imagery that worked for me. "God help me. God help me."

What I experienced was the warmth of God's embrace, and the pureness of my mother's love. I felt nothing and everything. White is merely an illusion after all. It takes every color combined together in equal parts to accomplish a perfect white palette. And I believe it is the same way with energy. All of the world's energy swirled about me in perfect balance to form the illusion of nothing. It had proved both soothing and terrifying at the same time. In fact, I had never felt so safe in all my life—or so scared. I had given myself over to the process so completely—so deeply—that return from the depths of a state of spirit-without-mind seemed more unreachable each time I meditated. In the past, I'd often experienced a drowning sensation in which I'd been terrified that I would never receive another breath. But in this case, I experienced contentment in the sensation that no outside influence would ever penetrate my being. At times, I was aware that other people were in the house—voices carried, toilets flushed, doors closed, or televisions droned—but I could hear nothing, even if I tried. Just as I might struggle in the past to regain the surface while water filled my lungs, I could now be content to drift ever deeper into a realm of total, protected isolation.

I sat in the bedroom one morning in a meditative trance and became aware of my need to surface, but felt no motivation to do so. The concept of time had been lost. I could not tell how long I'd been under or how close I'd wandered to the point of no return. I don't even know if there actually is a point of no return in meditative state, but I began to fear it, nonetheless. That fear finally brought me out, and for all the good I had realized from the practice, I chose to *stay* out. It's silly to think that I had become *too* good at meditation, but that's the way it seemed. My fears of the unknown convinced me to take what I had found there and just move on.

So, my days of meditation were over, but my journey of recovery continued to move forward with steady resolve and mounting reward. A period of time—perhaps six months or more—had passed, during which I probably would have told you that there had been no benefit borne of my effort, other than the in-the-moment gratification I'd experienced with each of the various therapeutic sessions. But, in fact, an unseen shift had occurred that would set off a slow and steady march of change that had a positive effect on every corner of my life.

It is unclear to me now—and may have been at the time—whether a slight decrease in the frequency of the nightmares had taken place, or a more reasonable reaction to them had begun to develop. At the same time, the significance of the heretofore-unnoticed changes had occurred to me. I'd awakened from a nightmare in which the Chinese faces of my pursuers had seemed especially clear and evil, yet I breathed easy. I lay on my back, opened my eyes, and looked at the ceiling. All of my blankets were in place, and Barbara slept soundly beside me. I thought about the dream for ten seconds or so—*Did I know the Marine?*—turned onto my left side, and then fell back to sleep with an arm draped over Barbara's waist. In the morning I pondered this welcome development. The last time I remembered waking up in terror had been three days before this dream. As I looked back on that event, however, I felt that the terror aspect had been less explosive than any other time I'd had one of my dreams during the past fifty-plus years. I now wondered about all of the times I'd had the dream in the prior few weeks. *Plenty.* But, even without a well-charted spreadsheet with careful and precise entries for confirmation, I was convinced that it had been fewer than usual. Or maybe I'd just slept right through a few dreams during those weeks. *Tomato, Tomahto.* I hadn't really given a crap. A hairline crack had been exposed in the once-impenetrable fortress that had protected my dark side for five decades, and I fully intended to chip away at the vulnerability until the stronghold had crumbled and light filled every corner of my being.

Some of the guys in our group considered the process hard work, and others a necessary evil. Still more, like me, loved every single minute of it—even the difficult minutes. The individual attention I'd received from Dr. Fredrickson made me feel like the most important person in the universe, while the group sessions provided communal healing in which others participated in mine, and I in theirs. When shared purpose and trust form the roots, the trees of brotherhood and fellowship grow lush and strong. That meeting room became my Garden of Eden.

Appointment days found me anxious to slip into my new orthopedic shoes and bounce out to the car for the half-hour drive to the VA. I couldn't wait to meet with my brothers. Before recovery, there had never been anyone in my life with whom I'd felt safe enough to share my feelings, doubts, or worries. For decades, I'd protected my own family from the truth about myself. In the military and on the police force, I'd feared being seen as weak. But in our counseling sessions, I'd found equals who had shared the trauma of war, and who had also held back all of their residual fears and anxiety from others. These men had slept in *my* bed, and there were no other people whom I trusted more. Together, we sloughed our protective blankets aside, placed our feet on the floor, and found the hidden strength we'd always had to stand on our own.

Vietnam veterans, with whom I'd had serious issues beforehand, actually became my close confidants and supporters. A long-overdue respect for their service had developed in my heart. I apologized to them for things they had no idea that I'd said and felt in the past. I thanked them for their service, and welcomed them home. At times, we'd engage in friendly debate over who'd had it worse during our respective wars. I'd insisted with certainty and sincerity that the Vietnam War had been worse than Korea. But the Nam boys seemed genuinely convinced that Korea—the Chosin—had been the greater evil. In the end, it had been a mutual show of respect for each other's service, and the actual degree of suffering during our respective wars hadn't really mattered all that much. *I do think they'd had it worse, though.*

Over the next couple years, while no given calendar month would have shown any significant or measurable improvement in my well being, the accumulated months revealed astonishing results. I would go weeks without a nightmare, and when they did arrive, they were simply powerless. I'd gotten to the point in my recovery where I no longer even considered them nightmares—they were just dreams. Most of the time, they wouldn't even wake me up, and in the morning, I simply shrugged off any lingering thoughts of them. The identity of the Marine did not concern me. The fate of the soldier was sad, but it was just a dream, and I no longer took it literally. Thankfully, I continue in this light today—with rare dreams and indifferent reactions to them.

While I hadn't been paying attention, my anger held its head low and tiptoed away. I guess it understood it was no longer welcome. Oh, for sure, some things still pissed me off. But, today, I can see them for what they are, judge their significance and weight, and deal with them in an appropriate manner. I have given up my high explosives, and people are no longer afraid to talk to me—or spill a glass of milk.

For my family and friends, I am now all too happy to share a tale or two about the Korean War. The stories I choose depends on the level of maturity of my audience, but a sweet verse or two of *Arirang* is always a crowd pleaser. And to *Float Through The Keyhole* is guaranteed to bring the house down at any family gathering. Paul Kreiger is still the funniest guy, even when he's not there.

But what may be most important of all my achievements during recovery is that I have gained a better understanding of people and what makes them tick. Every single person in this life who we encounter has his or her own challenges, and when we learn to stop living deep inside our own frailties, we are better prepared to recognize and understand the difficulties that others live with. I will never again make the mistake of ignoring the life challenges that other people dear to me endure. When I think about the past, I merely remember where it has taken me, and I thank God for these blessings.

One day recently, my afternoon nap was assaulted—not by a nightmare, but by the sound of a hammer outside the bedroom. I came out to find my son, Christopher, standing in the hallway that leads to my office and the living room. He set the hammer aside, picked up a large frame from the floor in front of him, and hung it on a freshly-placed picture hanger.

"What's this?"

"Take a look."

I walked over to him and looked at the framed, sepia-toned photograph. Thirteen young men knelt side-by-side in two rows in a small clearing on a hill. Their hands were folded in prayer. In front of them was another young man in a similar pose alongside a Catholic priest who knelt behind a make-shift altar that had been fashioned from a military cot. An abandoned Korean village spread out beyond the hill. I inhaled deeply and tears welled in my eyes. It was the photo of my first field mass in Sachon—the photo that had appeared in the New York newspaper over sixty years ago.

Christopher explained that my daughter-in-law, Laura, had found this original wire photo on an auction website, and purchased it from a seller in Spain, of all places. My eighty-three year old eyes examined the impossibly young version of myself. My head was turned down slightly, and I appeared somber. John Gruber, whom I dearly miss, was over my right shoulder. His t-shirt appeared sweaty and his hair was a mess. Sergeant Buckles knelt upright, tall, and straight-backed. Months after the photo had been taken, he was seriously injured during the ambush at the Chosin, where it was left to me to keep him alive, just as he had kept me alive during the months between that mass and the ambush. In the framed photo, Father Sporrer was deep in prayer. As I stood there in the hall with Christopher, I could hear the Padre ask God to watch over us, as well as all the Marines in the Pusan Perimeter.

I looked down the hall. That framed field-mass photo was the final entry to the small memory gallery of my time in the Marine Corps that had gone up over the past couple of years. Nearby is a photo of the 11th Marines boarding the USS Henrico in San Diego. It was a gift to me from employees of the VA hospital. Another photo shows Able Battery spread out on either side of a Howitzer at Camp Pendleton a few months before we'd deployed to Korea. My friends who'd come home are all there—Digger O'Dell, Stanley Zabodyn, Paul Kreiger, John Gruber, and so many others. The sergeants who cared for us at our gun—Buckles and McAbee—sit in the front row. And, of course, the heroes who did not make it—Denny Flom, Donald Miles, Bryan Simmons, Patrick Parrish, Donald Foster, Leland Godfrey, and Angelo De Stefano—finish off our proud field. Still another photo shows Platoon 37's graduation day at Parris Island on May 5, 1948. With the Eagle, Globe, and Anchor on my hat, I look like the most serious sixteen-year old anyone has ever seen. Timothy Sheehan, Jr. stands directly in front of me, relieved that his left foot led his right on that day. I wish that he could have stood beside me. I know he made a great Marine.

As I scanned the seventy-four other faces, including Sergeants Nethery and Dean, I considered the bed I'd made for myself. It was a nice bed. I wouldn't change a thing. I believed that my mother wouldn't either. I believe that when I leave this earth, I will rest with God who will grant me everlasting peace. But I am eternally grateful that, during my final years among the living, I have been given a head start.

With glassy eyes, I took one last look at the field-mass photo, turned to Christopher, and placed a hand on his shoulder.

"You're a good boy. I love you."

Then, with my brown, wooden cane (just like the one my father had used) to steady me, I walked to the kitchen pantry in search of a Tootsie Roll.

In 2011, I visited my folks in California. One afternoon during that week, the house had been deserted except for my father—Joe—and me. He sat in the living room with the television on and a book in his hand.

"I'm gonna go out front for a while, Dad," I said.

"Okay, boy. Enjoy your cigar," he chuckled.

About five minutes after I'd settled in on the little porch with my laptop and cigar, I heard him come through the front door.

"Thought I'd sit with you for a bit."

"Good." I closed the computer.

We talked about the weather (which never changes), my mother, some of the grandkids (nieces and nephews to me), and then he picked me up by my ankles and dangled me upside down while all the blood rushed to my head. Or so it had seemed.

I don't remember when exactly our conversation had shifted, but somewhere around the time I'd been thinking, *He's really chilled out in his old age*, Dad said, "Well, you know, I learned at the PTSD clinic that blah, blah, blah, blah." Everything he'd said after "PTSD clinic" had sounded like Charlie Brown's teacher.

"Wait a minute," I said. "What?"

"What?"

"The PTSD clinic?"

"Yeah. Don't you know about that?"

What a shock. But I guess that's the way these things go with my mom and dad. Those of us who live close by, find out about things through proximity. Little things—like heart attacks and surgical procedures—are bound to come up in casual conversation during family dinners. For us geographically-distant relatives, we usually have to either stumble upon this sort of information or ask very direct questions during phone conversations. Apparently, I'd never thought to ask if he'd been receiving treatment for PTSD.

"No, I didn't know that."

"Oh, yeah. I have PTSD. Anyway—"

He'd said it as if he had a cold.

"What do you mean? Since when?"

"Since I got out of the Marine Corps. Didn't you ever notice how angry I always was?"

Like I was supposed to have known it had been PTSD all along. I searched for the right answer to his question. "Um, No?" That wasn't it.

"Ha ha! Yeah. I go to meetings every week down at the VA. Counseling. You know, with other vets."

"Like Vietnam vets?" I said, *Vietnam* very carefully.

"Yeah. A couple of Korea and World War Two guys, too. All the wars. Great guys."

"When did this start? How did it start?"

"My psychiatrist got me into it."

"Your what?"

"Ha. My psychiatrist. I see a psychiatrist. Nice lady. I was having these awful nightmares. Just awful."

I figured they were recent. "When did that start?"

"Oh." He shrugged. "Fifty years ago. More. When I got out of the Marines. Like four, five, six nights a week. Awful dreams."

I stopped asking "What?", and let him speak. I went through two third-world-dictator-sized cigars while he told me everything. Now, understand: I'm the guy you hear with the sniffles in the dark movie theater during the coming attractions, so it had become difficult at times to remain stoic as I listened to his story. The night terrors and fights—to which my mother had fallen victim for years—were tough to hear. His descriptions of the dreams gave me chills. But the image of my father's car potentially crushed against one of Robert Moses's stone overpasses on the parkway, and him dead with his face against the steering wheel and a bullet in his head, had been too much. Yet, I'd kept it together. I'd been further shocked by the news of The Missing Days.

"I tried for so long to remember what had happened during those days," he said. "Figured that was the answer."

"The psychiatrist couldn't help?"

"I told her that if I could remember, it'd probably help me get rid of the dreams. She said, 'No.' Said it may be nothing, but it also might be something that I don't want to know. Maybe it'll make things worse."

"So, that's it?"

"That's it. She's probably right. I mean, I'd like to know what happened, but I don't worry myself about it. What's done is done. And this is all old news now. I'm good now."

"Like you're cured?"

"Oh, no. That doesn't happen. I still have PTSD. Always will. I just know how to cope with it."

"And the nightmares? You don't have them anymore?"

"Yeah. Sometimes. Hardly ever. They're just dreams, though. They don't bother me. I know they can't hurt me. I never die in the dreams, and I guess my subconscious now knows that I'm not gonna die."

"You still go to the meetings?"

"Sure. Wouldn't miss them. I love the meetings. And I love the guys. They've helped me a lot. I helped them, too. And now I get to help the new guys who come in—you know, just by showing them that there is a path to recovery, and that it works. I love it. Got a meeting tomorrow morning. You wanna drive me down?"

"Was this a two-hour setup just to ask me to take you to the VA?"

"Ha ha! You're funny."

"I try."

"No. I got plenty of people I can call. The VA will even send a van to pick me up."

"I'll be happy to take you down."

So, I drove him to the VA, and when the meeting let out, I met a couple of his friends. I witnessed the love he'd spoken of when Dad embraced Vincent, and they each said to the other, "I love you." A fellow named Ray—another Vietnam veteran—told me that all the guys look up to my father. Let me tell you, at that moment, I could not have been more proud to be his son. The look on my father's face made it apparent that he looked up to them, as well.

My father's recovery from PTSD has been as close to complete as may be possible. There'd been moments during the interviews with him for this book that the pain of his memories was evident, especially when he spoke of lost friends.

"Do you want to stop?"

"No. I'm okay."

"We don't have to do this."

"No. I want to. I want you to write this book."

There is nothing about Dad that leads me to believe he wanted this book written for his own benefit. Instead, he only wants other people to gain a better understanding of what PTSD does to lives. In a way, it is a continuation of the group therapy dynamic (at the PTSD clinic at the VA hospital in San Diego, California) in which he shared his innermost self—for his own benefit, but also for the betterment of those who followed him. Nobody knows better than he that a willingness to talk about PTSD is the only hope for recovery, and that there are people who are anxious to listen and to share their own experiences. Today, Dad is anxious to tell other veterans to stop avoiding the reality of PTSD, and to not waste so much of their lives hiding as he did.

During our interviews, Dad's cane or walker (compliments of the VA) always rests just off camera. His feet—ergo his walking—had become unreliable. He has been reminded of this a good half-dozen times when only the asphalt street, or the concrete driveway, or the tile floor had been there to break his fall. Talented doctors—and, perhaps, good fortune—have seen his bones heal well and quickly, though. The same determined spirit that guided him through his recovery at a late age seems to convince him that he can walk without the help of the VA-issued hardware. In this case, I wish he'd stifle that spirit.

When Dad had his first heart attack at the age of forty-five—I was nineteen years old, and I remember it well—he was given a life expectancy of five years. Today, he is eighty-six, with a "bullet," and not the kind that goes *Pop.* His cardiologist calls my father his "Miracle Patient." An implanted defibrillator has done its intended job a number of times. Years of congestive heart failure has done its best to take him away but, blessedly, to no avail. And say what you will about doctors who hand out prescriptions like Halloween candy, but there is nothing like the sight of this book's hero sitting at the kitchen table as he makes meticulous entries into his last-remaining hand-written spreadsheet of the dozens of pills he needs to swallow every day. Doctors monitor and change those drugs as needed. Dad pops the pills, makes his entries, and stays alive. But there may be no more efficacious medicine than the one known as grandchildren. While he may have fallen short of his mother-inspired goal of twelve children, even my Nana would be astonished by the sixty-plus grand and great-grand children that have emanated in concentric rings from Joe and Barbara's love for each other. Family reunions are a glorious madhouse, and I suspect that Dad enjoys them more than anyone.

Finally, it would appear that The Missing Days shall forever remain so. And, along with Dad, I am fine with that.

With regards to this book, I was unsure how to best portray The Missing Days. In our recorded interviews, Dad was unclear about exactly where in his Chosin Reservoir timeline those days fell. But when he told his story to my brother, Christopher, and me, he actually seemed most confused about the time that led up to the ambush. Dad's references to the disagreement with Stanley Zabodyn about his presence during the attack that killed Patrick Parrish (and left Stanley wounded) suggested that it included the time period that contained those days. Especially in light of his statement that Lieutenant Buckley had forgotten that he'd sent out the platoon on a patrol—which had ended in the ambush—four days later. I simply cannot be certain, however, but I do not think it matters, because The Missing Days were real, and I believe they are a key component—but likely not the only source—of Dad's PTSD.

During the research for this book, I set my computer aside and called my cousin, John Lynch, who is Dad's late, oldest brother, John's, son. My goal was to get details of the attack on the convoy that resulted in my uncle receiving a Purple Heart during World War Two. I explained to John why I needed this information.

"I understood from my father that your dad had a really rough time during the war," John said to me. "The Chosin Reservoir was really bad."

"Yeah. I don't know how any of them survived," I said. It was just small talk as prelude to the information I'd called about.

"He told me your dad had been captured, and held for a short time."

So much for small talk.

Wait. What? I couldn't get those words out of my mouth. I held the phone in stunned silence.

"He was lucky to get away," John continued. "They probably would have killed him."

My mind raced through scores of hours of recorded interviews in search of something that I already knew was not there. When it stopped on DVD number eleven, I hit play. "I never heard of any of our guys being captured. No." That is a direct quote from Joe Lynch.

"John, my dad never told me that," I said. "I'm sure he would have said something. That's pretty big."

"I'm sure that's what he told my father, Robert."

"How long did he say he'd been held?"

"I don't remember. It was a long time ago. God, my father's been gone for twenty-five years. I just remember him telling me that your dad had been captured and held for a short time. Maybe a day. Maybe two."

"But how would he have escaped?"

"I wish I could tell you."

After I'd hung up, I sat stunned and heavy in my office chair. For the next two weeks, I did not write a single word as my mind played the conversation over and over. *The Missing Days. Could this be it? Makes sense.* Or maybe my cousin had just mistakenly remembered what he'd been told by his father. There exists no record of Joe ever having been a POW. But, naturally, if there had been a capture and escape, there wouldn't be.

I did a quick online search, and discovered that, between December 2, 1950 and December 8 (the approximate time in question), forty-two Marines from the 7th Marine Regiment were listed as Missing In Action (MIA). Of these forty-two, eight had been assigned to Item Company, which was the specific unit Joe had been assigned to after he volunteered for the infantry. I found these numbers to be dramatic considering that the 7th Marines are only a small percentage of the total Marine Corps force engaged in the Chosin Reservoir Campaign. The idea that Joe could have been captured during this time is not unreasonable to me.

Of course, my only avenue was to ask my father about this revelation. Perhaps this would solve the mystery for him. But, just as often as my conversation with John had played out in my head, Dad's words from Dr. Fredrickson about The Missing Days repeated themselves:

Maybe it'll make things worse.

With the decision to leave it alone for a while, I got back to my writing. Soon enough, I came to the conclusion that I did not need to know what had happened during The Missing Days any more than my father did. He, obviously, has no memory of being captured and I have only hearsay evidence of such an occurrence. I could not, in good conscience, prod him to remember something that might easily undue what all his hard work had accomplished on behalf of his recovery.

Furthermore, I have no direct knowledge of any conversation between my father and his brother, John, related to Joe's experiences during the war, although it seems apparent that at least one conversation did take place. In the chapter *April Fools,* I have made reference to this assumed conversation. Dad did not tell me, however, that the conversation had taken place. I placed this reference only as an overture to what I have shared with you here.

And I offer this information now only as a *What if? What if* nineteen-year old Joe had been chased down and captured by two Chinese combatants? *What if* he'd felt that capture would mean certain death? *What if* he'd screamed and clawed and threw wild punches to save himself. *What if* Joe had attacked one of the Chinese soldiers after he'd been captured in an attempt to save the soldier and himself. *What if* the other Marine had been terrified into inaction? *What if* the smiling Chinaman had shot the soldier in the face? *What if* that young man had somehow managed to escape, or had simply been left to freeze to death?

Could all those *what ifs* add up to something that the mind would choose to suppress—only to be replayed over and over again in its dreams? You and I will never know. What if we don't ask Dad?

Joe with some of his Vietnam veteran PTSD buddies.

From left to right: Ted, David, Joe, Ruben, Brian, and Rick.

ACKNOWLEDGEMENTS

My village may be small, but I can assure you it was essential in order to make this book possible:

I could never have accomplished this lofty feat without the total support and encouragement of my wife, Laura. She believed in me whenever I faltered. She encouraged me to press on whenever I hit the wall. She read every word over and over through every edit and draft. She praised my successes, and gently encouraged me to dig deeper when my words fell short. And she put up with a husband whose life became consumed by his mission when she should have consumed it. Thank you, Laura. I love everything about you.

Over a period of six months, my brother, Christopher Lynch, spent scores of hours interviewing our dad in front of a video camera. Christopher's love for history and insightful questions provided me more bountiful jewels and humble trinkets than I had ever imagined possible. He and I spent countless hours on the phone discussing innumerable topics pertaining to this story. I only hope that I have done his hard work justice.

Marilyn Murray Willison has a way with words—even mine. Any writer worth his or her salt will concede that good writing means even better editing. Marilyn's precise attention to grammar and sentence structure is the polish on my new car—the spit shine on my wingtips. Marilyn makes me feel like a writer. Occasionally, I enjoyed sparring with Marilyn over the correct way to present some of my thoughts and admit that she usually won those friendly contests. I can assure you that any grammatical mistakes that remain are purely the fault of my occasional pigheadedness.

Even a great editor like Marilyn needs a proofreader. Especially when the author makes changes after the edit. The final gatekeeper before publication, my sister-in-law, Kelly Lynch, lent a keen eye for detail so that every "t" was crossed and each "i" was not spelled "Eye."

So many other people have supported this project from the beginning and stuck with it through its fruition. Lifelong friends and family, as well as new friends I have met along this journey, I thank each of you for your encouragement, ideas, critiques, and—most of all—your belief in the importance of this story:

James Simmons, who blew on those first sparks that, ultimately, lit the raging writing fire within me.

Todd Samuelson, Dave Young, and Renee Wright, who followed me, and supported and promoted this project through social media even though we have never met face-to-face.

Katrina Lakey, Marley Andretti, Jenny Lasala, Ray Calhoun, Diane Goodridge, Matthew Lynch, Ellen Ferraro, Marianne Landau, Joseph Lynch, Kathleen Lynn, Schanna McDonald, Christopher Lynch, and Mark Lynch, who all read THE BED I MADE in its early, humble, and somewhat embarrassing drafts.

The men who shared their fears and hopes with my dad at the San Diego VA PTSD clinic, without whom Joe's recovery could not have been possible. It has been my honor to have finally met some of you: Frank Maurer (April 13, 1925 – January 11, 2017), Willie Frieheit, Ray Calhoun, Rick Salde, Sr., Ted, David, Ruben, Brian, and many others for whom I do not have names. Your uplifting service to each other is matched only by your courageous sacrifices to country.

And finally, my new Korean friends who have found and followed me through social media: Your heartfelt gratitude for the United Nations forces who served to keep your country free touches me each day. A special thanks to Sungyong Park, a modern-day KATUSA and ROK Army veteran from Seoul, South Korea who has taken the time to express his gratitude directly to my dad, and who lent me his name for this book when Joe could not remember the name of the KATUSA he befriended in the Pusan Perimeter. For every question I've asked and each favor I've begged, you have responded without hesitation. Your excessive kindness and generous friendship means more to me than you will ever know.

REFERENCES

THE FOLLOWING RESOURCES WERE EMPLOYED to help me date events, determine unit locations during Joe's service, provide general information on the war and specific battles, and pinpoint dates and locations for Joe's friends who were killed in action:

FIRE BRIGADE: U.S. Marines in the Pusan Perimeter. By Captain John C. Chapin, U.S. Marine Corps Reserve, Retired

OVER THE SEAWALL: U.S. Marines at Inchon. By Brigadier General Edwin H. Simmons, USMC (Ret)

ASSAULT FROM THE SEA: The Amphibious Landing at Inchon. By Curtis A. Utz

BATTLE OF THE BARRICADES: U.S. Marines in the Recapture of Seoul. By Colonel Joseph H. Alexander, USMC (Ret)

FROZEN CHOSIN: U.S. Marines at the Changjin Reservoir. By Brigadier General Edwin H. Simmons, USMC (Ret)

THE CHOSIN CHRONOLOGY: Battle of the Changjin Reservoir, 1950. By George A. Rasula

COUNTEROFFENSIVE: U.S. Marines from Pohang to No Name Line. By Lieutenant Colonel Ronald J. Brown, USMCR (Ret)

FOR GOD'S SAKE, DO SOMETHING! An Autobiography. By The Reverend Monsignor Otto E. Sporrer

KOREAN WAR PROJECT (WEB): http://www.koreanwar.org. Editors: Hal Barker and Ted Barker, Korean War Project

KOREAN WAR EDUCATOR (WEB): http://www.koreanwar-educator.org

Joseph A. Lynch, Sr.

Barbara P. Lynch

Author, Robert M. Lynch

Historian, Christopher B. Lynch

92002605R00212

Made in the USA
Columbia, SC
23 March 2018